2900+ Inspirational Quotations for a

Better Living

By

Guggu V

Copyright 2013 Guggu V

1. "You've gotta dance like there's nobody watching,
   Love like you'll never be hurt,
   Sing like there's nobody listening,
   And live like it's heaven on earth."— William W. Purkey

2. "Be yourself; everyone else is already taken."— Oscar Wilde

3. "Be the change that you wish to see in the world."— Mahatma Gandhi

4. "No one can make you feel inferior without your consent."— Eleanor Roosevelt,
   This is My Story

5. "Live as if you were to die tomorrow. Learn as if you were to live forever."—
   Mahatma Gandhi

6. "Darkness cannot drive out darkness: only light can do that. Hate cannot drive
   out hate: only love can do that."— Martin Luther King Jr., A Testament of Hope:
   The Essential Writings and Speeches

7. "Without music, life would be a mistake."— Friedrich Nietzsche, Twilight of the
   Idols

8. "Imperfection is beauty, madness is genius and it's better to be absolutely
   ridiculous than absolutely boring."— Marilyn Monroe

9. "There are only two ways to live your life. One is as though nothing is a miracle.
   The other is as though everything is a miracle."— Albert Einstein

10. "Yesterday is history, tomorrow is a mystery, today is a gift of God, which is why
    we call it the present."— Bil Keane

11. "we accept the love we think we deserve."— Stephen Chbosky, The Perks of
    Being a Wallflower

12. "We are all in the gutter, but some of us are looking at the stars."— Oscar Wilde,
    Lady Windermere's Fan

13. "I am enough of an artist to draw freely upon my imagination. Imagination is more
    important than knowledge. Knowledge is limited. Imagination encircles the
    world."— Albert Einstein

14. "The opposite of love is not hate, its indifference. The opposite of art is not
    ugliness, its indifference.
    The opposite of faith is not heresy, its indifference. And the opposite of life is not
    death, its indifference."— Elie Wiesel

15. "I have not failed. I've just found 10,000 ways that won't work."— Thomas A.
    Edison

16. "You have brains in your head. You have feet in your shoes. You can steer yourself any direction you choose. You're on your own. And you know what you know. And YOU are the one who'll decide where to go..."— Dr. Seuss, Oh, the Places You'll Go!

17. "Fairy tales are more than true: not because they tell us that dragons exist, but because they tell us that dragons can be beaten."— Neil Gaiman, Coraline

18. "It is never too late to be what you might have been."— George Eliot

19. "This life is what you make it. No matter what, you're going to mess up sometimes, it's a universal truth. But the good part is you get to decide how you're going to mess it up. Girls will be your friends - they'll act like it anyway. But just remember, some come, some go. The ones that stay with you through everything - they're your true best friends. Don't let go of them. Also remember, sisters make the best friends in the world. As for lovers, well, they'll come and go too. And baby, I hate to say it, most of them - actually pretty much all of them are going to break your heart, but you can't give up because if you give up, you'll never find your soul mate. You'll never find that half who makes you whole and that goes for everything. Just because you fail once, doesn't mean you're gonna fail at everything. Keep trying, hold on, and always, always, always believe in yourself, because if you don't, then who will, sweetie? So keep your head high, keep your chin up, and most importantly, keep smiling, because life's a beautiful thing and there's so much to smile about."— Marilyn Monroe

20. "Do what you can, with what you have, where you are."— Theodore Roosevelt

21. "Everything you can imagine is real."— Pablo Picasso

22. "There is no greater agony than bearing an untold story inside you."— Maya Angelou

23. "Listen to the mustn'ts, child. Listen to the don'ts. Listen to the shouldn'ts, the impossibles, the won'ts. Listen to the never haves, then listen close to me... Anything can happen, child. Anything can be."— Shel Silverstein

24. "When one door of happiness closes, another opens; but often we look so long at the closed door that we do not see the one which has been opened for us."— Helen Keller

25. "I believe in pink. I believe that laughing is the best calorie burner. I believe in kissing, kissing a lot. I believe in being strong when everything seems to be going wrong. I believe that happy girls are the prettiest girls. I believe that tomorrow is another day and I believe in miracles."— Audrey Hepburn

26. "To the well-organized mind, death is but the next great adventure."— J.K. Rowling, Harry Potter and the Sorcerer's Stone

27. "You may say I'm a dreamer, but I'm not the only one. I hope someday you'll join us. And the world will live as one."— John Lennon

28. "Success is not final, failure is not fatal: it is the courage to continue that counts."— Winston Churchill

29. "Our deepest fear is not that we are inadequate. Our deepest fear is that we are powerful beyond measure. It is our light, not our darkness that most frightens us. We ask ourselves, 'Who am I to be brilliant, gorgeous, talented, and fabulous?' Actually, who are you not to be? You are a child of God. You're playing small does not serve the world. There is nothing enlightened about shrinking so that other people won't feel insecure around you. We are all meant to shine, as children do. We were born to make manifest the glory of God that is within us. It's not just in some of us; it's in everyone. And as we let our own light shine, we unconsciously give other people permission to do the same. As we are liberated from our own fear, our presence automatically liberates others."— Marianne Williamson, Return to Love: Reflections on the Principles of "A Course in Miracles"

30. "A person's a person, no matter how small."— Dr. Seuss, Horton Hears a Who!

31. "You can never get a cup of tea large enough or a book long enough to suit me."— C.S. Lewis

32. "Life isn't about finding yourself. Life is about creating yourself."— George Bernard Shaw

33. "If you don't like something, change it. If you can't change it, change your attitude. Don't complain."— Maya Angelou

34. "You can't live your life for other people. You've got to do what's right for you, even if it hurts some people you love."— Nicholas Sparks, The Notebook

35. "And, when you want something, the entire universe conspires in helping you to achieve it."— Paulo Coelho, The Alchemist

36. "When we honestly ask ourselves which person in our lives means the most to us, we often find that it is those who, instead of giving advice, solutions, or cures, have chosen rather to share our pain and touch our wounds with a warm and tender hand.
The friend who can be silent with us in a moment of despair or confusion, who can stay with us in an hour of grief and bereavement, who can tolerate not knowing, not curing, not healing and face with us the reality of our powerlessness, that is a friend who cares."— Henri J.M. Nouwen, The Road to Daybreak: A Spiritual Journey

37. "Well-behaved women seldom make history."— Laurel Thatcher Ulrich, Well-Behaved Women Seldom Make History

38. "A bird doesn't sing because it has an answer, it sings because it has a song."— Maya Angelou

39. "Nothing is impossible; the word itself says 'I'm possible'!"— Audrey Hepburn

40. "It's the possibility of having a dream come true that makes life interesting."— Paulo Coelho, Alchemist

41. "For Attractive lips, speak words of kindness.
For lovely eyes, seek out the good in people.
For a slim figure, share your food with the hungry.
For beautiful hair, let a child run their fingers through it once a day.
For poise, walk with the knowledge that you never walk alone.
People, more than things, have to be restored, renewed, revived, reclaimed, and redeemed. Remember, if you ever need a helping hand, you will find one at the end of each of your arms.
As you grow older, you will discover that you have two hands, one for helping yourself and the other for helping others."— Sam Levenson

42. "Peace begins with a smile..."— Mother Teresa

43. "Do what you feel in your heart to be right – for you'll be criticized anyway."— Eleanor Roosevelt

44. "Two wrongs don't make a right, but they make a good excuse."— Thomas Stephen Szasz

45. "Happiness is not something readymade. It comes from your own actions."— Dalai Lama XIV

46. "When I despair, I remember that all through history the way of truth and love has always won. There have been tyrants and murderers, and for a time, they can seem invincible, but in the end, they always fall. Think of it--always."— Mahatma Gandhi

47. "What lies behind us and what lies before us are tiny matters compared to what lies within us."— Ralph Waldo Emerson

48. "First they ignore you, then they ridicule you, then they fight you, and then you win."— Mahatma Gandhi

49. "Never doubt that a small group of thoughtful, committed, citizens can change the world. Indeed, it is the only thing that ever has."— Margaret Mead

50. "Whatever you are, be a good one."— Abraham Lincoln

51. "Do not read, as children do, to amuse yourself, or like the ambitious, for the purpose of instruction.
No, read in order to live."— Gustave Flaubert

52. "I believe that imagination is stronger than knowledge. That myth is more potent than history. That dreams are more powerful than facts. That hope always triumphs over experience. That laughter is the only cure for grief. And I believe that love is stronger than death."— Robert Fulghum, All I Really Need to Know I Learned in Kindergarten

53. "May you live every day of your life."— Jonathan Swift

54. "Always do what you are afraid to do."— Ralph Waldo Emerson

55. "Isn't it nice to think that tomorrow is a new day with no mistakes in it yet?"— L.M. Montgomery

56. "A book without words is like love without a kiss; it's empty."— Andrew Wolfe

57. "There is neither happiness nor misery in the world; there is only the comparison of one state with another, nothing more. He who has felt the deepest grief is best able to experience supreme happiness. We must have felt what it is to die, moral, that we may appreciate the enjoyments of life." Live, then, and be happy, beloved children of my heart, and never forget, that until the day God will deign to reveal the future to man, all human wisdom is contained in these two words, 'Wait and Hope."— Alexandre Dumas

58. "Our lives begin to end the day we become silent about things that matter."— Martin Luther King Jr., I Have a Dream: Writings and Speeches That Changed the World

59. "In the end, we will remember not the words of our enemies, but the silence of our friends."— Martin Luther King Jr.

60. "The Chinese use two brush strokes to write the word 'crisis.' One brush stroke stands for danger; the other for opportunity. In a crisis, be aware of the danger-- but recognize the opportunity."— John F. Kennedy

61. "So, this is my life. And I want you to know that I am both happy and sad and I'm still trying to figure out how that could be."— Stephen Chbosky, The Perks of Being a Wallflower

62. "He's not perfect. You aren't either, and the two of you will never be perfect. But if he can make you laugh at least once, causes you to think twice, and if he admits to being human and making mistakes, hold onto him and give him the most you can. He isn't going to quote poetry, he's not thinking about you every moment, but he will give you a part of him that he knows you could break. Don't hurt him, don't change him, and don't expect for more than he can give. Don't analyze. Smile when he makes you happy, yell when he makes you mad, and miss him when he's not there. Love hard when there is love to be had. Because perfect guys don't exist, but there's always one guy that is perfect for you."— Bob Marley

63. "I can't go back to yesterday because I was a different person then."— Lewis Carroll, Alice in Wonderland

64. "the only people for me are the mad ones, the ones who are mad to live, mad to talk, mad to be saved, desirous of everything at the same time, the ones who never yawn or say a commonplace thing, but burn, burn, burn like fabulous yellow roman candles exploding like spiders across the stars."— Jack Kerouac, On the Road

65. "Friendship is unnecessary, like philosophy, like art.... It has no survival value; rather it is one of those things which give value to survival."— C.S. Lewis, The Four Loves

66. "Talent hits a target no one else can hit. Genius hits a target no one else can see."— Arthur Schopenhauer

67. "Do not let your fire go out, spark by irreplaceable spark in the hopeless swamps of the not-quite, the not-yet, and the not-at-all. Do not let the hero in your soul perish in lonely frustration for the life you deserved and have never been able to reach. The world you desire can be won. It exists... it is real... it is possible... it's yours."— Ayn Rand, Atlas Shrugged

68. "Hope is the thing with feathersThat perches in the soulAnd sings the tune without the wordsAnd never stops at all."— Emily Dickinson

69. "I can be changed by what happens to me. But I refuse to be reduced by it."— Maya Angelou

70. "Waiting is painful. Forgetting is painful. But not knowing which to do is the worst kind of suffering."— Paulo Coelho, By the River Piedra I Sat Down and Wept" And, in the end The love you take is equal to the love you make."— Paul McCartney, The Beatles Illustrated Lyrics

71. "I am not sure exactly what heaven will be like, but I know that when we die and it comes time for God to judge us, he will not ask, 'How many good things have you done in your life?' rather he will ask, 'How much love did you put into what you did?"— Mother Teresa

72. "If you can't fly then run, if you can't run then walk, if you can't walk then crawl, but whatever you do you have to keep moving forward."— Martin Luther King Jr.

73. "Do not go where the path may lead, go instead where there is no path and leave a trail."— Ralph Waldo Emerson

74. "None but ourselves can free our minds."— Bob Marley

75. "Sometimes our light goes out, but is blown again into instant flame by an encounter with another human being."— Albert Schweitzer

76. "Don't judge each day by the harvest you reap but by the seeds that you plant."— Robert Louis Stevenson

77. "When you have eliminated all which is impossible, then whatever remains, however improbable, must be the truth."— Arthur Conan Doyle, The Case-Book of Sherlock Holmes

78. "Fantasy is hardly an escape from reality. It's a way of understanding it."— Lloyd Alexander

79. "It's kind of fun to do the impossible."— Walt Disney Company

80. "Turn your wounds into wisdom."— Oprah Winfrey

81. "A woman's heart should be so hidden in God that a man has to seek Him just to find her."— Max Lucado

82. "What I need is the dandelion in the spring. The bright yellow that means rebirth instead of destruction. The promise that life can go on, no matter how bad our losses. That it can be good again."— Suzanne Collins, Mockingjay

83. "When I was a little girl I used to read fairy tales. In fairy tales you meet Prince Charming and he's everything you ever wanted. In fairy tales the bad guy is very easy to spot. The bad guy is always wearing a black cape so you always know who he is. Then you grow up and you realize that Prince Charming is not as easy to find as you thought. You realize the bad guy is not wearing a black cape and he's not easy to spot; he's really funny, and he makes you laugh, and he has perfect hair."— Taylor Swift

84. "All the darkness in the world cannot extinguish the light of a single candle."— St. Francis of Assisi, The Little Flowers of St. Francis of Assisi

85. "A painter should begin every canvas with a wash of black, because all things in nature are dark except where exposed by the light."— Leonardo da Vinci

86. "Stories never really end...even if the books like to pretend they do. Stories always go on. They don't end on the last page, any more than they begin on the first page."— Cornelia Funke, Inkspell

87. "The secret of health for both mind and body is not to mourn for the past, nor to worry about the future, but to live the present moment wisely and earnestly."— Gautama Buddha

88. "Once you have tasted flight, you will forever walk the earth with your eyes turned skyward, for there you have been, and there you will always long to return."— Leonardo da Vinci

89. "Try a little harder to be a little better."— Gordon B. Hinckley

90. "Imagining the future is a kind of nostalgia. (...) You spend your whole life stuck in the labyrinth, thinking about how you'll escape it one day, and how awesome it will be, and imagining that future keeps you going, but you never do it. You just use the future to escape the present."— John Green, Looking for Alaska

91. "So we beat on, boats against the current, borne back ceaselessly into the past."— F. Scott Fitzgerald, The Great Gatsby

92. "I hope she'll be a fool -- that's the best thing a girl can be in this world, a beautiful little fool."— F. Scott Fitzgerald, The Great Gatsby

93. "When I was 5 years old, my mother always told me that happiness was the key to life. When I went to school, they asked me what I wanted to be when I grew

up. I wrote down 'happy'. They told me I didn't understand the assignment, and I told them they didn't understand life."— John Lennon

94. "You don't love someone for their looks, or their clothes, or for their fancy car, but because they sing a song only you can hear."— Oscar Wilde

95. "If my life is going to mean anything, I have to live it myself."— Rick Riordan, The Lightning Thief

96. "The future belongs to those who believe in the beauty of their dreams."— Eleanor Roosevelt

97. "The world is indeed full of peril and in it there are many dark places. But still there is much that is fair. And though in all lands, love is now mingled with grief, it still grows, perhaps, the greater."— J.R.R. Tolkien, The Lord of the Rings

98. "I love to see a young girl go out and grab the world by the lapels. Life's a bitch. You've got to go out and kick ass."— Maya Angelou

99. "Prayer is not asking. It is a longing of the soul. It is daily admission of one's weakness. It is better in prayer to have a heart without words than words without a heart."— Mahatma Gandhi

100. "Don't say you don't have enough time. You have exactly the same number of hours per day that were given to Helen Keller, Pasteur, Michelangelo, Mother Teresa, Leonardo da Vinci, Thomas Jefferson, and Albert Einstein."— H. Jackson Brown Jr.

101. "To me, Fearless is not the absence of fear. It's not being completely unafraid. To me, Fearless is having fears. Fearless is having doubts. Lots of them. To me, Fearless is living in spite of those things that scare you to death."— Taylor Swift

102. "You never fail until you stop trying."— Albert Einstein

103. "One love, one heart, one destiny."— Bob Marley

104. "You're off to Great Places! Today is your day! Your mountain is waiting,so... get on your way!"— Dr. Seuss, Oh, the Places You'll Go!

105. "Live in the present, remember the past, and fear not the future, for it doesn't exist and never shall. There is only now."— Christopher Paolini, Eldest

106. "Hope Smiles from the threshold of the year to come,Whispering 'it will be happier'..."— Alfred Tennyson

107. "You should never be surprised when someone treats you with respect, you should expect it."— Sarah Dessen, Keeping the Moon

108. "Why didn't I learn to treat everything like it was the last time? My greatest regret was how much I believed in the future."— Jonathan Safran Foer, Extremely Loud and Incredibly Close

109. "Simplicity, patience, compassion. These three are your greatest treasures. Simple in actions and thoughts, you return to the source of being. Patient with both friends and enemies,you accord with the way things are. Compassionate toward yourself,you reconcile all beings in the world."— Lao Tzu, Tao Te Ching

110. "It is not the critic who counts; not the man who points out how the strong man stumbles, or where the doer of deeds could have done them better. The credit belongs to the man who is actually in the arena, whose face is marred by dust and sweat and blood; who strives valiantly; who errs, who comes short again and again, because there is no effort without error and shortcoming; but who does actually strive to do the deeds; who knows great enthusiasms, the great devotions; who spends himself in a worthy cause; who at the best knows in the end the triumph of high achievement, and who at the worst, if he fails, at least fails while daring greatly, so that his place shall never be with those cold and timid souls who neither know victory nor defeat."— Theodore Roosevelt

111. "The unreal is more powerful than the real. Because nothing is as perfect as you can imagine it. Because its only intangible ideas, concepts, beliefs, fantasies that last. Stone crumbles. Wood rots. People, well, they die. But things as fragile as a thought, a dream, a legend, they can go on and on. If you can change the way people think. The way they see themselves. The way they see the world. You can change the way people live their lives. That's the only lasting thing you can create."— Chuck Palahniuk, Choke

112. "It was, he thought, the difference between being dragged into the arena to face a battle to the death and walking into the arena with your head held high. Some people, perhaps, would say that there was little to choose between the two ways, but Dumbledore knew - and so do I, thought Harry, with a rush of fierce pride, and so did my parents - that there was all the difference in the world."— J.K. Rowling, Harry Potter and the Half-Blood Prince

113. "Courage is not the absence of fear, but rather the judgment that

114. something else is more important than fear."— Meg Cabot

115. "I meant what I said and I said what I meant. An elephant's faithful one-hundred percent!"— Dr. Seuss, Horton Hatches the Egg

116. "Remember, darkness does not always equate to evil, just as light does not always bring good."— P.C. Cast, Betrayed

117. "And in the end it is not the years in your life that count, it's the life in your years."— Abraham Lincoln

118. "The mind is its own place, and in itself can make a heaven of hell, a hell of heaven..."— John Milton, Paradise Lost

119. "A ship is safe in harbor, but that's not what ships are for."— William G.T. Shedd

120. "Great heroes need great sorrows and burdens, or half their greatness goes unnoticed. It is all part of the fairy tale."— Peter S. Beagle, The Last Unicorn

121. "Promise Yourself

To be so strong that nothing
can disturb your peace of mind.
To talk health, happiness, and prosperity
to every person you meet.
To make all your friends feel
that there is something in them
To look at the sunny side of everything
and make your optimism come true.
To think only the best, to work only for the best,and to expect only the best.
To be just as enthusiastic about the success of others
as you are about your own.
To forget the mistakes of the past
and press on to the greater achievements of the future.
To wear a cheerful countenance at all times
and give every living creature you meet a smile.
To give so much time to the improvement of yourself
that you have no time to criticize others.
To be too large for worry, too noble for anger, too strong for fear, and too happy
to permit the presence of trouble.
To think well of yourself and to proclaim this fact to the world, not in loud words
but great deeds.
To live in faith that the whole world is on your side
so long as you are true to the best that is in you."— Christian D. Larson, Your
Forces and How to Use Them

122. Pain is inevitable. Suffering is optional."— Haruki Murakami, What I Talk About
When I Talk About Running

123. "He who controls the past controls the future. He who controls the present
controls the past."— George Orwell, 1984

124. "Pain is temporary. Quitting lasts forever."— Lance Armstrong, Every Second
Counts

125. "It's not the face, but the expressions on it. It's not the voice, but what you say.
It's not how you look in that body, but the thing you do with it. You are
beautiful."— Stephenie Meyer, The Host

126. "You can't stay in your corner of the Forest waiting for others to come to you. You
have to go to them sometimes."— A.A. Milne, Winnie-the-Pooh

127. "The most important kind of freedom is to be what you really are. You trade in
your reality for a role. You trade in your sense for an act. You give up your ability
to feel, and in exchange, put on a mask. There can't be any large-scale
revolution until there's a personal revolution, on an individual level. It's got to
happen inside first."— Jim Morrison

128. "Is 'fat' really the worst thing a human being can be? Is 'fat' worse than
'vindictive', 'jealous', 'shallow', 'vain', 'boring' or 'cruel'? Not to me."— J.K. Rowling

129. "So be sure when you step, Step with care and great tact. And remember that life's A Great Balancing Act. And will you succeed? Yes! You will, indeed! (98 and ¾ percent guaranteed) Kid, you'll move mountains."— Dr. Seuss, Oh, The Places You'll Go!

130. "War is peace.Freedom is slavery.Ignorance is strength."— George Orwell, 1984

131. "The thing about growing up with Fred and George," said Ginny thoughtfully, "is that you sort of start thinking anything's possible if you've got enough nerve."— J.K. Rowling, Harry Potter and the Half-Blood Prince

132. "You is kind. You is smart. You is important."— Kathryn Stockett, The Help

133. "It doesn't interest me what you do for a living. I want to know what you ache for, and if you dare to dream of meeting your heart's longing. It doesn't interest me how old you are. I want to know if you will risk looking like a fool for love, for your dream, for the adventure of being alive.It doesn't interest me what planets are squaring your moon. I want to know if you have touched the center of your own sorrow, if you have been opened by life's betrayals or have become shriveled and closed from fear of further pain! I want to know if you can sit with pain, mine or your own, without moving to hide it or fade it, or fix it.I want to know if you can be with joy, mine or your own, if you can dance with wildness and let the ecstasy fill you to the tips of your fingers and toes without cautioning us to be careful, to be realistic, to remember the limitations of being human.It doesn't interest me if the story you are telling me is true. I want to know if you can disappoint another to be true to yourself; if you can bear the accusation of betrayal and not betray your own soul; if you can be faithless and therefore trustworthy.I want to know if you can see beauty even when it's not pretty, every day, and if you can source your own life from its presence.I want to know if you can live with failure, yours and mine, and still stand on the edge of the lake and shout to the silver of the full moon, "Yes!" It doesn't interest me to know where you live or how much money you have. I want to know if you can get up, after the night of grief and despair, weary and bruised to the bone, and do what needs to be done to feed the children.It doesn't interest me who you know or how you came to be here. I want to know if you will stand in the center of the fire with me and not shrink back.It doesn't interest me where or what or with whom you have studied. I want to know what sustains you, from the inside, when all else falls away.I want to know if you can be alone with yourself and if you truly like the company you keep in the empty moments."— Oriah Mountain Dreamer

134. "I do not fear death. I had been dead for billions and billions of years before I was born, and had not suffered the slightest inconvenience from it."— Mark Twain

135. "Anyone can hide. Facing up to things, working through them, that's what makes you strong."— Sarah Dessen

136. "If you think you are too small to make a difference, try sleeping with a mosquito."— Dalai Lama XIV

137. "If you are irritated by every rub, how will your mirror be polished?"— Rumi

138. "Change will not come if we wait for some other person, or if we wait for some other time. We are the ones we've been waiting for. We are the change that we seek."— Barack Obama

139. "In the end these things matter most:How well did you love? How fully did you live? How deeply did you let go?"— Gautama Buddha

140. "It's not the size of the dog in the fight; it's the size of the fight in the dog." — Mark Twain

141. "Others have seen what is and asked why. I have seen what could be and asked why not. "— Pablo Picasso, Pablo Picasso: Metamorphoses of the Human Form: Graphic Works, 1895-1972

142. "I sought to hear the voice of God and climbed the topmost steeple, but God declared: "Go down again - I dwell among the people."— John Henry Newman

143. "We don't need a list of rights and wrongs, tables of dos and don'ts: we need books, time, and silence. Thou shalt not is soon forgotten, but Once upon a time lasts forever."— Philip Pullman

144. "However many holy words you read, however many you speak, what good will they do you if you do not act on upon them?"— Gautama Buddha

145. "I have never met a man so ignorant that I couldn't learn something from him."— Galileo Galilee

146. "Ladies and gentlemen of the class of '97:Wear sunscreen. If I could offer you only one tip for the future, sunscreen would be it. The long-term benefits of sunscreen have been proved by scientists, whereas the rest of my advice has no basis more reliable than my own meandering experience. I will dispense this advice now. Enjoy the power and beauty of your youth. Oh, never mind. You will not understand the power and beauty of your youth until they've faded. But trust me, in 20 years, you'll look back at photos of yourself and recall in a way you can't grasp now how much possibility lay before you and how fabulous you really looked. You are not as fat as you imagine. Don't worry about the future. Or worry, but know that worrying is as effective as trying to solve an algebra equation by chewing bubble gum. The real troubles in your life are apt to be things that never crossed your worried mind, the kind that blindside you at 4 p.m. on some idle Tuesday."— Mary Schmich

147. "Whatever you can do or dream you can, begin it. Boldness has genius, power and magic in it!"— Johann Wolfgang von Goethe

148. "Ask for what you want and be prepared to get it!"— Maya Angelou

149. "There is nothing more dreadful than the habit of doubt. Doubt separates people. It is a poison that disintegrates friendships and breaks up pleasant relations. It is a thorn that irritates and hurts; it is a sword that kills."— Gautama Buddha

150. "True love is not so much a matter of romance as it is a matter of anxious concern for the well-being of one's companion."— Gordon B. Hinckley, Stand a Little Taller

151. "If you're reading this... Congratulations, you're alive. If that's not something to smile about,then I don't know what is."— Chad Sugg, Monsters Under Your Head

152. "I was smiling yesterday, I am smiling today and I will smile tomorrow. Simply because life is too short to cry for anything."— Santosh Kalwar, Quote Me Everyday

153. "The things you do for yourself are gone when you are gone, but the things you do for others remain as your legacy."— Kalu Ndukwe Kalu

154. "I do not trust people who don't love themselves and yet tell me, 'I love you.' There is an African saying which is: Be careful when a naked person offers you a shirt."— Maya Angelou

155. "Hell is empty and all the devils are here."— William Shakespeare, The Tempest

156. "Only in the darkness can you see the stars."— Martin Luther King Jr.

157. "Maybe everyone can live beyond what they're capable of."— Markus Zusak, I Am the Messenger

158. "Rules for Happiness:something to do,someone to love,something to hope for."— Immanuel Kant

159. "I'd rather be hated for who I am, than loved for who I am not."— Kurt Cobain

160. "When people don't express themselves, they die one piece at a time."— Laurie Halse Anderson, Speak

161. "Kindness is a language which the deaf can hear and the blind can see."— Mark Twain

162. "Go on with what your heart tells you, or you will lose all."— Rick Riordan, The Lightning Thief

163. "So many people walk around with a meaningless life. They seem half-asleep, even when they're busy doing things they think are important. This is because they're chasing the wrong things. The way you get meaning into your life is to devote yourself to loving others, devote yourself to your community around you, and devote yourself to creating something that gives you purpose and meaning."— Mitch Albom, Tuesdays With Morrie

164. "Shoot for the moon. Even if you miss, you'll land among the stars."— Les Brown

165. "A woman's heart should be so hidden in God that a man has to seek Him just to find her."— Maya Angelou

166. "Jane, be still; don't struggle so like a wild, frantic bird, that is rending its own plumage in its desperation."

167. "I am no bird; and no net ensnares me; I am a free human being, with an independent will; which I now exert to leave you."— Charlotte Brontë, Jane Eyre

168. "Whatever you do, you need courage. Whatever course you decide upon, there is always someone to tell you that you are wrong. There are always difficulties arising that tempt you to believe your critics are right. To map out a course of action and follow it to an end requires some of the same courage that a soldier needs. Peace has its victories, but it takes brave men and women to win them."— Ralph Waldo Emerson

169. "why are trying so hard to fit in, when you're born to stand out"— Oliver James

170. "No matter how your heart is grieving, if you keep on believing, the dreams that you wish will come true."— Walt Disney Company

171. "If you make a mistake and do not correct it, this is called a mistake."— Confucius

172. "The best thing to hold onto in life is each other."— Audrey Hepburn

173. "Just because you can doesn't mean you should."— Sherrilyn Kenyon

174. "To-morrow, and to-morrow, and to-morrow,Creeps in this petty pace from day to day,To the last syllable of recorded time;and all our yesterdays have lighted fools the way to dusty death. Out, out, brief candle! Life's but a walking shadow, a poor player,that struts and frets his hour upon the stage,and then is heard no more. It is a tale Told by an idiot, full of sound and fury,signifying nothing."— William Shakespeare, Macbeth

175. "I never want to change so much that people can't recognize me."— Taylor Swift

176. "Sometimes God allows what he hates to accomplish what he loves."— Joni Eareckson Tada, The God I Love

177. "Happiness is like a butterfly which, when pursued, is always beyond our grasp, but, if you will sit down quietly, may alight upon you."— Nathaniel Hawthorne

178. "All that we are is the result of what we have thought. If a man speaks or acts with an evil thought, pain follows him. If a man speaks or acts with a pure thought, happiness follows him, like a shadow that never leaves him."— Gautama Buddha

179. "In the name of God, stop a moment, cease your work, look around you." — Leo Tolstoy

180. "Every man is a damn fool for at least five minutes every day; wisdom consists in not exceeding the limit."— Elbert Hubbard, The Roycroft Dictionary Concocted by Ali Baba and the Bunch on Rainy Days

181. "My heart is warm with the friends I make,And better friends I'll not be knowing,Yet there isn't a train I wouldn't take,No matter where it's going."— Edna St. Vincent Millay, The Selected Poetry

182. "It is so hard to leave—until you leave. And then it is the easiest goddamned thing in the world."— John Green, Paper Towns

183. "Better to be strong than pretty and useless."— Lilith Saintcrow, Strange Angels

184. "Well, now If little by little you stop loving me
    I shall stop loving you Little by little
    If suddenly you forget me
    Do not look for me
    For I shall already have forgotten you
    If you think it long and mad the wind of banners that passes through my life
    And you decide to leave me at the shore of the heart where I have roots
    Remember
    That on that day, at that hour, I shall lift my arms
    And my roots will set off to seek another land"— Pablo Neruda, Selected Poems

185. "The past has no power over the present moment."— Eckhart Tolle

186. "HAPPINESS [is] ONLY REAL WHEN SHARED"— Jon Krakauer, Into the Wild

187. "Nothing in the world is ever completely wrong. Even a stopped clock is right twice a day."— Paulo Coelho, Brida

188. "There are some things you can't share without ending up liking each other, and knocking out a twelve-foot mountain troll is one of them."— J.K. Rowling, Harry Potter and the Sorcerer's Stone

189. "You were born with wings, why prefer to crawl through life?"— Rumi

190. "All parents damage their children. It cannot be helped. Youth, like pristine glass, absorbs the prints of its handlers. Some parents smudge, others crack, a few shatter childhoods completely into jagged little pieces, beyond repair."— Mitch Albom, The Five People You Meet in Heaven

191. "I will love you always. When this red hair is white, I will still love you. When the smooth softness of youth is replaced by the delicate softness of age, I will still want to touch your skin. When your face is full of the lines of every smile you have ever smiled, of every surprise I have seen flash through your eyes, when every tear you have ever cried has left its mark upon your face, I will treasure you all the more, because I was there to see it all. I will share your life with you, Meredith, and I will love you until the last breath leaves your body or mine."— Laurell K. Hamilton, A Lick of Frost

192. "My concern is not whether God is on our side; my greatest concern is to be on God's side, for God is always right."— Abraham Lincoln

193. "If we listened to our intellect we'd never have a love affair. We'd never have a friendship. We'd never go in business because we'd be cynical: "It's gonna go wrong." Or "She's going to hurt me." Or, "I've had a couple of bad love affairs, so therefore . . ." Well, that's nonsense. You're going to miss life. You've got to jump off the cliff all the time and build your wings on the way down."— Ray Bradbury

194. "If we have no peace, it is because we have forgotten that we belong to each other."— Mother Teresa

195. "If you don't go after what you want, you'll never have it. If you don't ask, the answer is always no. If you don't step forward, you're always in the same place."— Nora Roberts

196. "Have courage for the great sorrows of life and patience for the small ones; and when you have laboriously accomplished your daily task, go to sleep in peace. God is awake."— Victor Hugo

197. "Only people who are capable of loving strongly can also suffer great sorrow, but this same necessity of loving serves to counteract their grief and heals them."— Leo Tolstoy

198. "Life sucks, and then you die..."— Stephenie Meyer, Breaking Dawn

199. "It's not what you look at that matters, it's what you see."— Henry David Thoreau

200. "I like living. I have sometimes been wildly, despairingly, acutely miserable, racked with sorrow; but through it all I still know quite certainly that just to be alive is a grand thing."— Agatha Christie

201. "Above all else, guard your heart for it affects everything else you do."— Anonymous, Holy Bible: New International Version

202. "We don't make mistakes, just happy little accidents."— Bob Ross

203. "Any book that helps a child to form a habit of reading, to make reading one of his deep and continuing needs, is good for him."— Maya Angelou

204. "Well, we all make mistakes, dear, so just put it behind you. We should regret our mistakes and learn from them, but never carry them forward into the future with us."— L.M. Montgomery, Anne of Avonlea

205. "A Penny Saved is a Penny Earned"— Benjamin Franklin

206. "He that can have patience can have what he will."— Benjamin Franklin

207. "Dumbledore will only leave from Hogwarts when there are none loyal to him!"— J.K. Rowling, Harry Potter and the Half-Blood Prince

208. "Don't let the bastards grind you down."— Margaret Atwood, The Handmaid's Tale

209. "There's more to life than dating the boy on the football team."— Taylor Swift

210. "It does not matter how slowly you go as long as you do not stop."— Confucius

211. "The love that moves the sun and the other stars."— Elizabeth Gilbert

212. "You see things; you say, 'Why?' But I dream things that never were; and I say 'Why not?'"— George Bernard Shaw, Back to Methuselah

213. "We're all seeking that special person who is right for us. But if you've been through enough relationships, you begin to suspect there's no right person, just different flavors of wrong. Why is this? Because you yourself are wrong in some way, and you seek out partners who are wrong in some complementary way. But it takes a lot of living to grow fully into your own wrongness. And it isn't until you finally run up against your deepest demons, your unsolvable problems—the ones that make you truly who you are—that we're ready to find a lifelong mate. Only then do you finally know what you're looking for. You're looking for the wrong person. But not just any wrong person: the right wrong person—someone you lovingly gaze upon and think, "This is the problem I want to have." I will find that special person who is wrong for me in just the right way. Let our scars fall in love."— Galway Kinnell

214. "Wanting to be someone else is a waste of the person you are."— Marilyn Monroe

215. "People say nothing is impossible, but I do nothing every day."— A.A. Milne, Winnie-the-Pooh

216. "The worst part of success is trying to find someone who is happy for you."— Bette Midler

217. "I figured something out. The future is unpredictable."— John Green, An Abundance of Katherines

218. "I wonder how many people don't get the one they want, but end up with the one they're supposed to be with."— Fannie Flagg, Fried Green Tomatoes at the Whistle Stop Cafe

219. "She seems so cool, so focused, so quiet, yet her eyes remain fixed upon the horizon. You think you know all there is to know about her immediately upon meeting her, but everything you think you know is wrong. Passion flows through her like a river of blood.She only looked away for a moment, and the mask slipped, and you fell. All your tomorrows start here."— Neil Gaiman, Fragile Things: short fictions and wonders

220. "If you want to be happy, be."— Leo Tolstoy

221. "It is easy in the world to live after the world's opinion; it is easy in solitude to live after our own; but the great man is he who in the midst of the crowd keeps with perfect sweetness the independence of solitude."— Ralph Waldo Emerson, The Complete Prose Works of Ralph Waldo Emerson

222. "A fight is going on inside me," said an old man to his son. "It is a terrible fight between two wolves. One wolf is evil. He is anger, envy, sorrow, regret, greed, arrogance, self-pity, guilt, resentment, inferiority, lies, false pride, superiority, and ego. The other wolf is good. he is joy, peace, love, hope, serenity, humility, kindness, benevolence, empathy, generosity, truth, compassion, and faith. The same fight is going on inside you."The son thought about it for a minute and then asked, "Which wolf will win?"The old man replied simply, "The one you feed."— Wendy Mass, Jeremy Fink and the Meaning of Life

223. "Because paper has more patience than people."— Anne Frank

224. "Death is not the greatest loss in life. The greatest loss is what dies inside while still alive. Never surrender."— Tupac Shakur

225. "I must be willing to give up what I am in order to become what I will be."— Albert Einstein

226. "The biggest adventure you can ever take is to live the life of your dreams."— Oprah Winfrey

227. "Only after disaster can we be resurrected. It's only after you've lost everything that you're free to do anything. Nothing is static, everything is evolving, everything is falling apart."— Chuck Palahniuk, Fight Club

228. "Aim higher in case you fall short."— Suzanne Collins, Catching Fire

229. "Scar tissue is stronger than regular tissue. Realize the strength, move on."— Henry Rollins

230. "It is always the false that makes you suffer, the false desires and fears, the false values and ideas, the false relationships between people. Abandon the false and you are free of pain; truth makes happy, truth liberates."— Sri Nisargadatta Maharaj

231. "For like a shaft, clear and cold, the thought pierced him that in the end the Shadow was only a small and passing thing: there was light and high beauty forever beyond its reach."— J.R.R. Tolkien, The Return of the King

232. "Any emotion, if it is sincere, is involuntary."— Mark Twain

233. "Nothing great was ever achieved without enthusiasm."— Ralph Waldo Emerson

234. "What's the world's greatest lie? It's this: that at a certain point in our lives, we lose control of what's happening to us, and our lives become controlled by fate."— Paulo Coelho

235. "Those who bring sunshine to the lives of others cannot keep it from themselves."— J.M. Barrie

236. "With all its sham, drudgery, and broken dreams,it is still a beautiful world. Be cheerful. Strive to be happy.""For I am an optimist - it does not seem to be much use to be anything else."— Winston Churchill

237. "But life is a battle: may we all be enabled to fight it well!"— Charlotte Brontë, The Letters of Charlotte Brontë

238. "Let us rise up and be thankful, for if we didn't learn a lot at least we learned a little, and if we didn't learn a little, at least we didn't get sick, and if we got sick, at least we didn't die; so, let us all be thankful."— Gautama Buddha

239. "Whether you live to be 50 or 100 makes no difference, if you made no difference in the world."— Jarod Kintz, Great Listener Series Mute Women

240. "Remember, if you ever need a helping hand, it's at the end of your arm, as you get older, remember you have another hand: The first is to help yourself, the second is to help others."— Sam Levenson

241. "It isn't what you have or who you are or where you are or what you are doing that makes you happy or unhappy. It is what you think about it."— Dale Carnegie, How to Win Friends and Influence People

242. "You can talk with someone for years, every day, and still, it won't mean as much as what you can have when you sit in front of someone, not saying a word, yet you feel that person with your heart, you feel like you have known the person for forever.... connections are made with the heart, not the tongue."— C. JoyBell C.

243. "please believe that things are good with me, and even when they're not, they will be soon enough. And I will always believe the same about you."— Stephen Chbosky, The Perks of Being a Wallflower

244. "Dance, when you're broken open. Dance, if you've torn the bandage off. Dance in the middle of the fighting. Dance in your blood. Dance when you're perfectly free."— Rumi

245. "Never be bullied into silence. Never allow yourself to be made a victim. Accept no one's definition of your life, but define yourself."— Harvey Fierstein

246. "Parents can only give good advice or put them on the right paths, but the final forming of a person's character lies in their own hands."— Anne Frank

247. "The mouth is made for communication, and nothing is more articulate than a kiss."— Jarod Kintz, It Occurred to Me

248. "The purpose of life is to live it, to taste experience to the utmost, to reach out eagerly and without fear for newer and richer experience."— Eleanor Roosevelt

249. "The brick walls are there for a reason. The brick walls are not there to keep us out. The brick walls are there to give us a chance to show how badly we want something. Because the brick walls are there to stop the people who don't want it

badly enough. They're there to stop the other people."— Randy Pausch, The Last Lecture

250. "No matter how plain a woman may be, if truth and honesty are written across her face, she will be beautiful."— Eleanor Roosevelt

251. "All thinking men are atheists."— Ernest Hemingway, A Farewell to Arms

252. "Two roads diverged in a wood, and I took the one less traveled by, And that has made all the difference."— Robert Frost

253. "The desire to reach for the stars is ambitious. The desire to reach hearts is wise."— Maya Angelou

254. "The damage was permanent; there would always be scars. But even the angriest scars faded over time until it was difficult to see them written on the skin at all, and the only thing that remained was the memory of how painful it had been."— Jodi Picoult

255. "Dear God," she prayed, "let me be something every minute of every hour of my life. Let me be gay; let me be sad. Let me be cold; let me be warm. Let me be hungry...have too much to eat. Let me be ragged or well dressed. Let me be sincere - be deceitful. Let me be truthful; let me be a liar. Let me be honorable and let me sin. Only let me be something every blessed minute. And when I sleep, let me dream all the time so that not one little piece of living is ever lost."— Betty Smith, A Tree Grows in Brooklyn

256. "In the end you should always do the right thing even if it's hard."— Nicholas Sparks, The Last Song

257. "When I let go of what I am, I become what I might be."— Lao Tzu

258. "There is no good and evil, there is only power and those too weak to seek it."— J.K. Rowling, Harry Potter and the Sorcerer's Stone

259. "Do not seek the because - in love there is no because, no reason, no explanation, no solutions."— Anaïs Nin, Henry And June

260. "May the forces of evil become confused on the way to your house?"— George Carlin

261. "I'd rather learn from one bird how to singthan teach ten thousand stars how not to dance"— E.E. Cummings

262. "Music melts all the separate parts of our bodies together."— Anaïs Nin

263. "Around here, however, we don't look backwards for very long. We keep moving forward, opening up new doors and doing new things, because we're curious...and curiosity keeps leading us down new paths."— Walt Disney Company

264. "Those who look for the bad in people will surely find it."— Abraham Lincoln

265. "I'd rather be a rising ape than a falling angel."— Terry Pratchett

266. "Dream as if you will live forever; Live as if you will die today."— James Dean

267. "I dreamed I spoke in another's language,I dreamed I lived in another's skin,I dreamed I was my own beloved,I dreamed I was a tiger's kin.
    I dreamed that Eden lived inside me,
    And when I breathed a garden came,
    I dreamed I knew all of Creation,
    I dreamed I knew the Creator's name.
    I dreamed--and this dream was the finest--
    That all I dreamed was real and true,And we would live in joy forever,You in me, and me in you."— Clive Barker, Days of Magic, Nights of War

268. "What you have to decide... is how you want your life to be. If your forever was ending tomorrow, would this be how you'd want to have spent it? Listen, the truth is, nothing is guaranteed. You know that more than anybody. So don't be afraid. Be alive."— Sarah Dessen, The Truth About Forever

269. "Life was meant to be lived, and curiosity must be kept alive. One must never, for whatever reason, turn his back on life."— Eleanor Roosevelt

270. "If I saw you hitchhiking, I'd smile and return your thumbs up, just for you doing such a great job of being a positive roadside influence."— Jarod Kintz

271. "To see a World in a Grain of SandAnd a Heaven in a Wild Flower,Hold Infinity in the palm of your handAnd Eternity in an hour."— William Blake, Auguries of Innocence

272. "The truth is, unless you let go, unless you forgive yourself, unless you forgive the situation, unless you realize that the situation is over, you cannot move forward."— Steve Maraboli, Unapologetically You: Reflections on Life and the Human Experience

273. "If you remember me, then I don't care if everyone else forgets."— Haruki Murakami, Kafka on the Shore

274. "Understanding is the first step to acceptance, and only with acceptance can there be recovery.""Love: a single word, a wispy thing, a word no bigger or longer than an edge. That's what it is: an edge; a razor. It draws up through the center of your life, cutting everything in two. Before and after. The rest of the world falls away on either side." — Lauren Oliver, Delirium

275. "Stepping onto a brand-new path is difficult, but not more difficult than remaining in a situation, which is not nurturing to the whole woman."— Maya Angelou

276. "Every book, every volume you see here, has a soul. The soul of the person who wrote it and of those who read it and lived and dreamed with it. Every time a

book changes hands, every time someone runs his eyes down its pages, its spirit grows and strengthens."— Carlos Ruiz Zafón, The Shadow of the Wind

277. "I don't think of all the misery, but of the beauty that still remains."— Anne Frank, The Diary of a Young Girl

278. "Imagination is everything. It is the preview of life's coming attractions."— Albert Einstein

279. "We're so self-important. So arrogant. Everybody's going to save something now. Save the trees, save the bees, save the whales, save the snails. And the supreme arrogance? Save the planet! Are these people kidding? Save the planet? We don't even know how to take care of ourselves; we haven't learned how to care for one another. We're gonna save the fuckin' planet? . . . And, by the way, there's nothing wrong with the planet in the first place. The planet is fine. The people are fucked! Compared with the people, the planet is doing' great. It's been here over four billion years . . . The planet isn't going' anywhere, folks. We are! We're going' away. Pack your shit, we're going' away. And we won't leave much of a trace. Thank God for that. Nothing left. Maybe a little Styrofoam. The planet will be here, and we'll be gone. Another failed mutation; another closed-end biological mistake."— George Carlin

280. "Never look back unless you are planning to go that way."— Henry David Thoreau

281. "I must be a mermaid, Rango. I have no fear of depths and a great fear of shallow living."— Anaïs Nin

282. "Earth provides enough to satisfy every man's needs, but not every man's greed."— Mahatma Gandhi

283. "any fool can be happy. It takes a man with real heart to make beauty out of the stuff that makes us weep."— Clive Barker, Days of Magic, Nights of War

284. "Write it on your heart that every day is the best day in the year."— Ralph Waldo Emerson

285. "Wanting to be someone else is a waste of who you are"— Kurt Cobain

286. "I am not a teacher, but an awakener."— Robert Frost

287. "Men are from Earth, women are from Earth. Deal with it."— George Carlin

288. "God allows us to experience the low points of life in order to teach us lessons that we could learn in no other way."— C.S. Lewis

289. "The reason birds can fly and we can't is simply because they have perfect faith, for to have faith is to have wings."— J.M. Barrie, The Little White Bird

290. "Don't be afraid of enemies who attack you. Be afraid of the friends who flatter you."— Dale Carnegie, How to Win Friends and Influence People

291. "Because,' she said, 'when you're scared but you still do it anyway, that's brave."— Neil Gaiman, Coraline

292. "Oh the places you'll go! There is fun to be done! There are points to be scored. There are games to be won. And the magical things you can do with that ball will make you the winning-est winner of all."— Dr. Seuss, Oh, The Places You'll Go! Yellow Back Book

293. "If a man is called to be a street sweeper, he should sweep streets even as a Michelangelo painted, or Beethoven composed music or Shakespeare wrote poetry. He should sweep streets so well that all the hosts of heaven and earth will pause to say, 'Here lived a great street sweeper who did his job well."— Martin Luther King Jr.

294. "What would come, would come...and you would have to meet it, when it did."— J.K. Rowling, Harry Potter and the Goblet of Fire

295. "There are two ways to reach me: by way of kisses or by way of the imagination. But there is a hierarchy: the kisses alone don't work."— Anaïs Nin, Henry And June

296. "Getting something and having the wits to use it...those are two different things."— Rick Riordan, The Battle of the Labyrinth

297. "Government exists to protect us from each other. Where government has gone beyond its limits is in deciding to protect us from ourselves."— Ronald Reagan

298. "Being brave is when you have to do something because you know it is right, but at the same time, you are afraid to do it, because it might hurt or whatever. But you do it anyway."— Meg Cabot, All-American Girl

299. "I trust that everything happens for a reason, even if we are not wise enough to see it."— Oprah Winfrey

300. "When things break, it's not the actual breaking that prevents them from getting back together again. It's because a little piece gets lost - the two remaining ends couldn't fit together even if they wanted to. The whole shape has changed."— John Green, Will Grayson, Will Grayson

301. "Courage isn't having the strength to go on - it is going on when you don't have strength."— Napoleon Bonaparte

302. "Even strength must bow to wisdom sometimes."— Rick Riordan, The Lightning Thief

303. "Death is no more than passing from one room into another. But there's a difference for me, you know. Because in that other room I shall be able to see."— Helen Keller

304. "No one really knows why they are alive until they know what they'd die for."— Martin Luther King Jr.

305. "Every day, think as you wake up, today I am fortunate to be alive, I have a precious human life, I am not going to waste it. I am going to use all my energies to develop myself, to expand my heart out to others; to achieve enlightenment for the benefit of all beings. I am going to have kind thoughts towards others, I am not going to get angry or think badly about others. I am going to benefit others as much as I can."― Dalai Lama XIV

306. "I was suffering the easily foreseeable consequences. Addiction is the hallmark of every infatuation-based love story. It all begins when the object of your adoration bestows upon you a heady, hallucinogenic dose of something you never dared to admit you wanted-an emotional speedball, perhaps, of thunderous love and roiling excitement. Soon you start craving that intense attention, with a hungry obsession of any junkie. When the drug is withheld, you promptly turn sick, crazy, and depleted (not to mention resentful of the dealer who encouraged this addiction in the first place but now refuses to pony up the good stuff anymore-- despite the fact that you know he has it hidden somewhere, goddamn it, because he used to give it to you for free). Next stage finds you skinny and shaking in a corner, certain only that you would sell your soul or rob your neighbors just to have 'that thing' even one more time. Meanwhile, the object of your adoration has now become repulsed by you. He looks at you like you're someone he's never met before, much less someone he once loved with high passion. The irony is, you can hardly blame him. I mean, check yourself out. You're a pathetic mess, unrecognizable even to your own eyes. So that's it. You have now reached infatuation's final destination-- the complete and merciless devaluation of self." - pg. 20-21"― Elizabeth Gilbert

307. "Believe you can and you're halfway there."― Theodore Roosevelt

308. "What are you going to do with your life?" In one way or another it seemed that people had been asking her this forever; teachers, her parents, friends at three in the morning, but the question had never seemed this pressing and still she was no nearer an answer... "Live each day as if it's your last', that was the conventional advice, but really, who had the energy for that? What if it rained or you felt a bit glandy? It just wasn't practical. Better by far to be good and courageous and bold and to make difference. Not change the world exactly, but the bit around you. Cherish your friends, stay true to your principles, live passionately and fully and well. Experience new things. Love and be loved, if you ever get the chance."― David Nicholls, One Day

309. "What makes the desert beautiful,' said the little prince, 'is that somewhere it hides a well...'"― Antoine de Saint-Exupéry, The Little Prince

310. "Without fear there cannot be courage."― Christopher Paolini

311. "Make the most of yourself....for that is all there is of you."― Ralph Waldo Emerson

312. "I never said it would be easy, I only said it would be worth it."― Mae West

313. "A mathematical formula for happiness: Reality divided by Expectations. There were two ways to be happy: improve your reality or lower your expectations."— Jodi Picoult, Nineteen Minutes

314. "We meet no ordinary people in our lives."— C.S. Lewis

315. "Be more concerned with your character than your reputation, because your character is what you really are, while your reputation is merely what others think you are."— John Wooden

316. "My father had taught me to be nice first, because you can always be mean later, but once you've been mean to someone, they won't believe the nice anymore. So be nice, be nice, until it's time to stop being nice, then destroy them."— Laurell K. Hamilton, A Stroke of Midnight

317. "And out of that hopeless attempt has come nearly all that we call human history—money, poverty, ambition, war, prostitution, classes, empires, slavery— the long terrible story of man trying to find something other than God which will make him happy."— C.S. Lewis, Mere Christianity

318. "A dream is a wish your heart makes, when you're fast asleep."— Walt Disney Company, Walt Disney's Cinderella

319. "It is by no means an irrational fancy that, in a future existence, we shall look upon what we think our present existence, as a dream."— Edgar Allan Poe

320. "No life is a waste," the Blue Man said. "The only time we waste is the time we spend thinking we're alone."— Mitch Albom

321. "If you don't have any shadows you're not in the light"— Lady Gaga

322. "All The Woulda-Coulda-Shouldas
    Layin' In The Sun,
    Talkin' 'Bout The Things
    They Woulda-Coulda-Shoulda Done...
    But All Those Woulda-Coulda-Shouldas
    All Ran Away And Hid
    From One Little Did."— Shel Silverstein

323. "You are, after all, what you think. Your emotions are the slaves to your thoughts, and you are the slave to your emotions."— Elizabeth Gilbert, Eat, Pray, Love

324. "To the world you may be one person but to one person you may be the world."— Bill Wilson

325. "My task, which I am trying to achieve, is, by the power of the written word, to make you hear, to make you feel--it is, before all, to make you see."— Joseph Conrad, Lord Jim

326. "You save yourself or you remain unsaved."— Alice Sebold

327. "Words can never fully say what we want them to say, for they fumble, stammer, and break the best porcelain. The best one can hope for is to find along the way someone to share the path, content to walk in silence, for the heart communes best when it does not try to speak."— Margaret Weis, Dragons of a Lost Star

328. "You need to find a way to live your life, that it doesn't make a mockery of your values."— Bill Ayers

329. "Never let your sense of morals prevent you from doing what is right."— Isaac Asimov, Foundation

330. "If people refuse to look at you in a new light and they can only see you for what you were, only see you for the mistakes you've made, if they don't realize that you are not your mistakes, then they have to go."— Steve Maraboli, Life, the Truth, and Being Free

331. "I want to be in a relationship where you telling me you love me is just a ceremonious validation of what you already show me."— Steve Maraboli, Life, the Truth, and Being Free

332. "I've been fighting to be who I am all my life. What's the point of being who I am, if I can't have the person who was worth all the fighting for?"— Stephanie Lennox, I Don't Remember You

333. "If you win, you need not have to explain...If you lose, you should not be there to explain!"— Adolf Hitler

334. "You'll never find a rainbow if you're looking down"— Charles Chaplin

335. "I like nonsense; it wakes up the brain cells. Fantasy is a necessary ingredient in living; it's a way of looking at life through the wrong end of a telescope. Which is what I do, And that enables you to laugh at life's realities."— Dr. Seuss

336. "Atticus, he was real nice."
"Most people are, Scout, when you finally see them."— Harper Lee, To Kill a Mockingbird

337. "Many of life's failures are people who did not realize how close they were to success when they gave up."— Thomas A. Edison

338. "Excellence is never an accident. It is always the result of high intention, sincere effort, and intelligent execution; it represents the wise choice of many alternatives - choice, not chance, determines your destiny."— Aristotle

339. "Don't think. Thinking is the enemy of creativity. It's self-conscious and anything self-conscious is lousy. You can't "try" to do things. You simply "must" do things."— Ray Bradbury

340. "I know that pain is the most important thing in the universes. Greater than survival, greater than love, greater even than the beauty it brings about. For without pain, there can be no pleasure. Without sadness, there can be no

happiness. Without misery there can be no beauty. And without these, life is endless, hopeless, doomed and damned.Adult. You have become adult."— Harlan Ellison, Paingod and Other Delusions

341. "Never dull your shine for somebody else."— Tyra Banks

342. "Wherever you go, go with all your heart."— Confucius

343. "I have a dream that one day little black boys and girls will be holding hands with little white boys and girls."— Martin Luther King Jr., I Have A Dream

344. "I heard a definition once: Happiness is health and a short memory! I wish I'd invented it, because it is very true."— Audrey Hepburn

345. "No! Try not. Do, or do not. There is no try."— George Lucas, Star Wars Trilogy

346. "All I can be is me- whoever that is."— Bob Dylan

347. "Though the road's been rocky it sure feels good to me."— Bob Marley

348. "After all," Anne had said to Marilla once, "I believe the nicest and sweetest days are not those on which anything very splendid or wonderful or exciting happens but just those that bring simple little pleasures, following one another softly, like pearls slipping off a string."— L.M. Montgomery, Anne of Avonlea

349. "Any intelligent fool can make things bigger, more complex, and more violent. It takes a touch of genius — and a lot of courage to move in the opposite direction."— E.F. Schumacher

350. "A hero is no braver than an ordinary man, but he is brave five minutes longer."— Ralph Waldo Emerson

351. "Do not worry about your difficulties in Mathematics. I can assure you mine are still greater."— Albert Einstein

352. "Weekends don't count unless you spend them doing something completely pointless."— Bill Watterson

353. "Wasn't that the point of the book? For women to realize, We are just two people. Not that much separates us. Not nearly as much as I'd thought."— Kathryn Stockett, The Help

354. "See, as much as you want to hold on to the bitter sore memory that someone has left this world, you are still in it"— Jodi Picoult, My Sister's Keeper

355. "I know because I read...Your mind is not a cage. It's a garden. And it requires cultivating."— Libba Bray

356. "What does it mean to be the best? It means you have to be better than the number two guy. But what gratification is there in that? He's a loser—that's why he's number two."— Jarod Kintz, This Book is Not for Sale

357. "If we ever forget that we're one nation under God, then we will be one nation gone under."— Ronald Reagan

358. "The minute I stopped trying to find the right girl, and started trying to become the right guy...the girl came."— Jonathan Antin

359. "Dare to Be
When a new day begins, dare to smile gratefully.
When there is darkness, dare to be the first to shine a light.
When there is injustice, dare to be the first to condemn it.
When something seems difficult, dare to do it anyway.
When life seems to beat you down, dare to fight back.
When there seems to be no hope, dare to find some.
When you're feeling tired, dare to keep going.
When times are tough, dare to be tougher.
When love hurts you, dare to love again.
When someone is hurting, dare to help them heal.
When another is lost, dare to help them find the way.
When a friend falls, dare to be the first to extend a hand.
When you cross paths with another, dare to make them smile.
When you feel great, dare to help someone else feels great too.
When the day has ended, dare to feel as you've done your best.
Dare to be the best you can –
At all times, Dare to be!"— Steve Maraboli, Life, the Truth, and Being Free

360. "If you want to forget something or someone, never hate it, or never hate him/her. Everything and everyone that you hate is engraved upon your heart; if you want to let go of something, if you want to forget, you cannot hate."— C. JoyBell C.

361. "Keep your thoughts positive because your thoughts become your words. Keep your words positive because your words become your behavior. Keep your behavior positive because your behavior becomes your habits. Keep your habits positive because your habits become your values. Keep your values positive because your values become your destiny."— Mahatma Gandhi

362. "Just be yourself, there is no one better."— Taylor Swift

363. "Keep your face always toward the sunshine - and shadows will fall behind you."— Walt Whitman

364. "There is a candle in your heart, ready to be kindled.

365. There is a void in your soul, ready to be filled.

366. You feel it, don't you?"— Rumi

367. "Where there is ruin, there is hope for a treasure."— Rumi

368. "I shall look at you out of the corner of my eye, and you will say nothing. Words are the source of misunderstandings." -from the Fox-"— Antoine de Saint-Exupéry, The Little Prince

369. "People where you live," the little prince said, "grow five thousand roses in one garden... yet they don't find what they're looking for...

370. They don't find it," I answered.

371. And yet what they're looking for could be found in a single rose, or a little water..."

372. Of course," I answered.

373. And the little prince added, "But eyes are blind. You have to look with the heart."— Antoine de Saint-Exupéry, The Little Prince

374. "The great thing to remember is that though our feelings come and go God's love for us does not."— C.S. Lewis

375. "The higher we soar the smaller we appear to those who cannot fly."— Friedrich Nietzsche, Thus Spoke Zarathustra

376. "Always dream and shoot higher than you know you can do. Do not bother just to be better than your contemporaries or predecessors. Try to be better than yourself."— William Faulkner

377. "Responsibility to yourself means refusing to let others do your thinking, talking, and naming for you...it means that you do not treat your body as a commodity with which to purchase superficial intimacy or economic security; for our bodies to be treated as objects, our minds are in mortal danger. It means insisting that those to whom you give your friendship and love are able to respect your mind. It means being able to say, with Charlotte Bronte's Jane Eyre: "I have an inward treasure born with me, which can keep me alive if all the extraneous delights should be withheld or offered only at a price I cannot afford to give. Responsibility to yourself means that you don't fall for shallow and easy solutions--predigested books and ideas...marrying early as an escape from real decisions, getting pregnant as an evasion of already existing problems. It means that you refuse to sell your talents and aspirations short...and this, in turn, means resisting the forces in society which say that women should be nice, play safe, have low professional expectations, drown in love and forget about work, live through others, and stay in the places assigned to us. It means that we insist on a life of meaningful work, insist that work be as meaningful as love and friendship in our lives. It means, therefore, the courage to be "different"...The difference between a life lived actively, and a life of passive drifting and dispersal of energies, is an immense difference. Once we begin to feel committed to our lives, responsible to ourselves, we can never again be satisfied with the old, passive way."— Adrienne Rich

378. "People who say it cannot be done should not interrupt those who are doing it."— George Bernard Shaw

379. "Do not go gentle into that good night,Old age should burn and rave at close of day;Rage, rage against the dying of the light."— Dylan Thomas, Do Not Go Gentle Into That Good Night

380. "No matter who you are, no matter what you did, no matter where you've come from, you can always change, become a better version of yourself."— Madonna

381. "Remember that everyone you meet is afraid of something, loves something and has lost something."— H. Jackson Brown Jr.

382. "Certain thoughts are prayers. There are moments when, whatever be the attitude of the body, the soul is on its knees."— Victor Hugo

383. "We are like sculptors, constantly carving out of others the image we long for, need, love or desire, often against reality, against their benefit, and always, in the end, a disappointment, because it does not fit them."— Anaïs Nin

384. "Whatever comes," she said, "cannot alter one thing. If I am a princess in rags and tatters, I can be a princess inside. It would be easy to be a princess if I were dressed in cloth of gold, but it is a great deal more of a triumph to be one all the time when no one knows it."— Frances Hodgson Burnett, A Little Princess

385. "You buy furniture. You tell yourself, this is the last sofa I will ever need in my life. Buy the sofa, then for a couple years you're satisfied that no matter what goes wrong, at least you've got your sofa issue handled. Then the right set of dishes. Then the perfect bed. The drapes. The rug. Then you're trapped in your lovely nest, and the things you used to own, now they own you."— Chuck Palahniuk, Fight Club

386. "Live today. Not yesterday. Not tomorrow. Just today. Inhabit your moments. Don't rent them out to tomorrow. Do you know what you're doing when you spend a moment wondering how things are going to turn out with Perry?

387. You're cheating yourself out of today. Today is calling to you, trying to get your attention, but you're stuck on tomorrow, and today trickles away like water down a drain. You wake up the next morning and that today you wasted is gone forever. It's now yesterday. Some of those moments may have had wonderful things in store for you, but now you'll never know."— Jerry Spinelli, Love, Stargirl

388. "There are two kinds of teachers: the kind that fills you with so much quail shot that you can't move, and the kind that just gives you a little prod behind and you jump to the skies."— Robert Frost

389. "Art is the proper task of life."— Friedrich Nietzsche

390. "I've been lucky. Opportunities don't often come along. So, when they do, you have to grab them."— Audrey Hepburn

391. "Surround yourself only with people who are going to take you higher."— Oprah Winfrey

392. "Do your own thing on your own terms and get what you came here for"— Oliver James

393. "Friendship with oneself is all important, because without it one cannot be friends with anyone else in the world."— Eleanor Roosevelt

394. "The only position that leaves me with no cognitive dissonance is atheism. It is not a creed. Death is certain, replacing both the siren-song of Paradise and the dread of Hell. Life on this earth, with all its mystery and beauty and pain, is then to be lived far more intensely: we stumble and get up, we are sad, confident, insecure, feel loneliness and joy and love. There is nothing more; but I want nothing more."— Ayaan Hirsi Ali, Infidel

395. "Hearts are breakable," Isabelle said. "And I think even when you heal, you're never what you were before"."— Cassandra Clare, City of Fallen Angels

396. "Just because you fall once, doesn't mean you're fall at everything. Keep trying, hold on, and always trust yourself, because if you don't then who will??"— Marilyn Monroe

397. "Go placidly amid the noise and the haste, and remember what peace there may be in silence. As far as possible without surrender, be on good terms with all persons. Speak your truth quietly and clearly, and listen to others, even the dull and ignorant; they too have their story. Be yourself. Especially do not feign affection. Neither be cynical about love – for in the face of all aridity and disenchantment is it perennial as the grass. Take kindly the counsel of the years, gracefully surrendering the things of youth. Nurture strength of spirit to shield you from misfortune. But do not distress yourself with imaginings. Many fears are born of fatigue and loneliness. Beyond a wholesome discipline, be gentle with yourself. You are a child of the universe no less than the trees and the stars; you have a right to be here. And whether or not it is clear to you, no doubt the universe is unfolding as it should. Therefore be at peace with God, whatever you conceive Him to be, and whatever your labors and aspirations, in the noisy confusion of life keep peace with your soul. With all its sham, drudgery and broken dreams, it is still a beautiful world."— Max Ehrmann, Desiderata: A Poem for a Way of Life

398. "I thank you God for this most amazing day, for the leaping greenly spirits of trees, and for the blue dream of sky and for everything which is natural, which is infinite, which is yes."— E.E. Cummings

399. "Once we accept our limits, we go beyond them."— Albert Einstein

400. "We either make ourselves miserable, or we make ourselves strong. The amount of work is the same."— Carlos Castaneda

401. "I said to my soul, be still and wait without hope, for hope would be hope for the wrong thing; wait without love, for love would be love of the wrong thing; there is yet faith, but the faith and the love are all in the waiting. Wait without thought, for you are not ready for thought: So the darkness shall be the light, and the stillness the dancing."— T.S. Eliot

402. "I have a dream that my four little children will one day live in a nation where they will not be judged by the color of their skin but by the content of their character."— Martin Luther King Jr.

403. "Man cannot discover new oceans unless he has the courage to lose sight of the shore."— André Gide

404. "A man with outward courage dares to die; a man with inner courage dares to live."— Lao Tzu, Tao Te Ching

405. "If you do follow your bliss you put yourself on a kind of track that has been there all the while, waiting for you, and the life that you ought to be living is the one you are living. Follow your bliss and don't be afraid, and doors will open where you didn't know they were going to be."— Joseph Campbell

406. "I sustain myself with the love of family."— Maya Angelou

407. "The easiest thing to be in the world is you. The most difficult thing to be is what other people want you to be. Don't let them put you in that position."— Leo Buscaglia

408. "Not knowing you can't do something, is sometimes all it takes to do it."— Ally Carter

409. "But remember, boy, that a kind act can sometimes be as powerful as a sword."— Rick Riordan, The Battle of the Labyrinth

410. "The rights of every man are diminished when the rights of one man are threatened."— John F. Kennedy

411. "Get up, stand up, Stand up for your rights. Get up, stand up, Don't give up the fight."— Bob Marley, Bob Marley - Legend

412. "Life is a process of becoming, a combination of states we have to go through. Where people fail is that they wish to elect a state and remain in it. This is a kind of death."— Anaïs Nin

413. "It's not about how to achieve your dreams, it's about how to lead your life, ... If you lead your life the right way, the karma will take care of itself, the dreams will come to you."— Randy Pausch, The Last Lecture

414. "When I was growing up I always wanted to be someone. Now I realize I should have been more specific."— Lily Tomlin

415. "Where your treasure is, there will your heart be also."— Anonymous, Holy Bible: King James Version

416. "Every great dream begins with a dreamer. Always remember, you have within you the strength, the patience, and the passion to reach for the stars to change the world."— Harriet Tubman

417. "Down on the lake rosy reflections of celestial vapor appeared, and I said, "God, I love you" and looked to the sky and really meant it."I have fallen in love with you, God. Take care of us all, one way or the other." To the children and the innocent it's all the same."— Jack Kerouac, The Dharma Bums

418. "The way I see it, if you want the rainbow, you gotta put up with the rain!"— Dolly Parton

419. "So tonight I reach for my journal again. This is the first time I've done this since I came to Italy. What I write in my journal is that I am weak and full of fear. I explain that Depression and Loneliness have shown up, and I'm scared they will never leave. I say that I don't want to take the drugs anymore, but I'm frightened I will have to. I am terrified that I will never really pull my life together.In response, somewhere from within me, raises a now-familiar presence, offering me all the certainties I have always wished another person would say to me when I was troubled. This is what I find myself writing on the page:I'm here. I love you. I don't care if you need to stay up crying all night long. I will stay with you. If you need the medication again, go ahead and take it—I will love you through that, as well. If you don't need the medication, I will love you, too. There's nothing you can ever do to lose my love. I will protect you until you die, and after your death I will still protect you. I am stronger than Depression and Braver than Loneliness and nothing will ever exhaust me.Tonight, this strange interior gesture of friendship— the lending of a hand from me to myself when nobody else is around to offer solace—reminds me of something that happened to me once in New York City. I walked into an office building one afternoon in a hurry, dashed into the waiting elevator. As I rushed in, I caught an unexpected glance of myself in a security mirror's reflection. In that moment, my brain did an odd thing—it fired off this split-second message: "Hey! You know her! That's a friend of yours!" And I actually ran forward toward my own reflection with a smile, ready to welcome that girl whose name I had lost but whose face was so familiar. In a flash instant of course, I realized my mistake and laughed in embarrassment at my almost doglike confusion over how a mirror works. But for some reason that incident comes to mind again tonight during my sadness in Rome, and I find myself writing this comforting reminder at the bottom of the page.Never forget that once upon a time, in an unguarded moment, you recognized yourself as a FRIEND... I fell asleep holding my notebook pressed against my chest, open to this most recent assurance. In the morning when I wake up, I can still smell a faint trace of depression's lingering smoke, but he himself is nowhere to be seen. Somewhere during the night, he got up and left. And his buddy loneliness beat it, too."— Elizabeth Gilbert

420. "To live is so startling it leaves little time for anything else."— Emily Dickinson

421. "The place to improve the world is first in one's own heart and head and hands, and then work outward from there."— Robert M. Pirsig, Zen and the Art of Motorcycle Maintenance: An Inquiry Into Values

422. "Step follows step,Hope follows Courage,Set your face towards danger,Set your heart on victory."— Gail Carson Levine, The Two Princesses of Bamarre

423. "We are afraid of losing what we have, whether it's our life or our possessions and property. But this fear evaporates when we understand that our life stories and the history of the world were written by the same hand."— Paulo Coelho

424. "Don't be afraid of your fears. They're not there to scare you. They're there to let you know that something is worth it."— C. JoyBell C.

425. "Shoot for the moon, even if you fail, you'll land among the stars"— Cecelia Ahern, P.S. I Love You

426. "We must live together as brothers or perish together as fools."— Martin Luther King Jr.

427. "Don't ever take a fence down until you know why it was put up."— Robert Frost

428. "People don't realize how a man's whole life can be changed by one book."— Malcolm X

429. "There is a way to be good again..."— Khaled Hosseini, The Kite Runner

430. "If a problem is fixable, if a situation is such that you can do something about it, then there is no need to worry. If it's not fixable, then there is no help in worrying. There is no benefit in worrying whatsoever."— Dalai Lama XIV

431. "The power of finding beauty in the humblest things makes home happy and life lovely."— Louisa May Alcott

432. "In the long run, the sharpest weapon of all is a kind and gentle spirit."— Anne Frank, The Diary of Anne Frank

433. "I'll think of it tomorrow, at Tara. I can stand it then. Tomorrow, I'll think of some way to get him back. After all, tomorrow is another day."— Margaret Mitchell, Gone with the Wind

434. "Write it. Shoot it. Publish it. Crochet it, sauté it, whatever. MAKE."— Joss Whedon

435. "Bitch (noun): A woman who won't bang her head against the wall obsessing over someone else's opinion - be it a man or anyone else in her life. She understands that if someone does not approve of her, it's just one person's opinion; therefore, it's of no real importance. She doesn't try to live up to anyone else's standards - only her own. Because of this, she relates to a man very differently."— Sherry Argov, Why Men Love Bitches: From Doormat to Dreamgirl - A Woman's Guide to Holding Her Own in a Relationship

436. "the time is always right to do the right thing"— Martin Luther King Jr.

437. "Believe nothing, no matter where you read it, or who said it, no matter if I have said it, unless it agrees with your own reason and your own common sense."— Gautama Buddha

438. "Well done is better than well said."— Benjamin Franklin

439. "It is the possibility that keeps me going, and though you may call me a dreamer or a fool or any other thing, I believe that anything is possible."— Nicholas Sparks

440. "Of all creatures that breathe and move upon the earth, nothing is bred that is weaker than man."— Homer, The Odyssey

441. "I postpone death by living, by suffering, by error, by risking, by giving, by losing."— Anaïs Nin

442. "A Woman in harmony with her spirit is like a river flowing. She goes where she will without pretense and arrives at her destination prepared to be herself and only herself"— Maya Angelou

443. "The Reality of The Other Person Lies Not In What He Reveals To You, But What He Cannot Reveal To You.

444. Therefore, If You Would Understand Him, Listen Not To What He Says, But Rather To What He Does Not Say."— Kahlil Gibran

445. "I am always doing that which I cannot do, in order that I may learn how to do it."— Pablo Picasso

446. "Sometimes you can see things happen right in front of your eyes and still jump to the wrong conclusions."— Jodi Picoult, Keeping Faith

447. "I want to thank you, Lord, for life and all that's in it.Thank you for the day and for the hour, and the minute. "— Maya Angelou

448. "We are all worms, But I do believe that I am a glow worm."— Winston Churchill, Never Give In! The Best of Winston Churchill's Speeches

449. "I long to accomplish a great and noble task, but it is my chief duty to accomplish small tasks as if they were great and noble."— Helen Keller

450. "No one can go back and make a brand new start, my friend, but anyone can start from here and make a brand new end."— Dan Zadra

451. "Grace is the face that love wears when it meets imperfection."— Joseph R. Cooke

452. "The further you go, the more you have to be proud of. At the same time, in order to come a long way, you have to be behind to begin with. IN the end, though maybe it's not how you reach a place that matters. Just that you get there at all."— Sarah Dessen, Lock and Key

453. "Tears are words that need to be written."— Paulo Coelho

454. "Incredible change happens in your life when you decide to take control of what you do have power over instead of craving control over what you don't."— Steve Maraboli, Life, the Truth, and Being Free

455. "There is the great lesson of 'Beauty and the Beast,' that a thing must be loved before it is lovable."— G.K. Chesterton

456. "Bottom line is, even if you see 'em coming, you're not ready for the big moments. No one asks for their life to change, not really. But it does. So what are we, helpless? Puppets? No. The big moments are gonna come. You can't help that. It's what you do afterwards that counts. That's when you find out who you are."— Joss Whedon

457. "Do not stop thinking of life as an adventure. You have no security unless you can live bravely, excitingly, imaginatively; unless you can choose a challenge instead of competence."— Eleanor Roosevelt, The Autobiography of Eleanor Roosevelt

458. "Equality is not a concept. It's not something we should be striving for. It's a necessity. Equality is like gravity. We need it to stand on this earth as men and women, and the misogyny that is in every culture is not a true part of the human condition. It is life out of balance, and that imbalance is sucking something out of the soul of every man and woman who's confronted with it. We need equality. Kinda now."— Joss Whedon

459. "We come spinning out of nothingness, scattering stars like dust."— Rumi

460. "I'm not saying I'm gonna change the world, but I guarantee that I will spark the brain that will change the world."— Tupac Shakur

461. "When each day is the same as the next, it's because people fail to recognize the good things that happen in their lives every day that the sun rises."— Paulo Coelho, The Alchemist

462. "We are products of our past, but we don't have to be prisoners of it."— Rick Warren, The Purpose Driven Life: What on Earth Am I Here for?

463. "Nothing is permanent in this wicked world, not even our troubles."— Charles Chaplin

464. "Shallow men believe in luck or in circumstance. Strong men believe in cause and effect."— Ralph Waldo Emerson

465. "If you dare nothing, then when the day is over, nothing is all you will have gained."— Neil Gaiman, The Graveyard Book

466. "One life is all we have and we live it as we believe in living it. But to sacrifice what you are and to live without belief, that is a fate more terrible than dying."— Joan of Arc

467. "That which God said to the rose, and caused it to laugh in full-blown beauty, He said to my heart, and made it a hundred times more beautiful."— Rumi

468. "Heaven can be found in the most unlikely corners."— Mitch Albom, The Five People You Meet in Heaven - Meniti Bianglala

469. "For beauty is nothing but the beginning of terror which we are barely able to endure, and it amazes us so,because it serenely disdains to destroy us. Every angel is terrible."— Rainer Maria Rilke, Duino Elegies

470. "We are saved by faith alone, but the faith that saves is never alone."— Martin Luther

471. "Without leaps of imagination or dreaming, we lose the excitement of possibilities. Dreaming, after all is a form of planning."— Gloria Steinem

472. "Things die. But they don't always stay dead. Believe me, I know."— Richelle Mead, Frostbite

473. "Success is not the key to happiness. Happiness is the key to success. If you love what you are doing, you will be successful."— Albert Schweitzer

474. "Remake the world, a little at a time, each in your own corner of the world."— Rick Riordan

475. "Nothing will work unless you do."— Maya Angelou

476. "Yesterday is not ours to recover, but tomorrow is ours to win or lose."— Lyndon B. Johnson

477. "Are you on our side...and want to be different, or are you on that side and want to throw a football at my head!?"— Gerard Way

478. "Love yourself first and everything else falls into line. You really have to love yourself to get anything done in this world."— Lucille Ball

479. "Each person deserves a day away in which no problems are confronted, no solutions searched for."— Maya Angelou

480. "It is not the failure of others to appreciate your abilities that should trouble you, but rather your failure to appreciate theirs."— Confucius

481. "Rise to the occasion which is life!"— Virginia Euwer Wolff

482. "One Choice
One Choice, decided your friends.
One Choice, defines your beliefs.
One Choice, determines your loyalties - Forever.
ONE CHOICE CAN TRANSFORM YOU"— Veronica Roth, Divergent

483. "Be empty of worrying.
Think of who created thought!

Why do you stay in prison
When the door is so wide open?"— Rumi, The Essential Rumi

484. "In the end, you have to choose whether or not to trust someone."— Sophie Kinsella, Shopaholic & Baby

485. "We all need to be mocked from time to time, lest we take ourselves too seriously."— George R.R. Martin

486. "You're never given a dream without also being given the power to make it true."— Richard Bach, Illusions: The Adventures of a Reluctant Messiah

487. "The best discoveries always happened to the people who weren't looking for them."— Morgan Matson, Amy and Roger's Epic Detour

488. "A goal without a plan is just a wish."— Antoine de Saint-Exupéry

489. "Life moves on, whether we act as cowards or heroes. Life has no other discipline to impose, if we would but realize it, than to accept life unquestioningly. Everything we shut our eyes to, everything we run away from, everything we deny, denigrate or despise, serves to defeat us in the end. What seems nasty, painful, evil, can become a source of beauty, joy, and strength, if faced with an open mind. Every moment is a golden one for him who has the vision to recognize it as such"— Henry Miller

490. "I have come home at last! This is my real country! I belong here. This is the land I have been looking for all my life, though I never knew it till now...Come further up, come further in!"— C.S. Lewis, The Last Battle

491. "I offer you peace. I offer you love. I offer you friendship. I see your beauty. I hear your need. I feel your feelings."— Mahatma Gandhi

492. "If you´re lucky enough to be different from everyone else, don't change."— Taylor Swift

493. "If you once forfeit the confidence of your fellow citizens, you can never regain their respect and esteem. It is true that you may fool all of the people some of the time; you can even fool some of the people all of the time; but you can't fool all of the people all of the time. -Speech at Clinton, Illinois, September 8, 1854."— Abraham Lincoln

494. "Reality is wrong. Dreams are for the real."— Tupac Shakur

495. "It was like the beginning of life and laughter. It was the real meaning of the sun"— Charles Bukowski, Factotum

496. "I've missed more than 9000 shots in my career. I've lost almost 300 games. 26 times, I've been trusted to take the game winning shot and missed. I've failed over and over and over again in my life. And that is why I succeed."— Michael Jordan

497. "Your problem is how you are going to spend this one and precious life you have been issued. Whether you're going to spend it trying to look good and creating the illusion that you have power over circumstances, or whether you are going to taste it, enjoy it and find out the truth about who you are."— Anne Lamott

498. "If you enter this world knowing you are loved and you leave this world knowing the same, then everything that happens in between can be dealt with."— Michael Jackson

499. "Start by doing what is necessary, then what is possible, and suddenly you are doing the impossible."— St. Francis of Assisi

500. "You come of the Lord Adam and the Lady Eve," said Aslan. "And that is both honor enough to erect the head of the poorest beggar, and shame enough to bow the shoulders of the greatest emperor on earth. Be content."— C.S. Lewis, Prince Caspian

501. "Keep your eyes on the stars, and your feet on the ground."— Theodore Roosevelt

502. "He who would learn to fly one day must first learn to walk and run and climb and dance; one cannot fly into flying."— Friedrich Nietzsche

503. "If you have to dry the dishes (Such an awful boring chore)
If you have to dry the dishes ('Stead of going to the store)
If you have to dry the dishes.
And you drop one on the floor.
Maybe they won't let you
Dry the dishes anymore"— Shel Silverstein, A Light in the Attic

504. "You get in life what you have the courage to ask for."— Oprah Winfrey

505. "Fault always lies in the same place: with him weak enough to lay blame."— Stephen King

506. "Life's like a movie, write your own ending. Keep believing, keep pretending."— Jim Henson

507. "I wish I could've lived my life without making any wrong turns. But that's impossible. A path like that doesn't exist. We fail. We trip. We get lost. We make mistakes. And little by little, one step at a time, we push forward. It's all we can do.
On our own two feet."— Natsuki Takaya, Fruits Basket, Volume 21

508. "God is subtle but he is not malicious."— Albert Einstein

509. "If you can't you must, and if you must you can."— Anthony Robbins

510. "You have to, take a deep breath. and allow the music to flow through you. Revel in it, allow yourself to awe. When you play allow the music to break your heart with its beauty."— Kelly White

511. "Champions have the courage to keep turning the pages because they know a better chapter lies ahead."— Paula White

512. "I have come to accept the feeling of not knowing where I am going. And I have trained myself to love it. Because it is only when we are suspended in mid-air with no landing in sight, that we force our wings to unravel and alas begin our flight. And as we fly, we still may not know where we are going to. But the miracle is in the unfolding of the wings. You may not know where you're going, but you know that so long as you spread your wings, the winds will carry you."— C. JoyBell C.

513. "Not being heard is no reason for silence."— Victor Hugo, Les Misérables

514. "The best things in life make you sweaty."— Edgar Allan Poe

515. "Be like the sun for grace and mercy. Be like the night to cover others' faults. Be like running water for generosity. Be like death for rage and anger. Be like the Earth for modesty. Appear as you are. Be as you appear."— Rumi

516. "Too often we underestimate the power of a touch, a smile, a kind word, a listening ear, an honest compliment, or the smallest act of caring, all of which have the potential to turn a life around."— Leo Buscaglia

517. "I've come to believe that each of us has a personal calling that's as unique as a fingerprint - and that the best way to succeed is to discover what you love and then find a way to offer it to others in the form of service, working hard, and also allowing the energy of the universe to lead you."— Oprah Winfrey

518. "We are just an advanced breed of monkeys on a minor planet of a very average star. But we can understand the Universe. That makes us something very special."— Stephen Hawking

519. "Darling, when things go wrong in life, you lift your chin, put on a ravishing smile, mix yourself a little cocktail..."— Sophie Kinsella

520. "It was always the becoming he dreamed of, never the being."— F. Scott Fitzgerald

521. "Don't ask what the world needs. Ask what makes you come alive, and go do it. Because what the world needs is people who have come alive."— Howard Thurman

522. "Freedom is never more than one generation away from extinction. We didn't pass it to our children in the bloodstream. It must be fought for, protected, and handed on for them to do the same, or one day we will spend our sunset years telling our children and our children's children what it was once like in the United States where men were free."— Ronald Reagan

523. "And if my heart be scarred and burned,The safer, I, for all I learned."— Dorothy Parker, Sunset Gun

524. "When I find myself in times of trouble, mother Mary comes to me,speaking words of wisdom, let it be.
And in my hour of darkness she is standing right in front of me,speaking words of wisdom, let it be.
Let it be, let it be, let it be, let it be.
Whisper words of wisdom, let it be.
And when the broken hearted people living in the world agree,there will be an answer, let it be.
For though they may be parted there is still a chance that they will see,there will be an answer. let it be.
Let it be, let it be,And when the night is cloudy, there is still a light, that shines on me,shine until tomorrow, let it be.
I wake up to the sound of music, mother Mary comes to me,speaking words of wisdom, let it be.
Let it be, let it be,"— Paul McCartney

525. "Hearing voices no one else can hear isn't a good sign, even in the wizarding world."— J.K. Rowling, Harry Potter and the Chamber of Secrets

526. "Always be yourself, there's no one better!"— Selena Gomez

527. "Time weighs down on you like an old, ambiguous dream. You keep on moving, trying to sleep through it. But even if you go to the ends of the earth, you won't be able to escape it. Still, you have to go there- to the edge of the world. There's something you can't do unless you get there."— Haruki Murakami, Kafka on the Shore

528. "Reputation is what other people know about you. Honor is what you know about yourself."— Lois McMaster Bujold, A Civil Campaign

529. "That proves you are unusual,' returned the Scarecrow; 'and I am convinced that the only people worthy of consideration in this world are the unusual ones. For the common folks are like the leaves of a tree, and live and die unnoticed."— L. Frank Baum, The Land Of Oz

530. "Question with boldness even the existence of God; because, if there be one, he must more approve of the homage of reason than that of blindfolded fear."— Thomas Jefferson

531. "Never bend your head. Hold it high. Look the world straight in the eye."— Helen Keller

532. "No matter how ugly the world gets or how stupid it shows me it is, I always have faith"— Gerard Way

533. "Even if you are on the right track, you'll get run over if you just sit there."— Will Rogers

534. "Every person, all the events of your life are there because you have drawn them there. What you choose to do with them is up to you."— Richard Bach

535. "I was born into Bolívar's labyrinth, and so I must believe in the hope of Rabelais' Great Perhaps."— John Green

536. "To be in your children's memories tomorrow,You have to be in their lives today."— Barbara Johnson

537. "Everyone has his own reality in which, if one is not too cautious, timid or frightened, one swims. This is the only reality there is."— Henry Miller, Stand Still Like the Hummingbird

538. "To those who will see, the world waits."— Libba Bray

539. "Try, reach, want, and you may fall. But even if you do, you might be okay anyway.If you don't try, you save nothing, because you might as well be dead."— Ann Brashares, Girls In Pants: The Third Summer of the Sisterhood

540. "Someday is now."— Gaddy Bergmann

541. "The only person who can pull me down is myself, and I'm not going to let myself pull me down anymore."— C. JoyBell C.

542. "You may tell a tale that takes up residence in someone's soul, becomes their blood and self and purpose. That tale will move them and drive them and who knows that they might do because of it, because of your words. That is your role, your gift."— Erin Morgenstern, The Night Circus

543. "We travel, some of us forever, to seek other states, other lives, other souls."— Anaïs Nin, The Diary of Anaïs Nin, Vol. 7: 1966-1974

544. "Get Off The Scale!
You are beautiful. Your beauty, just like your capacity for life, happiness, and success, is immeasurable. Day after day, countless people across the globe get on a scale in search of validation of beauty and social acceptance.
Get off the scale! I have yet to see a scale that can tell you how enchanting your eyes are. I have yet to see a scale that can show you how wonderful your hair looks when the sun shines its glorious rays on it. I have yet to see a scale that can thank you for your compassion, sense of humor, and contagious smile. Get off the scale because I have yet to see one that can admire you for your perseverance when challenged in life.
It's true, the scale can only give you a numerical reflection of your relationship with gravity. That's it. It cannot measure beauty, talent, purpose, life force, possibility, strength, or love. Don't give the scale more power than it has earned. Take note of the number, then get off the scale and live your life. You are beautiful!"— Steve Maraboli, Life, the Truth, and Being Free

545. "In the end you can't always choose what to keep. You can only choose how you let it go."— Ally Condie, Crossed

546. "I am a happy camper so I guess I'm doing something right. Happiness is like a butterfly; the more you chase it, the more it will elude you, but if you turn your

attention to other things, it will come and sit softly on your shoulder."— Henry David Thoreau

547. "Fear doesn't shut you down; it wakes you up. I've seen it. It's fascinating." He releases me but doesn't pull away, his hand grazing my jaw, my neck. "Sometimes I just...want to see it again. Want to see you awake."— Veronica Roth, Divergent

548. "Behind every trial and sorrow that He makes us shoulder, God has a reason."— Khaled Hosseini, A Thousand Splendid Suns

549. "I do not care so much what I am to others as I care what I am to myself."

550. — Michel de Montaigne

551. "You can avoid reality, but you cannot avoid the consequences of avoiding reality."— Ayn Rand

552. "People say that eyes are windows to the soul."— Khaled Hosseini, The Kite Runner

553. "No act of kindness, no matter how small, is ever wasted."— Aesop

554. "Attitude is a little thing that makes a big difference."— Winston Churchill

555. "My happiness is not the means to any end. It is the end. It is its own goal. It is its own purpose."— Ayn Rand, Anthem

556. "Fake it 'till you make it."— Gayle Forman, If I Stay

557. "Dripping water hollows out stone, not through force but through persistence."— Ovid

558. "Desiderata" Go placidly amid the noise and the haste,
and remember what peace there may be in silence. As far as possible, without surrender, be on good terms with all persons.
Speak your truth quietly and clearly, and listen to others,
even to the dull and ignorant;
they too have their story.
Avoid loud and aggressive persons;
they are vexatious to the spirit.
If you compare yourself with others,
you may become vain or bitter,
for always there will be
greater and lesser persons than yourself.
Enjoy your achievements as well as your plans.
Keep interested in your own career
however humble;
it is a real possession in the changing fortunes of time.
Exercise caution in your business affairs,
for the world is full of trickery.

But let this not blind you
to what virtue there is;
many persons strive for high ideals,
and everywhere life is full of heroism.
Be yourself.
Especially do not feign affection.
Neither be cynical about love,
for in the face of all aridity and disenchantment,
it is as perennial as the grass.
Take kindly the counsel of the years,
gracefully surrendering the things of youth.
Nurture strength of spirit
to shield you in sudden misfortune.
But do not distress yourself with dark imaginings.
Many fears are born of fatigue and loneliness.
Beyond a wholesome discipline,
be gentle with yourself.
You are a child of the universe
no less than the trees and the stars;
you have a right to be here.
And whether or not it is clear to you,
no doubt the universe is unfolding as it should.
Therefore, be at peace with God,
whatever you conceive Him to be.
And whatever your labors and aspirations,
in the noisy confusion of life,
keep peace in your soul.
With all its sham,
drudgery, and broken dreams,
it is still a beautiful world.
Be cheerful.
Strive to be happy."— Max Ehrmann

559. "Instead of cursing the darkness, light a candle."— Benjamin Franklin

560. "So early in my life, I had learned that if you want something, you had better make some noise."— Malcolm X, The Autobiography Of Malcolm X

561. "I disregard the proportions, the measures, the tempo of the ordinary world. I refuse to live in the ordinary world as ordinary women. To enter ordinary relationships. I want ecstasy. I am a neurotic — in the sense that I live in my world. I will not adjust myself to the world. I am adjusted to myself."— Anaïs Nin, The Diary of Anaïs Nin, Vol. 1: 1931-1934

562. "The tears of the world are a constant quantity. For each one who begins to weep somewhere else another stops. The same is true of the laugh."— Samuel Beckett, Waiting for Godot

563. "Things do not change; we change."— Henry David Thoreau

564. "Believe there is a great power silently working all things for good, behave yourself and never mind the rest."— Beatrix Potter

565. "These were the lovely bones that had grown around my absence: the connections-sometimes tenuous, sometimes made at great cost, but often magnificent-that happened after I was gone. And I began to see things in a way that let me hold the world without me in it. The events that my death wrought were merely the bones of a body that would become whole at some unpredictable time in the future. The price of what I came to see as this miraculous body had been my life."— Alice Sebold, The Lovely Bones

566. "She lacks confidence, she craves admiration insatiably. She lives on the reflections of herself in the eyes of others. She does not dare to be herself."— Anaïs Nin

567. "What do we live for, if it is not to make life less difficult for each other?"— George Eliot

568. "Chaos is more freedom; in fact, total freedom. But no meaning. I want to be free to act, and I also want my actions to mean something."— Audrey Niffenegger, The Time Traveler's Wife

569. "I live my life in widening circles That reach out across the world."— Rainer Maria Rilke, Rilke's Book of Hours: Love Poems to God

570. "Nothing's a better cure for writer's block than to eat ice cream right out of the carton."— Don Roff

571. "I am no king, and I am no lord,And I am no soldier at-arms," said he.
"I'm none but a harper, and a very poor harper,That am come hither to wed with ye."
"If you were a lord, you should be my lord,And the same if you were a thief," said she.
"And if you are a harper, you shall be my harper,For it makes no matter to me, to me,For it makes no matter to me."
"But what if it prove that I am no harper?
That I lied for your love most monstrously?"
"Why, then I'll teach you to play and sing,
For I dearly love a good harp," said she."— Peter S. Beagle, The Last Unicorn

572. "Just because I liked something at one point in time doesn't mean I'll always like it, or that I have to go on liking it at all points in time as an unthinking act of loyalty to who I am as a person, based solely on who I was as a person. To be loyal to myself is to allow myself to grow and change, and challenge who I am and what I think. The only thing I am for sure is unsure, and this means I'm growing, and not stagnant or shrinking."— Jarod Kintz, At even one penny, this book would be overpriced. In fact, free is too expensive, because you'd still waste time by reading it.

573. "Everybody is special. Everybody. Everybody is a hero, a lover, a fool, a villain. Everybody. Everybody has their story to tell."— Alan Moore, V for Vendetta

574. "Sometimes life knocks you on your ass... get up, get up, get up!!! Happiness is not the absence of problems; it's the ability to deal with them."— Steve Maraboli, Life, the Truth, and Being Free

575. "Change the way you look at things and the things you look at change."— Wayne W. Dyer

576. "I just hope I remember to tell my kids that they are as happy as I look in my old photographs. And I hope that they believe me."— Stephen Chbosky, The Perks of Being a Wallflower

577. "In friendship...we think we have chosen our peers. In reality a few years' difference in the dates of our births, a few more miles between certain houses, the choice of one university instead of another...the accident of a topic being raised or not raised at a first meeting--any of these chances might have kept us apart. But, for a Christian, there are, strictly speaking no chances. A secret master of ceremonies has been at work. Christ, who said to the disciples, "Ye have not chosen me, but I have chosen you," can truly say to every group of Christian friends, "Ye have not chosen one another but I have chosen you for one another." The friendship is not a reward for our discriminating and good taste in finding one another out. It is the instrument by which God reveals to each of us the beauties of others."— C.S. Lewis, The Four Loves

578. "The stupid neither forgive nor forget; the naive forgive and forget; the wise forgive but do not forget."— Thomas Stephen Szasz

579. "Being happy doesn't mean that everything is perfect. It means that you've decided to look beyond the imperfections."— Gerard Way

580. "Do not wait for leaders; do it alone, person to person."— Mother Teresa

581. "The dog is a gentleman; I hope to go to his heaven not man's."— Mark Twain

582. "Think, Believe, Dream, and Dare."— Walt Disney Company

583. "Stop feeling sorry for yourself and you will be happy."— Stephen Fry

584. "Nothing ever really goes away--it just changes into something else. Something beautiful."— Sarah Ockler, Twenty Boy Summer

585. "I kept always two books in my pocket, one to read, one to write in."— Robert Louis Stevenson, Essays of Robert Louis Stevenson

586. "We lay there and looked up at the night sky and she told me about stars called blue squares and red swirls and I told her I'd never heard of them. Of course not, she said, the really important stuff they never tell you. You have to imagine it on your own."— Brian Andreas

587. "All great achievements require time."— Maya Angelou

588. "The soul should always stand ajar, ready to welcome the ecstatic experience."— Emily Dickinson

589. "He not busy being born is busy dying."— Bob Dylan

590. "Be yourself; no base imitator of another, but your best self. There is something which you can do better than another. Listen to the inward voice and bravely obey that. Do the things at which you are great, not what you were never made for."— Ralph Waldo Emerson, Self-Reliance and Other Essays

591. "God, grant me the serenity to accept the things I cannot change, the courage to change the things I can, and the wisdom to know the difference."— Reinhold Niebuhr

592. "The pure present is an ungraspable advance of the past devouring the future. In truth, all sensation is already memory."— Haruki Murakami, Kafka on the Shore

593. "I love you, in my mind where my thoughts reside, in my heart where my emotions live, and in my soul where my dreams are born. I love you."— Dee Henderson, The Healer

594. "Sticking feathers up your butt does not make you a chicken!"— Chuck Palahniuk, Fight Club

595. "What saves a man is to take a step. Then another step."— Antoine de Saint-Exupéry

596. "Be steady and well-ordered in your life so that you can be fierce and original in your work."— Gustave Flaubert

597. "May I share with you a formula that in my judgment will help you and help me to journey well through mortality... First, fill your mind with truth; second, fill your life with service; and third, fill your heart with love."— Thomas S. Monson

598. "Too much sanity may be madness — and maddest of all: to see life as it is, and not as it should be!"— Dale Wasserman, Man of La Mancha

599. "The man who writes about himself and his own time is the only man who writes about all people and all time."— George Bernard Shaw

600. "You could do a lot worse."— Suzanne Collins, Catching Fire

601. "All I ask is this: Do something. Try something. Speaking out, showing up, writing a letter, a check, a strongly worded e-mail. Pick a cause – there are few unworthy ones. And nudge yourself past the brink of tacit support to action. Once a month, once a year, or just once...Even just learning enough about a subject so you can speak against an opponent eloquently makes you an unusual personage. Start with that. Any one of you would have cried out, would have intervened, had you been in that crowd in Bashiqa. Well thanks to digital technology, you're all in it now."— Joss Whedon

602. "The unhappiest people in this world, are those who care the most about what other people think."— C. JoyBell C.

603. "Clouds come floating into my life, no longer to carry rain or usher storm, but to add color to my sunset sky."— Rabindranath Tagore, Stray Birds

604. "Everything can be taken from a man but one thing: the last of the human freedoms—to choose one's attitude in any given set of circumstances, to choose one's own way."— Viktor E. Frankl, Man's Search for Meaning

605. "Always bear in mind that your own resolution to succeed is more important than any one thing."— Abraham Lincoln

606. "Every blessing ignored becomes a curse."— Paulo Coelho, The Alchemist

607. "We are going to die, and that makes us the lucky ones. Most people are never going to die because they are never going to be born. The potential people who could have been here in my place but who will in fact never see the light of day outnumber the sand grains of Arabia. Certainly those unborn ghosts include greater poets than Keats, scientists greater than Newton. We know this because the set of possible people allowed by our DNA so massively exceeds the set of actual people. In the teeth of these stupefying odds it is you and I, in our ordinariness, that are here.We privileged few, who won the lottery of birth against all odds, how dare we whine at our inevitable return to that prior state from which the vast majority have never stirred?"— Richard Dawkins, Unweaving the Rainbow: Science, Delusion and the Appetite for Wonder

608. "Start a huge, foolish project, like Noah…it makes absolutely no difference what people think of you."— Rumi

609. "Amateurs sit and wait for inspiration, the rest of us just get up and go to work."— Stephen King, On Writing

610. "You must find the place inside yourself where nothing is impossible."— Deepak Chopra

611. "This life is yours. Take the power to choose what you want to do and do it well. Take the power to love what you want in life and love it honestly. Take the power to walk in the forest and be a part of nature. Take the power to control your own life. No one else can do it for you. Take the power to make your life happy."— Susan Polis Schutz

612. "Amor Fati – "Love Your Fate", which is in fact your life."— Friedrich Nietzsche

613. "Although I'm only fourteen, I know quite well what I want, I know who is right and who is wrong. I have my opinions, my own ideas and principles, and although it may sound pretty mad from an adolescent, I feel more of a person than a child, I feel quite independent of anyone."— Anne Frank, The Diary of Anne Frank

614. "Do you really want to be happy? You can begin by being appreciative of who you are and what you've got."— Benjamin Hoff, The Tao of Pooh

615. "It [feminism] is mixed up with a muddled idea that women are free when they serve their employers but slaves when they help their husbands."— G.K. Chesterton

616. "Love is too precious to be ashamed of."— Laurell K. Hamilton, A Stroke of Midnight

617. "There are times when solitude is better than society, and silence is wiser than speech. We should be better Christians if we were more alone, waiting upon God, and gathering through meditation on His Word spiritual strength for labor in his service. We ought to muse upon the things of God, because we thus get the real nutriment out of them. . . . Why is it that some Christians, although they hear many sermons, make but slow advances in the divine life? Because they neglect their closets, and do not thoughtfully meditate on God's Word. They love the wheat, but they do not grind it; they would have the corn, but they will not go forth into the fields to gather it; the fruit hangs upon the tree, but they will not pluck it; the water flows at their feet, but they will not stoop to drink it. From such folly deliver us, O Lord. . . ."— Charles H. Spurgeon

618. "The fishermen know that the sea is dangerous and the storm terrible, but they have never found these dangers sufficient reason for remaining ashore."— Vincent van Gogh

619. "I have no right to say or do anything that diminishes a man in his own eyes. What matters is not what I think of him but what he thinks of himself. Hurting a man in his dignity is a crime."— Antoine de Saint-Exupéry

620. "An eye is meant to see things.
The soul is here for its own joy.
A head has one use: For loving a true love.
Feet: To chase after.
Love is for vanishing into the sky.
The mind,for learning what men have done and tried to do.
Mysteries are not to be solved:
The eye goes blind when it only wants to see why.
A lover is always accused of something.
But when he finds his love, whatever was lost
in the looking comes back completely changed."— Rumi, Night and Sleep

621. "Definitions belong to the definers, not the defined."— Toni Morrison, Beloved

622. "Intellectual growth should commence at birth and cease only at death."— Albert Einstein

623. "Only the gentle are ever really strong."— James Dean

624. "We dance round in a ring and suppose,But the Secret sits in the middle and knows."— Robert Frost

625. "Every time you do a good deed you shine the light a little farther into the dark. And the thing is, when you're gone that light is going to keep shining on, pushing the shadows back."— Charles de Lint

626. "I've had it with being nice, understanding, fair and hopeful. I feel like being negative all day. The chip on my shoulder could sink the QE2. I've got an attitude problem and nobody better get in my way...I'm in a bad mood and the whole stupid little world is gonna pay!"— John Waters, Crackpot: The Obsessions of John Waters

627. "Never let a problem to be solved, become more important than a person to be loved."— Thomas S. Monson

628. "There is no limit to the amount of good you can do if you don't care who gets the credit."— Ronald Reagan

629. "I think that one of these days," he said, "you're going to have to find out where you want to go. And then you've got to start going there. But immediately. You can't afford to lose a minute. Not you."— J.D. Salinger, The Catcher in the Rye

630. "I keep thinking about a tale my nurse used to read to me about a bird whose wings are pinned to the ground. In the end, when he finally frees himself, he flies so high he becomes a star. My nurse said the story was about how we all have something that keeps us down."— Shannon Hale, Princess Academy

631. "Women can fake an orgasm, but men can fake an entire relationship."— Sharon Stone

632. "The only way that we can live, is if we grow. The only way that we can grow is if we change. The only way that we can change is if we learn. The only way we can learn is if we are exposed. And the only way that we can become exposed is if we throw ourselves out into the open. Do it. Throw yourself."— C. JoyBell C.

633. "The real heroes anyway aren't the people doing things; the real heroes are the people NOTICING things, paying attention."— John Green, The Fault in Our Stars

634. "Life is too short to waste any amount of time on wondering what other people think about you. In the first place, if they had better things going on in their lives, they wouldn't have the time to sit around and talk about you. What's important to me is not others' opinions of me, but what's important to me is my opinion of myself."— C. JoyBell C.

635. "As my sufferings mounted I soon realized that there were two ways in which I could respond to my situation -- either to react with bitterness or seek to transform the suffering into a creative force. I decided to follow the latter course."— Martin Luther King Jr.

636. "Life doesn't get easier or more forgiving, we get stronger and more resilient."— Steve Maraboli, Life, the Truth, and Being Free

637. "Why Not You?

Today, many will awaken with a fresh sense of inspiration. Why not you?
Today, many will open their eyes to the beauty that surrounds them. Why not you?
Today, many will choose to leave the ghost of yesterday behind and seize the immeasurable power of today. Why not you?
Today, many will break through the barriers of the past by looking at the blessings of the present. Why not you?
Today, for many the burden of self-doubt and insecurity will be lifted by the security and confidence of empowerment. Why not you?
Today, many will rise above their believed limitations and make contact with their powerful innate strength. Why not you?
Today, many will choose to live in such a manner that they will be a positive role model for their children. Why not you?
Today, many will choose to free themselves from the personal imprisonment of their bad habits. Why not you?
Today, many will choose to live free of conditions and rules governing their own happiness. Why not you?
Today, many will find abundance in simplicity. Why not you?
Today, many will be confronted by difficult moral choices and they will choose to do what is right instead of what is beneficial. Why not you?
Today, many will decide to no longer sit back with a victim mentality, but to take charge of their lives and make positive changes. Why not you?
Today, many will take the action necessary to make a difference. Why not you?
Today, many will make the commitment to be a better mother, father, son, daughter, student, teacher, worker, boss, brother, sister, & so much more. Why not you?
Today is a new day!
Many will seize this day.
Many will live it to the fullest.
Why not you?"— Steve Maraboli, Life, the Truth, and Being Free

638. "When you arise in the morning think of what a privilege it is to be alive, to think, to enjoy, to love ..."— Marcus Aurelius, Meditations

639. "Love. Fall in love and stay in love. Write only what you love, and love what you write. The word is love. You have to get up in the morning and write something you love, something to live for."— Ray Bradbury

640. "I didn't come here of my own accord, and I can't leave that way.

641. Whoever brought me here will have to take me home."— Rumi

642. "If we all did the things we are capable of, we would astound ourselves."— Thomas A. Edison

643. "If you care about what you do and work hard at it, there isn't anything you can't do if you want to."— Jim Henson, It's Not Easy Being Green: And Other Things to Consider

644. "The place where you made your stand never mattered. Only that you were there...and still on your feet."— Stephen King, The Stand

645. "Know thyself."— Socrates

646. "Once you learn to quit, it becomes a habit"— Vince Lombardi

647. "It is amazing what you can accomplish if you do not care who gets the credit."— Harry S. Truman

648. "If my mind can conceive it, and my heart can believe it - then I can achieve it."— Muhammad Ali, The Soul of a Butterfly: Reflections on Life's Journey

649. "Somehow I can't believe that there are any heights that can't be scaled by a man who knows the secrets of making dreams come true. This special secret, it seems to me, can be summarized in four Cs. They are curiosity, confidence, courage, and constancy, and the greatest of all is confidence. When you believe in a thing, believe in it all the way, implicitly and unquestionable."— Walt Disney Company

650. "If you haven't the strength to impose your own terms upon life, then you must accept the terms it offers you."— T.S. Eliot

651. "E.L. Doctorow said once said that 'Writing a novel is like driving a car at night. You can see only as far as your headlights, but you can make the whole trip that way.' You don't have to see where you're going, you don't have to see your destination or everything you will pass along the way. You just have to see two or three feet ahead of you. This is right up there with the best advice on writing, or life, I have ever heard."— Anne Lamott, Bird by Bird: Some Instructions on Writing and Life

652. "Indeed, learning to write may be part of learning to read. For all I know, writing comes out of a superior devotion to reading."— Eudora Welty, On Writing

653. "Believe in yourself and there will come a day when others will have no choice but to believe with you."— Cynthia Kersey

654. "If I've learned one lesson from all that's happened to me, it's that there is no such thing as the biggest mistake of your existence. There's no such thing as ruining your life. Life's a pretty resilient thing, it turns out."— Sophie Kinsella, The Undomestic Goddess

655. "When you're screwing up and nobody says anything to you anymore, that means they've given up on you."— Randy Pausch

656. "I choose gentleness... Nothing is won by force. I choose to be gentle. If I raise my voice may it be only in praise. If I clench my fist, may it be only in prayer. If I make a demand, may it be only of myself."— Max Lucado

657. "How far you go in life depends on your being tender with the young, compassionate with the aged, sympathetic with the striving and tolerant of the

weak and strong. Because someday in your life you will have been all of these.
"— George Washington Carver

658. "The greatest discovery of any generation is that a human can alter his life by altering his attitude."— William James

659. "I've gotta get out of the basement. I've gotta see the world. I've gotta make a difference"— Gerard Way

660. "Music is an agreeable harmony for the honor of God and the permissible delights of the soul."— Johann Sebastian Bach

661. "It is better to be respected than it is to be popular. Popularity ends on yearbook day, but respect lasts forever."— John Bytheway

662. "And once the storm is over, you won't remember how you made it through, how you managed to survive. You won't even be sure, whether the storm is really over. But one thing is certain. When you come out of the storm, you won't be the same person who walked in. That's what this storm's all about."— Haruki Murakami

663. "We have to allow ourselves to be loved by the people who really love us, the people who really matter. Too much of the time, we are blinded by our own pursuits of people to love us, people that don't even matter, while all that time we waste and the people who do love us have to stand on the sidewalk and watch us beg in the streets! It's time to put an end to this. It's time for us to let ourselves be loved."— C. JoyBell C.

664. "Happiness is not the absence of problems; it's the ability to deal with them."— Steve Maraboli, Life, the Truth, and Being Free

665. "I read somewhere... how important it is in life not necessarily to be strong, but to feel strong... to measure yourself at least once."— Jon Krakauer, Into the Wild

666. "We are the music-makers,
And we are the dreamers of dreams,
Wandering by lone sea-breakers,
And sitting by desolate streams.
World-losers and world-forsakers,
Upon whom the pale moon gleams;
Yet we are the movers and shakers,
Of the world forever, it seems."— Arthur O'Shaughnessy, Poems of Arthur O'Shaughnessy

667. "It's strange how dreams get under your skin and give your heart a test for what's real and what's imaginary."— Jason Mraz

668. "If you start by promising what you don't even have yet, you'll lose your desire to work towards getting it."— Paulo Coelho, The Alchemist

669. "The only limits for tomorrow are the doubts we have today."— Pittacus Lore, The Power of Six

670. "How far that little candle throws his beams! So shines a good deed in a weary world."— William Shakespeare, The Merchant of Venice

671. "Our life is what our thoughts make it."— Marcus Aurelius, Meditations

672. "To each there comes in their lifetime a special moment when they are figuratively tapped on the shoulder and offered the chance to do a very special thing, unique to them and fitted to their talents. What a tragedy if that moment finds them unprepared or unqualified for that which could have been their finest hour."— Winston Churchill

673. "You're alive, Bod. That means you have infinite potential. You can do anything, make anything, dream anything. If you can change the world, the world will change. Potential. Once you're dead, it's gone. Over. You've made what you've made, dreamed your dream, written your name. You may be buried here, you may even walk. But that potential is finished."— Neil Gaiman, The Graveyard Book

674. "All I ask is one thing, and I'm asking this particularly of young people: please don't be cynical. I hate cynicism, for the record, it's my least favorite quality and it doesn't lead anywhere. Nobody in life gets exactly what they thought they were going to get. But if you work really hard and you're kind, amazing things will happen."— Conan O'Brien

675. "Luck is what happens when preparation meets opportunity."— Lucius Annaeus Seneca

676. "When you judge another, you do not define them, you define yourself."— Wayne W. Dyer

677. "You become what you think about all day long."— Ralph Waldo Emerson

678. "No man is an island, entire of itself; every man is a piece of the continent, a part of the main. If a clod be washed away by the sea, Europe is the less, as well as if a promontory were, as well as if a manor of thy friend's or of thine own were: any man's death diminishes me, because I am involved in mankind, and therefore never send to know for whom the bells tolls; it tolls for thee."— John Donne, No Man Is An Island

679. "Fairness means everyone gets what they need. And the only way to get what you need is to make it happen yourself."— Rick Riordan, The Red Pyramid

680. "I hated every minute of training, but I said, 'Don't quit. Suffer now and live the rest of your life as a champion'."— Muhammad Ali

681. "An individual has not started living until he can rise above the narrow confines of his individualistic concerns to the broader concerns of all humanity."— Martin Luther King Jr.

682. "I try to avoid looking forward or backward, and try to keep looking upward."—Charlotte Brontë

683. "You ask, what is our aim? I can answer in one word. It is victory, victory at all costs, victory in spite of all terror, victory, however long and hard the road may be; for without victory, there is no survival."— Winston Churchill

684. "If you want to catch beasts you don't see every day,
You have to go places quite out of the way,
You have to go places no others can get to.
You have to get cold and you have to get wet, too."— Dr. Seuss

685. "Determine never to be idle. No person will have occasion to complain of the want of time, who never loses any. It is wonderful how much may be done, if we are always doing."— Thomas Jefferson

686. "It is much easier to be brave if you do not know everything."— Lois Lowry

687. "That which we persist in doing becomes easier to do, not that the nature of the thing has changed but that our power to do has increased."— Ralph Waldo Emerson

688. "Wait long enough and people will surprise and impress. When you're pissed off at someone and you're angry at them, you just haven't given them enough time. Just give them a little more time and they almost always will impress you."—Randy Pausch

689. "And though I have the gift of prophecy, and understand all mysteries, and all knowledge; and though I have all faith, so that I could remove mountains, but have not love, I am nothing. (1 Cor. 13:2 New King James Version)"—Anonymous, Holy Bible: The New King James Version

690. "It is the time you have wasted for your rose that makes your rose so important."— Antoine de Saint-Exupéry, The Little Prince

691. "Make a pact with yourself today to not be defined by your past. Sometimes the greatest thing to come out of all your hard work isn't what you get for it, but what you become for it. Shake things up today! Be You...Be Free...Share."— Steve Maraboli, Life, the Truth, and Being Free

692. "You must learn to let go. Release the stress. You were never in control anyway."— Steve Maraboli, Life, the Truth, and Being Free

693. "We all make mistakes, have struggles, and even regret things in our past. But you are not your mistakes, you are not your struggles, and you are here NOW with the power to shape your day and your future."— Steve Maraboli, Unapologetically You: Reflections on Life and the Human Experience

694. "We have to create culture, don't watch TV, don't read magazines, don't even listen to NPR. Create your own roadshow. The nexus of space and time where

you are now is the most immediate sector of your universe, and if you're worrying about Michael Jackson or Bill Clinton or somebody else, then you are disempowered, you're giving it all away to icons, icons which are maintained by an electronic media so that you want to dress like X or have lips like Y. This is shit-brained, this kind of thinking. That is all cultural diversion, and what is real is you and your friends and your associations, your highs, your orgasms, your hopes, your plans, your fears. And we are told 'no', we're unimportant, we're peripheral. 'Get a degree, get a job, get a this, get a that.' And then you're a player, you don't want to even play in that game. You want to reclaim your mind and get it out of the hands of the cultural engineers who want to turn you into a half-baked moron consuming all this trash that's being manufactured out of the bones of a dying world."— Terence McKenna

695. "Be like melting snow -- wash yourself of yourself."— Rumi

696. "The Democracy will cease to exist when you take away from those who are willing to work and give to those who would not."— Thomas Jefferson

697. "Don't give up the fight,Stand up for your rights."— Bob Marley

698. "The duty of youth is to challenge corruption."— Kurt Cobain

699. "No man chooses evil because it is evil; he only mistakes it for happiness, the good he seeks."— Mary Shelley

700. "When I give, I give myself."— Walt Whitman

701. "Real magic can never be made by offering someone else's liver. You must tear out your own, and not expect to get it back."— Peter S. Beagle, The Last Unicorn

702. "As a single footstep will not make a path on the earth, so a single thought will not make a pathway in the mind. To make a deep physical path, we walk again and again. To make a deep mental path, we must think over and over the kind of thoughts we wish to dominate our lives."— Henry David Thoreau

703. "We are all of us born with a letter inside us, and that only if we are true to ourselves, may we be allowed to read it before we die."— Douglas Coupland

704. "What the caterpillar calls the end of the world, the master calls a butterfly."— Richard Bach, Illusions: The Adventures of a Reluctant Messiah

705. "What's most important in a friendship? Tolerance and loyalty."— J.K. Rowling

706. "I think joy and sweetness and affection are a spiritual path. We're here to know God, to love and serve God, and to be blown away by the beauty and miracle of nature. You just have to get rid of so much baggage to be light enough to dance, to sing, to play. You don't have time to carry grudges; you don't have time to cling to the need to be right."— Anne Lamott

707. "Life is wasted on the living."— Douglas Adams, The Restaurant at the End of the Universe

708. "When you chase a dream, you learn about yourself. You learn your capabilities and limitations, and the value of hard work and persistence."— Nicholas Sparks, Three Weeks With My Brother

709. "It is truth that liberates, not your effort to be free."— Jiddu Krishnamurti, The First and Last Freedom

710. "Let us live so that when we come to die even the undertaker will be sorry."— Mark Twain

711. "My heart, which is so full to overflowing, has often been solaced and refreshed by music when sick and weary."— Martin Luther

712. "That as long as we are being remembered, we remain alive."— Carlos Ruiz Zafón

713. "There is a time in every man's education when he arrives at the conviction that envy is ignorance; that imitation is suicide; that he must take himself for better, for worse, as his portion; that though the wide universe is full of good, no kernel of nourishing corn can come to him but through his toil bestowed on that plot of ground which is given to him to till. The power which resides in him is new in nature, and none but he knows what that is which he can do, nor does he know until he has tried."— Ralph Waldo Emerson, Self Reliance

714. "Many of us are slaves to our minds. Our own mind is our worst enemy. We try to focus, and our mind wanders off. We try to keep stress at bay, but anxiety keeps us awake at night. We try to be good to the people we love, but then we forget them and put ourselves first. And when we want to change our life, we dive into spiritual practice and expect quick results, only to lose focus after the honeymoon has worn off. We return to our state of bewilderment. We're left feeling helpless and discouraged. It seems we all agree that training the body through exercise, diet, and relaxation is a good idea, but why don't we think about training our minds?"— Sakyong Mipham

715. "Things work out, it isn't as bad as you sometimes think it is. It all works out, don't worry. I say that to myself every morning. It will all work out. If you do your best, it will all work out. Put your trust in God, and move forward with faith and confidence in the future. The Lord will not forsake us. If we will put our trust in him, if we will pray to him, if we will live worthy of his blessings, he will hear our prayers."— Gordon B. Hinckley

716. "Argue for your limitations and, sure enough, they're yours."— Richard Bach

717. "The caged bird sings with a fearful trill, of things unknown, but longed for still, and his tune is heard on the distant hill, for the caged bird sings of freedom."— Maya Angelou

718. "All paths are present, always... and we can but choose among them."— Jacqueline Carey, Kushiel's Chosen

719. "I want to be like Gandhi and Martin Luther King and John Lennon but I want to STAY ALIVE."— Madonna

720. "Pain is a pesky part of being human, I've learned it feels like a stab wound to the heart, something I wish we could all do without, in our lives here. Pain is a sudden hurt that can't be escaped. But then I have also learned that because of pain, I can feel the beauty, tenderness, and freedom of healing. Pain feels like a fast stab wound to the heart. But then healing feels like the wind against your face when you are spreading your wings and flying through the air! We may not have wings growing out of our backs, but healing is the closest thing that will give us that wind against our faces."— C. JoyBell C.

721. "There is some kind of a sweet innocence in being human- in not having to be just happy or just sad- in the nature of being able to be both broken and whole, at the same time."— C. JoyBell C.

722. "Only those who attempt the absurd can achieve the impossible."— Albert Einstein

723. "When you hold a grudge, you want someone else's sorrow to reflect your level of hurt but the two rarely meet."— Steve Maraboli, Unapologetically You: Reflections on Life and the Human Experience

724. "Do not go gentle."— Ally Condie, Matched

725. "There is no happiness like that of being loved by your fellow creatures, and feeling that your presence is an addition to their comfort."— Charlotte Brontë, Jane Eyre

726. "And I thought that all those little kids are going to grow up someday. And all of those little kids are going to do the things that we do. And they will all kiss someone someday. But for now, sledding is enough. I think it would be great if sledding were always enough, but it isn't."— Stephen Chbosky, The Perks of Being a Wallflower

727. "You can't outwit fate by standing on the sidelines placing little side bets about the outcome of life. either you wade in and risk everything you have to play the game or you don't play at all. and if u don't play u can't win."— Judith McNaught, Paradise

728. "Envy is ignorance, Imitation is Suicide."— Ralph Waldo Emerson, Self-Reliance

729. "The key to your happiness is to own your slippers, own who you are, own how you look, own your family, own the talents you have, and own the ones you don't. If you keep saying your slippers aren't yours, then you'll die searching, you'll die bitter, always feeling you were promised more. Not only our actions, but also our omissions, become our destiny."— Abraham Verghese, Cutting for Stone

730. "Nothing's perfect, the world's not perfect. But it's there for us, trying the best it can; that's what makes it so damn beautiful."— Hiromu Arakawa, Fullmetal Alchemist, Vol. 01

731. "Anything is possible. Anything can be."— Shel Silverstein

732. "You know what I can't understand? You have all these people telling you all the time how great you are, smart and funny and talented and all that, I mean endlessly, I've been telling you for years. So why don't you believe it? why do you think people say that stuff, Em? Do you think it's a conspiracy, people secretly ganging up to be nice about you?"— David Nicholls, One Day

733. "It's just that in the Deep South, women learn at a young age that when the world is falling apart around you, it's time to take down the drapes and make a new dress."— Karen Marie Moning, Faefever

734. "Everything happens for a reason and, something better will come along for me!"— Selena Gomez

735. "According to Aristophanes in Plato's The Banquet, in the ancient world of legend there were three types of people.
In ancient times people weren't simply male or female, but one of three types: male/male, male/female or female/female. In other words, each person was made out of the components of two people. Everyone was happy with this arrangement and never really gave it much thought. But then God took a knife and cut everyone in half, right down the middle. So after that the world was divided just into male and female, the upshot being that people spend their time running around trying to locate their missing half." — Haruki Murakami, Kafka on the Shore

736. "The truth knocks on the door and you say, "Go away, I'm looking for the truth," and so it goes away. Puzzling."— Robert M. Pirsig, Zen and the Art of Motorcycle Maintenance: An Inquiry Into Values

737. "I'd like to add some beauty to life," said Anne dreamily. "I don't exactly want to make people KNOW more... though I know that IS the noblest ambition... but I'd love to make them have a pleasanter time because of me... to have some little joy or happy thought that would never have existed if I hadn't been born."— L.M. Montgomery, Anne's House of Dreams

738. "But why think about that when all the golden lands ahead of you and all kinds of unforeseen events wait lurking to surprise you and make you glad you're alive to see?"— Jack Kerouac, On the Road

739. "Jessica. For god's sake," he said. "Allow me to do at least one common courtesy for you. In spite own what 'women's lib' teaches you, chivalry does not imply that women are powerless. On the contrary, chivalry is an admission of women's superiority. An acknowledgment of your power over us. This is the only form of servitude a Vladescu ever practices, and I perform it gladly for you. You, in turn, are obligated to accept graciously."— Beth Fantaskey, Jessica's Guide to Dating on the Dark Side

740. "It's your life-but only if you make it so."— Eleanor Roosevelt, You Learn by Living: Eleven Keys for a More Fulfilling Life

741. "Living well is an art that can be developed: a love of life and ability to take great pleasure from small offerings and assurance that the world owes you nothing and that every gift is exactly that, a gift."— Maya Angelou, Wouldn't Take Nothing for My Journey Now

742. "There's a hunger for stories in all of us, adults too. We need stories so much that we're even willing to read bad books to get them, if the good books won't supply them."— Philip Pullman

743. "An idea is salvation by imagination"— Frank Lloyd Wright

744. "Life is a series of surprises and would not be worth taking or keeping if it were not."— Ralph Waldo Emerson

745. "When men are pure, laws are useless; when men are corrupt, laws are broken."— Benjamin Disraeli

746. "Gratitude is a sign of maturity...Where there is appreciation: there is also courtesy and concern for the rights and property of others."— Gordon B. Hinckley

747. "I am a strong believer in the tyranny, the dictatorship, the absolute authority of the writer."— Philip Pullman

748. "I'm unpredictable, I never know where I'm going until I get there, I'm so random, I'm always growing, learning, changing, I'm never the same person twice. But one thing you can be sure of about me; is I will always do exactly what I want to do."— C. JoyBell C.

749. "Oh, what a tangled web we weave...when first we practice to deceive."— Walter Scott, Marmion

750. "I've come to the conclusion that people who wear headphones while they walk, are much happier, more confident, and more beautiful individuals than someone making the solitary drudge to work without acknowledging their own interests and power."— Jason Mraz

751. "But still, I find the need to remind myself of the temporariness of a day, to reassure myself that I got through yesterday, I'll get through today."— Gayle Forman, Where She Went

752. "I would rather make mistakes in kindness and compassion than work miracles in unkindness and hardness."— Mother Teresa, A Gift for God: Prayers and Meditations

753. "Ruin is a gift. Ruin is the road to transformation."— Elizabeth Gilbert, Eat, Pray, Love

754. "Adapt what is useful, reject what is useless, and add what is specifically your own."— Bruce Lee

755. "The problems of the world cannot possibly be solved by skeptics or cynics whose horizons are limited by the obvious realities. We need men who can dream of things that never were."— John Keats

756. "When a Stargirl cries, she sheds not tears but light."— Jerry Spinelli, Stargirl

757. "Look at children. Of course they may quarrel, but generally speaking they do not harbor ill feelings as much or as long as adults do. Most adults have the advantage of education over children, but what is the use of an education if they show a big smile while hiding negative feelings deep inside? Children don't usually act in such a manner. If they feel angry with someone, they express it, and then it is finished. They can still play with that person the following day."— Dalai Lama XIV

758. "To truly laugh, you must be able to take your pain, and play with it."— Charles Chaplin

759. "But beauty is about finding the right fit, the most natural fit, To be perfect, you have to feel perfect about yourself --- avoid trying to be something you're not. For a goddess, that's especially hard. We can change so easily.-Aphrodite"— Rick Riordan, The Lost Hero

760. "Nine requisites for contented living:Health enough to make work a pleasure.Wealth enough to support your needs.Strength to battle with difficulties and overcome them.Grace enough to confess your sins and forsake them.Patience enough to toil until some good is accomplished.Charity enough to see some good in your neighbor.Love enough to move you to be useful and helpful to others.Faith enough to make real the things of God.Hope enough to remove all anxious fears concerning the future."— Johann Wolfgang von Goethe

761. "Have you ever seen the stars in the night? See them closely, they will tell you, how to be open, how to love and how to shine and twinkle without any differences and jealousy of other stars."— Santosh Kalwar, Quote Me Everyday

762. "Frustration and Love can't exist in the same place at the same time, so get real and start doing what you would rather be doing in life. Love your life. All of it. Even the heavy shit that happened to you when you were 8. All of it was and IS perfect."— Jason Mraz

763. "I am who I am; no more, no less."— Terry Goodkind, Wizard's First Rule

764. "All the problem of women starts with men. All the problem of men ends with women."— Santosh Kalwar, Quote Me Everyday

765. "Laughter is carbonated holiness."— Anne Lamott

766. "A wind has blown the rain away & the sky away & all the leaves away, & the trees stand. I think I, too, have known autumn too long."— E.E. Cummings

767. "If nature has made you for a giver, your hands are born open, and so is your heart; and though there may be times when your hands are empty, your heart is

always full, and you can give things out of that--warm things, kind things, sweet things--help and comfort and laughter--and sometimes gay, kind laughter is the best help of all."— Frances Hodgson Burnett, A Little Princess

768. "A dog has no use for fancy cars or big homes or designer clothes. Status symbol means nothing to him. A waterlogged stick will do just fine. A dog judges others not by their color or creed or class but by who they are inside. A dog doesn't care if you are rich or poor, educated or illiterate, clever or dull. Give him your heart and he will give you his. It was really quite simple, and yet we humans, so much wiser and more sophisticated, have always had trouble figuring out what really counts and what does not. As I wrote that farewell column to Marley, I realized it was all right there in front of us, if only we opened our eyes. Sometimes it took a dog with bad breath, worse manners, and pure intentions to help us see."— John Grogan

769. "Our opportunities to give of ourselves are indeed limitless, but they are also perishable. There are hearts to gladden. There are kind words to say. There are gifts to be given. There are deeds to be done. There are souls to be saved.
As we remember that "when ye are in the service of your fellow beings ye are only in the service of your God," (Messiah 2:17) we will not find ourselves in the unenviable position of Jacob Marley's ghost, who spoke to Ebenezer Scrooge in Charles Dickens's immortal "Christmas Carol." Marley spoke sadly of opportunities lost. Said he: 'Not to know that any Christian spirit working kindly in its little sphere, whatever it may be, will find its mortal life too short for its vast means of usefulness. Not to know that no space of regret can make amends for one life's opportunity misused! Yet such was I! Oh! Such was I!'
Marley added: 'Why did I walk through crowds of fellow-beings with my eyes turned down, and never raise them to that blessed Star which led the Wise Men to a poor abode? Were there no poor homes to which its light would have conducted me!'
Fortunately, as we know, Ebenezer Scrooge changed his life for the better. I love his line, 'I am not the man I was.'
Why is Dickens' "Christmas Carol" so popular? Why is it ever new? I personally feel it is inspired of God. It brings out the best within human nature. It gives hope. It motivates change. We can turn from the paths which would lead us down and, with a song in our hearts, follow a star and walk toward the light. We can quicken our step, bolster our courage, and bask in the sunlight of truth. We can hear more clearly the laughter of little children. We can dry the tear of the weeping. We can comfort the dying by sharing the promise of eternal life. If we lift one weary hand which hangs down, if we bring peace to one struggling soul, if we give as did the Master, we can—by showing the way—become a guiding star for some lost mariner."— Thomas S. Monson

770. "Ah, but a man's reach should exceed his grasp, or what's a heaven for?"— Robert Browning, Men and Women and Other Poems

771. "If every life is a river, then it's little wonder that we do not even notice the changes that occur until we are far out in the darkest sea. One day you look around and nothing is familiar, not even your own face.
My name once meant daughter, granddaughter, friend, sister, beloved. Now those words mean only what their letters spell out; Star in the night sky. Truth in

the darkness.
I have crossed over to a place where I never thought I'd be. I am someone I would have never imagined. A secret. A dream. I am this, body and soul. Burn me. Drown me. Tell me lies. I will still be who I am."— Alice Hoffman, Incantation

772. "It is not so much the major events as the small day-to-day decisions that map the course of our living. . . Our lives are, in reality, the sum total of our seemingly unimportant decisions and of our capacity to live by those decisions."— Gordon B. Hinckley

773. "Having an eye for beauty isn't the same thing as a weakness...except possibly when it comes to you."— Suzanne Collins

774. "Is it easy? Usually not. But you don't forgive people for their benefit. You do it for your benefit."— Andrew Matthews

775. "The world is wide, and I will not waste my life in friction when it could be turned into momentum."— Frances Willard

776. "Can't stand all these poisonous creatures, all these snakes and insects and fish and things. Wretched things, biting everybody. And then people expect me to tell them what to do about it. I'll tell them what to do. Don't get bitten in the first place. (quoting Dr. Struan Sutherland)"— Douglas Adams

777. "I just want you to know that you're very special... and the only reason I'm telling you is that I don't know if anyone else ever has."— Stephen Chbosky, The Perks of Being a Wallflower

778. "How would your life be different if...You stopped making negative judgmental assumptions about people you encounter? Let today be the day...You look for the good in everyone you meet and respect their journey."— Steve Maraboli, Life, the Truth, and Being Free

779. "Those who do not weep do not see."— Victor Hugo, Les Misérables

780. "If you're horrible to me, I'm going to write a song about it, and you won't like it. That's how I operate."— Taylor Swift

781. "Go confidently in the direction of your dreams. Live the life you've imagined."— Henry David Thoreau

782. "Resentment is like drinking poison and then hoping it will kill your enemies."— Nelson Mandela

783. "The greatest glory in living lies not in never falling, but in rising every time we fall."— Nelson Mandela

784. "It is not death that a man should fear, but he should fear never beginning to live."— Marcus Aurelius, Meditations

785. "The tragedy of life is what dies inside a man while he lives."— Albert Einstein

786. "The most important thing in life is to stop saying 'I wish' and start saying 'I will.' Consider nothing impossible, then treat possibilities as probabilities."— David Copperfield

787. "Desperation is the raw material of drastic change. Only those who can leave behind everything they have ever believed in can hope to escape. "— William S. Burroughs

788. "If you can't run, you crawl. If you can't crawl-- you find someone to carry you."— Joss Whedon

789. "We don't receive wisdom; we must discover it for ourselves after a journey that no one can take for us or spare us."— Marcel Proust

790. "Life begins on the other side of despair."— Jean-Paul Sartre

791. "Free at last, Free at last, Thank God almighty we are free at last."— Martin Luther King Jr., I Have a Dream: Writings and Speeches That Changed the World

792. "If you're not comfortable enough with yourself or with your own truth when entering a relationship, then you're not ready for that relationship."— Steve Maraboli, Life, the Truth, and Being Free

793. "A man who does not think for himself does not think at all."— Oscar Wilde

794. "Every man is more than just himself; he also represents the unique, the very special and always significant and remarkable point at which the world's phenomena intersect, only once in this way, and never again. That is why every man's story is important, eternal, sacred; that is why every man, as long as he lives and fulfills the will of nature, is wondrous, and worthy of consideration. In each individual the spirit has become flesh, in each man the creation suffers, within each one a redeemer is nailed to the cross."— Hermann Hesse, Demian

795. "If the only prayer you say throughout your life is "Thank You," then that will be enough."— Elie Wiesel

796. "It serves me right for putting all my eggs in one bastard."— Dorothy Parker, You Might as Well Live: The Life and Times of Dorothy Parker

797. "When they say the sky's the limit to me that's really true"— Michael Jackson

798. "Life is truly known only to those who suffer, lose, endure adversity, & stumble from defeat to defeat."— Anaïs Nin

799. "I am not a smart man, particularly, but one day, at long last, I stumbled from the dark woods of my own, and my family's, and my country's past, holding in my hands these truths: that love grows from the rich loam of forgiveness; that mongrels make good dogs; that the evidence of God exists in the roundness of things. This much, at least, I've figured out. I know this much is true."— Wally Lamb, I Know This Much Is True

800. "They say that every snowflake is different. If that were true, how could the world go on? How could we ever get up off our knees? How could we ever recover from the wonder of it?"— Jeanette Winterson

801. "Each of us has the right and the responsibility to assess the roads which lie ahead, and those over which we have traveled, and if the future road looms ominous or unpromising, and the roads back uninviting, then we need to gather our resolve and, carrying only the necessary baggage, step off that road into another direction. If the new choice is also unpalatable, without embarrassment, we must be ready to change that as well."— Maya Angelou, Wouldn't Take Nothing for My Journey Now

802. "The greatest pleasure in life is doing what people say you cannot do."— Walter Bagehot

803. "The culture of women in the church today is crippled by some very pervasive lies. "To be spiritual is to be busy. To be spiritual is to be disciplined. To be spiritual is to be dutiful." No, to be spiritual is to be in Romance with God. The desire to be romanced lies deep in the heart of every woman. It is for such that you were made. Are you ARE romanced, and ever will be."— John Eldredge

804. "If you are still breathing maybe it is not such a bad day after all..."— Darren E. Laws

805. "When one tugs at a single thing in nature, he finds it attached to the rest of the world."— John Muir

806. "You only need one man to love you. But him to love you free like a wildfire, crazy like the moon, always like tomorrow, sudden like an inhale and overcoming like the tides. Only one man and all of this."— C. JoyBell C.

807. "You've got this life and while you've got it, you'd better kiss like you only have one moment, try to hold someone's hand like you will never get another chance to, look into people's eyes like they're the last you'll ever see, watch someone sleeping like there's no time left, jump if you feel like jumping, run if you feel like running, play music in your head when there is none, and eat cake like it's the only one left in the world!"— C. JoyBell C.

808. "there is a place in the heart that will never be filled a space and even during the best moments and the greatest times we will know it we will know it more than ever there is a place in the heart that will never be filled and we will wait and wait in that space."— Charles Bukowski

809. "You're not obligated to win. You're obligated to keep trying. To the best you can do every day."— Jason Mraz

810. "Congratulations! Today is your day. You're off to Great Places! You're off and away!"— Dr. Seuss, Oh, the Places You'll Go!

811. "If you have good thoughts they will shine out of your face like sunbeams and you will always look lovely."— Roald Dahl

812. "There is no passion to be found playing small - in settling for a life that is less than the one you are capable of living."— Nelson Mandela

813. "People say that what we're all seeking is a meaning for life. I don't think that's what we're really seeking. I think that what we're seeking is an experience of being alive, so that our life experiences on the purely physical plane will have resonances with our own innermost being and reality, so that we actually feel the rapture of being alive."— Joseph Campbell, The Power of Myth

814. "Hope is important because it can make the present moment less difficult to bear. If we believe that tomorrow will be better, we can bear a hardship today."— Thích Nhất Hạnh, Peace Is Every Step: The Path of Mindfulness in Everyday Life

815. "Would you rather live one perfect day over and over or live your life with no perfect days but just decent ones?"— Jenny Han, The Summer I Turned Pretty

816. "Do not dare not to dare."— C.S. Lewis, The Horse and His Boy

817. "There is a legend about a bird which sings just once in its life, more sweetly than any other creature on the face of the earth. From the moment it leaves the nest it searches for a thorn tree, and does not rest until it has found one. Then, singing among the savage branches, it impales itself upon the longest, sharpest spine. And, dying, it rises above its own agony to outcarol the lark and the nightingale. One superlative song, existence the price. But the whole world stills to listen, and God in His heaven smiles. For the best is only bought at the cost of great pain... Or so says the legend."— Colleen McCullough, The Thorn Birds

818. "The butterfly counts not months but moments, and has time enough."— Rabindranath Tagore

819. "Love demands everything, they say, but my love demands only this: that no matter what happens or how long it takes, you`ll keep faith in me, you`ll remember who we are, and you`ll never feel despair."— Ann Brashares, My Name Is Memory

820. "Each morning when I awake, I experience again a supreme pleasure: that of being Salvador Dali."— Salvador Dalí

821. "A dead thing goes with the stream, but only a living thing can go against it."— G.K. Chesterton

822. "Whatever you see you gotta keep a sense of humor; you gotta be able to smile through all the bullshit."— Tupac Shakur

823. "It is not because things are difficult that we do not dare, it is because we do not dare that they are difficult."— Lucius Annaeus Seneca

824. "A thing of beauty is a joy forever: Its loveliness increases; it will never Pass into nothingness; but still will keep A bower quiet for us, and a sleep Full of sweet dreams, and health, and quiet breathing."— John Keats

825. "To have regret is to be disappointed with yourself and your choices. Those who are wise, see their life like stepping stones across a great river. Everyone misses a stone from time to time. No one can cross the river without getting wet. Success is measured by your arrival on the other side, not on how muddy your shoes are. Regrets are only felt by those who do not understand life's purpose. They become so disillusioned that they stand still in the river and do not take the next leap."— Colleen Houck

826. "I do not believe that sheer suffering teaches. If suffering alone taught, all the world would be wise, since everyone suffers. To suffering must be added mourning, understanding, patience, love, openness, and the willingness to remain vulnerable."— Anne Morrow Lindbergh, Gift from the Sea

827. "Someday we'll find it. The Rainbow Connection. The lovers, the dreamers, and me."— Jim Henson

828. "Whatsoever a man soweth, that shall he also reap."— Anonymous, Holy Bible: King James Version

829. "How sweet is the assurance, how comforting is the peace that comes from the knowledge that if we marry right and live right, our relationship will continue, notwithstanding the certainty of death and the passage of time. Men may write love songs and sing them. They may yearn and hope and dream. But all of this will be only a romantic longing unless there is an exercise of authority that transcends the powers of time and death."— Gordon B. Hinckley

830. "I know in my heart that man is good, that what is right will always eventually triumph, and there is purpose and worth to each and every life."— Ronald Reagan

831. "I'd heard of Evergreen Care Center before. Cass and I had always made fun of the stupid ads they ran on TV, featuring some dragged-out woman with a limp perm and big, painted-on circles under her eyes, downing vodka and sobbing uncontrollably. "We can't heal you at Evergreen", the very somber voiceover said. "But we can help you to heal yourself." It had become our own running joke, applicable to almost anything. "Hey Cass, "I'd say, "hand me that toothpaste." "Caitlin," she'd say, her voice dark and serious. "I can't hand you the toothpaste. But I CAN help you hand the toothpaste to yourself."— Sarah Dessen, Dreamland

832. "What the soul hardly realizes is that, unbeliever or not, his loneliness is really homesickness for God."— Dom Hubert Van Zeller

833. "Everyone is lonely, we have to remember that life is to be lived one day at a time. You cannot worry about the past or future. Happiness is in the now."— Claudia Gray

834. "I am a part of all that I have met."— Alfred Tennyson, The Complete Poetical Works of Tennyson

835. "You must take life the way it comes at you and make the best of it."— Yann Martel, Life of Pi

836. "I think that we are like stars. Something happens to burst us open; but when we burst open and think we are dying; we're actually turning into a supernova. And then when we look at ourselves again, we see that we're suddenly more beautiful than we ever were before!"— C. JoyBell C.

837. "I may not always be with you But when we're far apart Remember you will be with me Right inside my heart"— Marc Wambolt, Poems from the Heart

838. "These people fail to realize that it is on the inside that God must be defended, not on the outside. They should direct their anger at themselves. For evil in the open is but evil from within that has been let out. The main battlefield for good is not the open ground of the public arena but the small clearing of each heart."— Yann Martel, Life of Pi

839. "A rock pile ceases to be a rock pile the moment a single man contemplates it, bearing within him the image of a cathedral."— Antoine de Saint-Exupéry, The Little Prince

840. "It only takes a split second to smile and forget, yet to someone that needed it, it can last a lifetime. We should all smile more often."— Steve Maraboli, Life, the Truth, and Being Free

841. "If I must fall, may it be from a high place."— Paulo Coelho, By the River Piedra I Sat Down and Wept

842. "I remembered the fox. One runs the risk of crying a bit if one allows oneself to be tamed."— Antoine de Saint-Exupéry, The Little Prince

843. "Each suburban wife struggles with it alone. As she made the beds, shopped for groceries, matched slipcover material, ate peanut butter sandwiches with her children, chauffeured Cub Scouts and Brownies, lay beside her husband at night- she was afraid to ask even of herself the silent question-- 'Is this all?'"— Betty Friedan, The Feminine Mystique

844. "I give myself a good cry if I need it. But then I concentrate on the good things still in my life. I don't allow myself any more self-pity than that. A little each every morning, a few tears, and that's all. "— Mitch Albom, Tuesdays With Morrie

845. "When you have exhausted all possibilities, remember this - you haven't."— Thomas A. Edison

846. "I've had many enemies over the years. If there's one thing I've learned, it's never engage in a fight you're sure to lose. On the other hand, never let anyone who has insulted you get away with it. Bide your time and strike back when you're in a position of strength—even if you no longer need to strike back."— Stieg Larsson, The Girl with the Dragon Tattoo

847. "I cannot believe that the purpose of life is to be happy. I think the purpose of life is to be useful, to be responsible, to be compassionate. It is, above all to matter, to count, to stand for something, to have made some difference that you lived at all..."— Leo Rosten

848. "You should never assume. You know what happens when you assume. You make an ass out of you and me because that's how it's spelled."— Ellen DeGeneres

849. "No Difference
Small as a peanut,
Big as a giant,
We're all the same size
When we turn off the light.
Rich as a sultan,
Poor as a mite,
We're all worth the same
When we turn off the light.
Red, black or orange,
Yellow or white,We all look the same
When we turn off the light.
So maybe the way,To make everything right
Is for god to just reach out
And turn off the light!"— Shel Silverstein

850. "There's no limit to what you can dream. You expect the unexpected, you believe in magic, in fairy tales, and in possibilities. Then you grow older and that innocence is shattered and somewhere along the way the reality of life gets in the way and you're hit by the realization that you can't be all you wanted to be, you just might have to settle for a little bit less."— Cecelia Ahern

851. "To love is easy, to be in a relationship is extremely difficult."— Santosh Kalwar, Quote Me Everyday

852. "Men and women who turn their lives over to God will discover that He can make a lot more out of their lives than they can. He can deepen their joys, expand their vision, quicken their minds, strengthen their muscles, lift their spirits, multiply their blessings, increase their opportunities, comfort their souls, and pour out peace."— Ezra Taft Benson

853. "What if I'm in Slytherin?' The whisper was for his father alone, and Harry knew that only the moment of departure could have forced Albus to reveal how great and sincere that fear was. Harry crouched down so that Albus's face was slightly above his own. Alone of Harry's three children, Albus had inherited Lily's eyes. Albus Severus', Harry said quietly, so that nobody but Ginny could hear, and she was tactful enough to pretend to be waving to Rose, who was now on the train, 'you were named for two headmasters of Hogwarts. One of them was a Slytherin and he was probably the bravest man I ever knew'."— J.K. Rowling, Harry Potter and the Deathly Hallows

854. "Early to bed and early to rise makes a man healthy, wealthy, and wise."— Benjamin Franklin

855. "Many persons have a wrong idea of what constitutes true happiness. It is not attained through self-gratification but through fidelity to a worthy purpose."— Helen Keller

856. "Everything that is done in this world is done by hope."— Martin Luther

857. "Sometimes you have to steer away from the crowd in order to be a better person. It's not always easy, that's for sure. But it's right. And sometimes doing the right thing feels good, even if it does end up in a trip to the principal's office."— Simone Elkeles, Leaving Paradise

858. "If we don't change the direction we are headed, we will end up where we are going."— Jodi Picoult, Nineteen Minutes

859. "You are old beyond your years Zoeybird. Believe in yourself and you will find a way. But remember darkness does not always equate to evil just like light does not always bring good."— P.C. Cast, Marked

860. "To all that come to this happy place, welcome. Disneyland is your land. Here age relives fond memories of the past, and here youth may savor the challenge and promise of the future. Disneyland is dedicated to the ideals, the dreams, and the hard facts that have created America... with hope that it will be a source of joy and inspiration to all the world."— Walt Disney Company

861. "But what is life if you don't live it?"— James Patterson, Suzanne's Diary for Nicholas

862. "All you need is trust and a little bit of pixie dust!"— J.M. Barrie

863. "Your world is a living expression of how you are using and have used your mind."— Earl Nightingale

864. "Renew, release, let go. Yesterday's gone. There's nothing you can do to bring it back. You can't "should've" done something. You can only DO something. Renew yourself. Release that attachment. Today is a new day!"— Steve Maraboli, Unapologetically You: Reflections on Life and the Human Experience

865. "The universe is big, it's vast and complicated, and ridiculous. And sometimes, very rarely, impossible things just happen and we call them miracles. And that's the theory. Nine hundred years, never seen one yet, but this would do me."— Steven Moffat

866. "At the end of the day, let there be no excuses, no explanations, no regrets."— Steve Maraboli, Life, the Truth, and Being Free

867. "When you see a good person, think of becoming like her/him. When you see someone not so good, reflect on your own weak points."— Confucius

868. "Remember tonight... for it is the beginning of always"— Dante Alighieri

869. "It doesn't matter if a million people tell you what you can't do, or if ten million tell you no. If you get one yes from God that's all you need."— Tyler Perry

870. "The doubters said,
    "Man cannot fly,"
    The doers said,
    "Maybe, but we'll try,"
    And finally soared
    In the morning glow
    While non-believers
    Watched from below."— Bruce Lee

871. "There is no need to search; achievement leads to nowhere. It makes no difference at all, so just be happy now! Love is the only reality of the world, because it is all One, you see. And the only laws are paradox, humor and change. There is no problem, never was, and never will be. Release your struggle, let go of your mind, throw away your concerns, and relax into the world. No need to resist life, just do your best. Open your eyes and see that you are far more than you imagine. You are the world, you are the universe; you are yourself and everyone else, too! It's all the marvelous Play of God. Wake up, regain your humor. Don't worry, just be happy. You are already free!"— Dan Millman, Way of the Peaceful Warrior: A Book That Changes Lives

872. "In prayer it is better to have a heart without words than words without a heart."— John Bunyan

873. "Drink your tea slowly and reverently, as if it is the axis on which the world earth revolves - slowly, evenly, without rushing toward the future."— Thích Nhất Hạnh

874. "People pay for what they do, and still more for what they have allowed themselves to become. And they pay for it very simply; by the lives they lead."— James Baldwin, Go Tell It On The Mountain

875. "By hook or by crook, I hope that you will possess yourselves of money enough to travel and to idle, to contemplate the future or the past of the world, to dream over books and loiter at street corners and let the line of thought dip deep into the stream"— Virginia Woolf

876. "I am what I am, an' I'm not ashamed. 'Never be ashamed,' my ol' dad used ter say, 'there's some who'll hold it against you, but they're not worth botherin' with."— J.K. Rowling, Harry Potter and the Goblet of Fire

877. "Facing it, always facing it, that's the way to get through. Face it."— Joseph Conrad

878. "one must always be prepared for riotous and endless waves of transformation."— Elizabeth Gilbert, Eat, Pray, Love

879. "Fourscore and seven years ago our fathers brought forth on this continent, a new nation, conceived in Liberty, and dedicated to the proposition that all men are created equal."— Abraham Lincoln, The Gettysburg Address

880. "Arrange whatever pieces come your way."— Virginia Woolf

881. "Give me the Love that leads the way
The Faith that nothing can dismay
The Hope no disappointments tire
The Passion that'll burn like fire
Let me not sink to be a clod
Make me Thy fuel, Flame of God"— Amy Carmichael

882. "Maybe some things aren't meant to be known. maybe there just meant to be accepted."— Wendy Mass, Jeremy Fink and the Meaning of Life

883. "Do not give way to useless alarm; though it is right to be prepared for the worst, there is no occasion to look on it as certain."— Jane Austen, Pride and Prejudice

884. "Of all the wonders that I have heard,It seems to me most strange that men should fear;Seeing death, a necessary end,Will come when it will come. (Act II, Scene 2)"— William Shakespeare, Julius Caesar

885. "Courage and perseverance have a magical talisman, before which difficulties disappear and obstacles vanish into air."— John Quincy Adams

886. "For the things we have to learn before we can do them, we learn by doing them."— Aristotle, The Nicomachean Ethics

887. "Try to find pleasure in the speed that you're not used to. Changing the way you do routine things allows a new person to grow inside of you. But when all is said and done, you're the one who must decide how you handle it."— Paulo Coelho

888. "My life is very monotonous," the fox said. "I hunt chickens: men hunt me. All the chickens are just alike, and all the men are just alike. And, in consequence, I am a little bored. But if you tame me, it will be as if the sun came to shine on my life. I shall know the sound of a step that will be different from all the others. Other steps send me hurrying back underneath the ground. Yours will call me, like music, out of my burrow. And then look: you see the grain fields down yonder? [...] The wheat fields have nothing to say to me. And that is sad. But you have hair that is the color of gold. Think how wonderful that will be when you have tamed me! The grain, which is also golden, will bring me back to the thought of you. And I shall love to listen to the wheat in the wind..."— Antoine de Saint-Exupéry

889. "As for what it's against - the story is against those who pervert and misuse religion, or any other kind of doctrine with a holy book and a priesthood and an apparatus of power that wields unchallengeable authority, in order to dominate and suppress human freedoms."— Philip Pullman, His Dark Materials

890. "If I am truly to become an autonomous woman, then I must take over that role of being my own guardian...I not only have to become my own husband, but I need to be my own father, too."— Elizabeth Gilbert

891. "You are doing the best you can, and that best results in good to yourself and to others. Do not nag yourself with a sense of failure. Get on your knees and ask for the blessings of the Lord; then stand on your feet and do what you are asked to do."— Gordon B. Hinckley

892. "Rogerson," I asked him sweetly as we sat watching a video in the pool house, "where would I find the pelagic zone?" "In the open sea," he said. "Now shut up and eat your Junior Mints."— Sarah Dessen, Dreamland

893. "How would your life be different if...You walked away from gossip and verbal defamation? Let today be the day...You speak only the good you know of other people and encourage others to do the same."— Steve Maraboli, Life, the Truth, and Being Free

894. "Don't confuse poor decision-making with destiny. Own your mistakes. It's ok; we all make them. Learn from them so they can empower you!"— Steve Maraboli, Life, the Truth, and Being Free

895. "Do all the good you can. By all the means you can. In all the ways you can. In all the places you can. At all the times you can. To all the people you can. As long as ever you can."— John Wesley

896. "Let today be the day you stop being haunted by the ghost of yesterday. Holding a grudge & harboring anger/resentment is poison to the soul. Get even with people...but not those who have hurt us, forget them, instead get even with those who have helped us."— Steve Maraboli, Life, the Truth, and Being Free

897. "To call woman the weaker sex is a libel; it is man's injustice to woman. If by strength is meant brute strength, then, indeed, is woman less brute than man. If by strength is meant moral power, then woman is immeasurably man's superior. Has she not greater intuition, is she not more self-sacrificing, has she not greater powers of endurance, has she not greater courage? Without her, man could not be. If nonviolence is the law of our being, the future is with woman. Who can make a more effective appeal to the heart than woman?"— Mahatma Gandhi

898. "You may choose to look the other way but you can never say again that you did not know."— William Wilberforce

899. "...Next time you're faced with a choice, do the right thing. It hurts everyone less in the long run."— Wendelin Van Draanen, Flipped

900. "Faith is the bird that feels the light and sings when the dawn is still dark."— Rabindranath Tagore

901. "It does not matter how slowly you go so long as you do not stop."— Andy Warhol

902. "There is nothing more beautiful than seeing a person being themselves. Imagine going through your day being unapologetically you."— Steve Maraboli, Unapologetically You: Reflections on Life and the Human Experience

903. "She had been given a wonderful gift: life. Sometimes it was cruelly taken away too soon, but it's what you did with it that counted, not how long it lasted."— Cecelia Ahern, P.S. I Love You

904. "Life is short. If you doubt me, ask a butterfly. Their average life span is a mere five to fourteen days."— Ellen DeGeneres, The Funny Thing Is...

905. "Remind thyself, in the darkest moments, that every failure is only a step toward success, every detection of what is false directs you toward what is true, every trial exhausts some tempting form of error, and every adversity will only hide, for a time, your path to peace and fulfillment. "— Og Mandino

906. "It's not that some people have willpower and some don't... It's that some people are ready to change and others are not."— James Gordon

907. "Do not become someone else just because you are hurt. Be who you are & smile, it may solve, all problems you have got."— Santosh Kalwar, Quote Me Everyday

908. "If I had to choose between betraying my country and betraying my friend, I hope I should have the guts to betray my country"— E.M. Forster

909. "The second thing you have to do to be a writer is to keep on writing. Don't listen to people who tell you that very few people get published and you won't be one of them. Don't listen to your friend who says you are better that Tolkien and don't have to try any more. Keep writing, keep faith in the idea that you have unique stories to tell, and tell them. I meet far too many people who are going to be writers 'someday.' When they are out of high school, when they've finished college, after the wedding, when the kids are older, after I retire . . . That is such a trap You will never have any more free time than you do right now. So, whether you are 12 or 70, you should sit down today and start being a writer if that is what you want to do. You might have to write on a notebook while your kids are playing on the swings or write in your car on your coffee break. That's okay. I think we've all 'been there, done that.' It all starts with the writing. "— Robin Hobb

910. "Always tell what you feel. Do what you think..."— Gabriel Garcí¬a Márquez

911. "The whole summer lay ahead of us-time to rest, time to wait. And when the future comes-no matter what comes with it-I'll be smarter. I'll be stronger. I'll be ready."— Ally Carter, Cross My Heart and Hope to Spy

912. "being afraid to take chances is scarier than actually doing things that challenge you."— Simone Elkeles, Leaving Paradise

913. "We never know how high we are till we are called to rise. Then if we are true to form our statures touch the skies."— Emily Dickinson, Collected Poems of Emily Dickinson

914. "I'm beginning to think that maybe it's not just how much you love someone. Maybe what matters is who you are when you're with them."— Anne Tyler, The Accidental Tourist

915. "It takes as much courage to have tried and failed as it does to have tried and succeeded."— Anne Morrow Lindbergh

916. "Sometimes small things can become very large, indeed."— Rick Riordan

917. "It's been said that love finds you when you're ready."— James Patterson

918. "What she had long believed was not true, and now the world was wide open to discover what was.

919. It is like all my life I thought the sky was green."— Shannon Hale

920. "Love cures people, both the ones who give it and the ones who receive it."— Karl A. Menninger

921. "Were knowledge all, what were our need
    To thrill and faint and sweetly bleed?"— Christopher Brennan

922. "No matter what he does, every person on earth plays a central role in the history of the world. And normally he doesn't know it."— Paulo Coelho, The Alchemist

923. "People have to forgive. We don't have to like them, we don't have to be friends with them, we don't have to send them hearts in text messages, but we have to forgive them, to overlook, to forget. Because if we don't we are tying rocks to our feet, too much for our wings to carry!"— C. JoyBell C.

924. "You're beautiful, but you're empty...One couldn't die for you. Of course, an ordinary passerby would think my rose looked just like you. But my rose, all on her own, is more important than all of you together, since she's the one I've watered. Since she's the one I put under glass, since she's the one I sheltered behind the screen. Since she's the one for whom I killed the caterpillars (except the two or three butterflies). Since she's the one I listened to when she complained, or when she boasted, or even sometimes when she said nothing at all. Since she's my rose."— Antoine de Saint-Exupéry, The Little Prince

925. "Even if things don't unfold the way you expected, don't be disheartened or give up. One who continues to advance will win in the end."— Daisaku Ikeda

926. "Whatever the mind can conceive and believe, it can achieve."— Napoleon Hill, Think and Grow Rich: A Black Choice

927. "One of the most spiritual things you can do is embrace your humanity. Connect with those around you today. Say "I love you", "I'm sorry", "I appreciate you", "I'm proud of you"...whatever you're feeling. Send random texts, write a cute note, embrace your truth and share it...cause a smile today for someone else...and give plenty of hugs."— Steve Maraboli, Life, the Truth, and Being Free

928. "People who lack the clarity, courage, or determination to follow their own dreams will often find ways to discourage yours. When you change for the better, the people around you will be inspired to change also....but only after doing their best to make you stop. Live your truth and don't EVER stop."— Steve Maraboli, Life, the Truth, and Being Free

929. "Plant seeds of happiness, hope, success, and love; it will all come back to you in abundance. This is the law of nature."— Steve Maraboli, Unapologetically You: Reflections on Life and the Human Experience

930. "Maktub" (It is written.)"— Paulo Coelho, The Alchemist

931. "The only difference between you and God is that you have forgotten you are divine."— Dan Brown, The Lost Symbol

932. "Be not ashamed women, you are the gates of the body, and you are the gates of the soul."— Walt Whitman

933. "You have every right to a beautiful life."— Selena Gomez

934. "First you jump off the cliff and build your wings on the way down."— Ray Bradbury

935. "You can love a person dear to you with a human love, but an enemy can only be loved with divine love."— Leo Tolstoy, War and Peace

936. "All changes, even the most longed for, have their melancholy; for what we leave behind us is a part of ourselves; we must die to one life before we can enter another."— Anatole France

937. "When your will is God's will, you will have your will."— Charles H. Spurgeon

938. "Happiness is the object and design of our existence; and will be the end thereof, if we pursue the path that leads to it; and this path is virtue, uprightness, faithfulness, holiness, and keeping all the commandments of God."— Joseph Smith Jr.

939. "If you don't like the road you're walking, start paving another one."— Dolly Parton

940. "I realize that life is risks. It's acknowledging the past but looking forward. It's taking a chance that we will make mistakes but believing that we all deserve to be forgiven."— Carrie Ryan, The Dead-Tossed Waves

941. "Take wrong turns. Talk to strangers. Open unmarked doors. And if you see a group of people in a field, go find out what they are doing. Do things without always knowing how they'll turn out. You're curious and smart and bored, and all you see is the choice between working hard and slacking off. There are so many adventures that you miss because you're waiting to think of a plan. To find them, look for tiny interesting choices. And remember that you are always making up the future as you go."— Randall Munroe, xkcd: volume 0

942. "Yes, I have tricks in my pocket, I have things up my sleeve. But I am the opposite of a stage magician. He gives you illusion that has the appearance of truth. I give you truth in the pleasant disguise of illusion."— Tennessee Williams, The Glass Menagerie

943. "To touch the soul of another human being is to walk on holy ground."— Stephen R. Covey

944. "Each of us is full of shit in our own special way. We are all shitty little snowflakes dancing in the universe."— Lewis Black, Me of Little Faith

945. "How does one become a butterfly? They have to want to learn to fly so much that you are willing to give up being a caterpillar."— Trina Paulus, Hope for the Flowers

946. "Argue not concerning God,...re-examine all that you have been told at church or school or in any book, dismiss whatever insults your soul..."— Walt Whitman

947. "As long as you have life and breath, believe. Believe for those who cannot. Believe even if you have stopped believing. Believe for the sake of the dead, for love, to keep your heart beating, believe. Never give up, never despair, let no mystery confound you into the conclusion that mystery cannot be yours."— Mark Helprin, A Soldier of the Great War

948. "People are always telling me that I'm not like other girls...that I don't dress like other girls...that I don't act like other girls. But I'm my OWN person...I go to the beat of my own drum."— Miley Cyrus

949. "I do like the world quite a lot."— Shannon Hale, Book of a Thousand Days

950. "Avoid loud and aggressive persons, they are vexations to the spirit."— Max Ehrmann, Desiderata: A Poem for a Way of Life

951. "A star falls from the sky and into your hands. Then it seeps through your veins and swims inside your blood and becomes every part of you. And then you have to put it back into the sky. And it's the most painful thing you'll ever have to do and that you've ever done. But what's yours is yours. Whether it's up in the sky or here in your hands. And one day, it'll fall from the sky and hit you in the head real hard and that time, you won't have to put it back in the sky again."— C. JoyBell C.

952. "If I am to be fallen into love, I will. And if as a result I will appear to be stupid, disillusioned, and of poor judgment, I will. And I would be damned if I cared what other people think. For I would rather be thought of as all of these things, than not love. If in loving, I become the naked woman on the horse, I will ride that horse with my head held high. This is my spirit. I am unbreakable."— C. JoyBell C.

953. "Don't think about making life better for other people who don't even deserve you, rather, focus on making your life the best, for yourself and those who love you."— C. JoyBell C.

954. "If you hang out with chickens, you're going to cluck and if you hang out with eagles, you're going to fly."— Steve Maraboli, Unapologetically You: Reflections on Life and the Human Experience

955. "I'm going to paraphrase Thoreau here... rather than love, than money, than faith, than fame, than fairness... give me truth."— Jon Krakauer, Into the Wild

956. "Great things are not done by impulse, but by a series of small things brought together."— Vincent van Gogh

957. "No. Don't give up hope just yet. It's the last thing to go. When you have lost hope, you have lost everything. And when you think all is lost, when all is dire and bleak, there is always hope."— Pittacus Lore, I Am Number Four

958. "Don't find fault, find a remedy; anybody can complain"— Henry Ford

959. "Scars are not injuries, Tanner Sack. A scar is a healing. After injury, a scar is what makes you whole."— China Miéville, The Scar

960. "Always forgive, but never forget, else you will be a prisoner of your own hatred, and doomed to repeat your mistakes forever."— Wil Zeus, Sun Beyond the Clouds

961. "Everything changed the day she figured out there was exactly enough time for the important things in her life."— Brian Andreas

962. "The place God calls you to is the place where your deep gladness and the world's deep hunger meet."— Frederick Buechner, Wishful Thinking: A Theological ABC

963. "Whatever you think, be sure it is what you think; whatever you want, be sure that is what you want; whatever you feel, be sure that is what you feel."— T.S. Eliot

964. "Hard times build determination and inner strength. Through them we can also come to appreciate the uselessness of anger. Instead of getting angry nurture a deep caring and respect for troublemakers because by creating such trying circumstances they provide us with invaluable opportunities to practice tolerance and patience."— Dalai Lama XIV

965. "Complain and remain. Praise and be raised."— Joyce Meyer

966. "God save us from religion."— David Eddings

967. "The beauty of the world...has two edges, one of laughter, one of anguish, cutting the heart asunder."— Virginia Woolf

968. "The deeds you do may be the only sermon some persons will hear today"— St. Francis of Assisi

969. "Two wrongs don't make a right, but don't three lefts make a right? Two wrongs don't make a right, but don't two negatives make a positive?"— Andrew Clements, Things Not Seen

970. "You need just the right amount of 'Fuck the world' and the right amount of belief in something...and you need the right amount of love."— Gerard Way

971. "Wherever men and women are persecuted because of their race, religion, or political views, that place must — at that moment — become the center of the universe."— Elie Wiesel

972. "In his suicide note, Kurt Cobain wrote, "It's better to burn out than to fade away." He was quoting a Neil Young song about Johnny Rotten of the Sex Pistols. When I was twenty-four, I interviewed John Lennon. I asked him about this sentiment, one that pervades rock and roll. He took strong, outraged exception to it. "It's better to fade away like an old soldier than to burn out," he said. "I worship people who survive. I'll take the living and the healthy."— David Sheff, Beautiful Boy: A Father's Journey Through His Son's Addiction

973. "Never let anybody guess that you have a mind of your own. Above all be pure"— Virginia Woolf

974. "Self-esteem comes from being able to define the world in your own terms and refusing to abide by the judgments of others."— Oprah Winfrey

975. "When God had made The Man, he made him out of stuff that sung all the time and glittered all over. Some angels got jealous and chopped him into millions of pieces, but still he glittered and hummed. So they beat him down to nothing but sparks but each little spark had a shine and a song. So they covered each one over with mud. And the lonesomeness in the sparks makes them hunt for one another."— Zora Neale Hurston, Their Eyes Were Watching God

976. "Wanderer, your footsteps are the road, and nothing more; wanderer, there is no road, the road is made by walking. By walking one makes the road, and upon glancing behind one sees the path that never will be trod again. Wanderer, there is no road-- Only wakes upon the sea.

977. "Miracles do not, in fact, break the laws of nature."— C.S. Lewis, Miracles

978. "The cause of most of man's unhappiness is sacrificing what he wants most for what he wants now."— Gordon B. Hinckley

979. "Can a dream be wrong? Aren't dreams God's way of telling you things?"— Ellen Hopkins

980. "I can tell you I love you as many times as you can stand to hear it, but all it does is remind us that love is not enough. Not even close."— Mark Andrus

981. "How would your life be different if...You stopped allowing other people to dilute or poison your day with their words or opinions? Let today be the day...You stand strong in the truth of your beauty and journey through your day without

attachment to the validation of others"— Steve Maraboli, Life, the Truth, and Being Free

982. "Go into yourself. Find out the reason that commands you to write; see whether it has spread its roots into the very depths of your heart; confess to yourself whether you would have to die if you were forbidden to write.
This most of all: ask yourself in the most silent hour of your night: must I write? Dig into yourself for a deep answer. And if this answer rings out in assent, if you meet this solemn question with a strong, simple "I must," then build your life in accordance with this necessity; your whole life, even into its humblest and most indifferent hour, must become a sign and witness to this impulse. Then come close to Nature. Then, as if no one had ever tried before, try to say what you see and feel and love and lose...
...Describe your sorrows and desires, the thoughts that pass through your mind and your belief in some kind of beauty - describe all these with heartfelt, silent, humble sincerity and, when you express yourself, use the Things around you, the images from your dreams, and the objects that you remember. If your everyday life seems poor, don't blame it; blame yourself; admit to yourself that you are not enough of a poet to call forth its riches; because for the creator there is not poverty and no poor, indifferent place. And even if you found yourself in some prison, whose walls let in none of the world's sounds – wouldn't you still have your childhood, that jewel beyond all price, that treasure house of memories? Turn your attentions to it. Try to raise up the sunken feelings of this enormous past; your personality will grow stronger, your solitude will expand and become a place where you can live in the twilight, where the noise of other people passes by, far in the distance. - And if out of this turning-within, out of this immersion in your own world, poems come, then you will not think of asking anyone whether they are good or not. Nor will you try to interest magazines in these works: for you will see them as your dear natural possession, a piece of your life, a voice from it. A work of art is good if it has arisen out of necessity. That is the only way one can judge it."— Rainer Maria Rilke

983. "We've all started to put down the virtues of the other factions in the process of bolstering our own. I don't want to do that. I want to be brave, and selfless, and smart, and kind, and honest." He clears his throat. "I continually struggle with kindness."— Veronica Roth, Divergent

984. "Walk with the dreamers, the believers, the courageous, the cheerful, the planners, the doers, the successful people with their heads in the clouds and their feet on the ground. Let their spirit ignite a fire within you to leave this world better than when you found it..."— Wilferd Peterson

985. "Anything that's human is mentionable, and anything that is mentionable can be more manageable. When we can talk about our feelings, they become less overwhelming, less upsetting, and less scary. The people we trust with that important talk can help us know that we are not alone."— Fred Rogers

986. "I hate you."
I love you."
You're a freak, you know that? Everyone says so. They always have."
I'm trying not to be."— Stephen Chbosky, The Perks of Being a Wallflower

987. "Everything will turn out right, the world is built on that."— Mikhail Bulgakov, The Master and Margarita

988. "Everything stinks till it's finished."— Dr. Seuss

989. "The world is so empty if one thinks only of mountains, rivers & cities; but to know someone who thinks & feels with us, & who, though distant, is close to us in spirit, this makes the earth for us an inhabited garden."— Johann Wolfgang von Goethe

990. "In a strong relationship, you should love your companion more than you need them."— Steve Maraboli, Life, the Truth, and Being Free

991. "When I hear music, I fear no danger. I am invulnerable. I see no foe. I am related to the earliest times, and to the latest."— Henry David Thoreau

992. "One of the great liabilities of history is that all too many people fail to remain awake through great periods of social change. Every society has its protectors of status quo and its fraternities of the indifferent who are notorious for sleeping through revolutions. Today, our very survival depends on our ability to stay awake, to adjust to new ideas, to remain vigilant and to face the challenge of change."— Martin Luther King Jr.

993. "Don't limit a child to your own learning, for she was born in another time."— Rabindranath Tagore

994. "If people make fun of you, that probably means you're doing something right."— Evanescence

995. "O me! O life!... of the questions of these recurring;
Of the endless trains of the faithless—of cities fill'd with the foolish;
Of myself forever reproaching myself, (for who more foolish than I, and who more faithless?)
Of eyes that vainly crave the light—of the objects mean—of the struggle ever renew'd;
Of the poor results of all—of the plodding and sordid crowds I see around me;
Of the empty and useless years of the rest—with the rest me intertwined;
The question, O me! so sad, recurring—What good amid these, O me, O life?
Answer.That you are here—that life exists, and identity;
That the powerful play goes on, and you will contribute a verse."— Walt Whitman, Leaves of Grass

996. "Two years he walks the earth. No phone, no pool, no pets, no cigarettes. Ultimate freedom. An extremist. An aesthetic voyager whose home is the road. Escaped from Atlanta. Thou shalt not return, 'cause "the West is the best." And now after two rambling years comes the final and greatest adventure. The climactic battle to kill the false being within and victoriously conclude the spiritual pilgrimage. Ten days and nights of freight trains and hitchhiking bring him to the Great White North. No longer to be poisoned by civilization he flees, and walks alone upon the land to become lost in the wild.--Alexander Supertramp, May 1992"— Christopher McCandless

997. "There are scores of people waiting for someone just like us to come along; people who will appreciate our compassion, our encouragement, who will need our unique talents. Someone who will live a happier life merely because we took the time to share what we had to give."— Leo Buscaglia

998. "When I was alive, I believed — as you do — that time was at least as real and solid as myself, and probably more so. I said 'one o'clock' as though I could see it, and 'Monday' as though I could find it on the map; and I let myself be hurried along from minute to minute, day to day, year to year, as though I were actually moving from one place to another. Like everyone else, I lived in a house bricked up with seconds and minutes, weekends and New Year's Days, and I never went outside until I died, because there was no other door. Now I know that I could have walked through the walls. (...) You can strike your own time, and start the count anywhere. When you understand that — then any time at all will be the right time for you."— Peter S. Beagle, The Last Unicorn

999. "It is not enough to be industrious; so are the ants. What are you industrious about?"[Letter to Harrison Blake; November 16, 1857]"— Henry David Thoreau, Letters to Various Persons

1000. "Your children are not your children. They are the sons and daughters of Life's longing for itself...You may house their bodies but not their souls, for their souls dwell in the house of tomorrow, which you cannot visit, not even in your dreams."— Kahlil Gibran

1001. "Stand up and walk. Move on. After all, you have perfect legs to stand on."— Hiromu Arakawa

1002. "To invent your own life's meaning is not easy, but it's still allowed, and I think you'll be happier for the trouble."— Bill Watterson

1003. "The Lord is my shepherd. I shall not want for nothing. He makes me lie down in the green pastures. He greases up my head with oil. He gives me kung-Fu in the face of my enemies. Amen"— Stephen King, The Stand

1004. "energy and persistence conquers all things"— Benjamin Franklin

1005. "Love was that way. You could not render it in black or white. It always came down to the strange, blended shades of grey."— Jodi Picoult

1006. "It's not how old you are, it's how you are old."— Jules Renard

1007. "Life consists of what man is thinking about all day."— Ralph Waldo Emerson

1008. "(Captain Hammer)
It may not feel too classy, begging just to eat
But you know who does that?
Lassie, and she always gets a treat So you wonder what your part is Because you're homeless and depressed But home is where the heart is
So your real home's in your chest Everyone's a hero in their own way Everyone's

got villains they must face
They're not as cool as mine
But folks you know it's fine to know your place Everyone's a hero in their own way
In their own not-that-heroic way
So I thank my girlfriend Penny
Yeah, we totally had sex
She showed me there's so many different muscles I can flex
There's the deltoids of compassion, there's the abs of being kind
It's not enough to bash in heads, you've got to bash in minds Everyone's a hero in their own way Everyone's got something they can do Get up go out and fly
Especially that guy, he smells like poo
Everyone's a hero in their own way You and you and mostly me and you
I'm poverty's new sheriff And I'm bashing in the slums
A hero doesn't care if you're a bunch of scary alcoholic bums
Everybody! Everyone's a hero in their own way Everyone can blaze a hero's trail
Don't worry if it's hard, if you're not a friggin 'tard you will prevail Everyone's a hero in their own way Everyone's a hero in their..."— Joss Whedon, Dr Horrible's Sing-Along Blog Book

1009.   "If you can keep your head when all about you're losing theirs and blaming it on you,
If you can trust yourself when all men doubt you,
But make allowance for their doubting too;
If you can wait and not be tired by waiting,
Or being lied about, don't deal in lies,
Or being hated, don't give way to hating,
And yet don't look too good, nor talk too wise
If you can dream - and not make dreams your master;
If you can think - and not make thoughts your aim;
If you can meet with Triumph and Disaster
And treat those two impostors just the same;
If you can bear to hear the truth you've spoken
Twisted by knaves to make a trap for fools,
Or watch the things you gave your life to, broken,
And stoop and build 'em up with worn-out tools
If you can make one heap of all your winnings And risk it on one turn of pitch-and-toss,
And lose, and start again at your beginnings
And never breathe a word about your loss;
If you can force your heart and nerve and sinew
To serve your turn long after they are gone,
And so hold on when there is nothing in you
Except the will which says to them: 'Hold on!'
If you can talk with crowds and keep your virtue, Or walk with Kings - nor lose the common touch, If neither foes nor loving friends can hurt you, If all men count with you, but none too much; If you can fill the unforgiving minute
With sixty seconds' worth of distance run, Yours is the Earth and everything that's in it, And - which is more - you'll be a Man, my son!"— Rudyard Kipling, If: A Father's Advice to His Son

1010.　　　"Forget yesterday - it has already forgotten you. Don't sweat tomorrow - you haven't even met. Instead, open your eyes and your heart to a truly precious gift - today."— Steve Maraboli, Life, the Truth, and Being Free

1011.　　　"When you look for a man- what you want to look for is a man with the heart of a poor boy and the mind of a conqueror."— C. JoyBell C.

1012.　　　"Anger is like flowing water; there's nothing wrong with it as long as you let it flow. Hate is like stagnant water; anger that you denied yourself the freedom to feel, the freedom to flow; water that you gathered in one place and left to forget. Stagnant water becomes dirty, stinky, disease-ridden, poisonous, deadly; that is your hate. On flowing water travels little paper boats; paper boats of forgiveness. Allow yourself to feel anger, allow your waters to flow, along with all the paper boats of forgiveness. Be human."— C. JoyBell C.

1013.　　　"The best relationships in our lives are the best not because they have been the happiest ones, they are that way because they have stayed strong through the most tormentful of storms."— Pandora Poikilos, Excuse Me, My Brains Have Stepped Out

1014.　　　"So many people live within unhappy circumstances and yet will not take the initiative to change their situation because they are conditioned to a life of security, conformity, and conservatism, all of which may appear to give one peace of mind, but in reality nothing is more dangerous to the adventurous spirit within a man than a secure future. The very basic core of a man's living spirit is his passion for adventure. The joy of life comes from our encounters with new experiences, and hence there is no greater joy than to have an endlessly changing horizon, for each day to have a new and different sun."— Jon Krakauer, Into the Wild

1015.　　　"The most important decision you make is to be in a good mood."— Voltaire

1016.　　　"With your head full of brains and your shoes full of feet, you're too smart to go down any not-so-good street."— Dr. Seuss

1017.　　　"Ever since happiness heard your name, it has been running through the streets trying to find you."— Hafiz

1018.　　　"But what was there to say? Only that there were tears. Only that Quietness and Emptiness fitted together like stacked spoons. Only that there was a snuffling in the hollows at the base of a lovely throat. Only that a hard honey-colored shoulder had a semicircle of teeth marks on it. Only that they held each other close, long after it was over. Only that what they shared that night was not happiness, but hideous grief.Only that once again they broke the Love Laws. That lay down who should be loved. And how. And how much."— Arundhati Roy, The God of Small Things

1019.　　　"Anything under God's control is never out of control."— Charles R. Swindoll

1020.   "Give up to grace. The ocean takes care of each wave 'til it gets to shore. You need more help than you know."— Rumi, Words of Paradise: Selected Poems of Rumi

1021.   "Consider it: every person you have ever met, every person will suffer the loss of his friends and family. All are going to lose everything they love in this world. Why would one want to be anything but kind to them in the meantime?"— Sam Harris, The End of Faith: Religion, Terror, and the Future of Reason

1022.   "Seize the moments of happiness, love and be loved! That is the only reality in the world, all else is folly. It is the one thing we are interested in here."— Leo Tolstoy

1023.   "Distance can ruin even the best of intentions. But I suppose it depends on how you look at it. Distance just adds a richness you would not otherwise get. People come. People go. They will drift in and out of your life, almost like characters in a favorite book. When you finally close the cover, the characters have told their stories and you start up again with another book, complete with new characters and adventures. Then you find yourself focusing on the new ones. Not the ones from the past."— Nicholas Sparks, The Rescue

1024.   "The deepest secret is that life is not a process of discovery, but a process of creation. You are not discovering yourself, but creating yourself anew. Seek therefore, not to find out Who You Are, but seek to determine Who You Want to Be."— Neale Donald Walsch

1025.   "We judge ourselves by what we feel capable of doing, while others judge us by what we have already done."— Henry Wadsworth Longfellow

1026.   "I am still determined to be cheerful and happy, in whatever situation I may be; for I have also learned from experience that the greater part of our happiness or misery depends upon our dispositions, and not upon our circumstances."— Martha Washington

1027.   "A thousand words leave not the same deep impression as does a single deed."— Henrik Ibsen

1028.   "Time is what keeps things from happening all at once."— Ann Brashares, The Sisterhood of the Traveling Pants

1029.   "Never apologize for showing feeling. When you do so, you apologize for the truth."— Benjamin Disraeli

1030.   "If we admit that human life can be ruled by reason, then all possibility of life is destroyed."— Leo Tolstoy

1031.   "And if these mountains had eyes, they would wake to find two strangers in their fences, standing in admiration as a breathing red pours its tinge upon earth's shore. These mountains, which have seen untold sunrises, long to thunder praise but stand reverent, silent so that man's weak praise should be given God's attention."— Donald Miller, Through Painted Deserts: Light, God, and Beauty on the Open Road

1032.   "Do what you love, think what you feel and live the way you want."— Santosh Kalwar, Quote Me Everyday

1033.   "If you want something you can have it, but only if you want everything that goes with it, including all the hard work and the despair, and only if you're willing to risk failure."— Philip Pullman, Clockwork

1034.   "None of us will ever accomplish anything excellent or commanding except when he listens to this whisper which is heard by him alone."— Ralph Waldo Emerson

1035.   "Status quo, you know, is Latin for 'the mess we're in'."— Ronald Reagan

1036.   "The heart may freeze, or it can burn. The pain will ease and I can learn. There is no future, there is no past. I live this moment as, my last."— Jonathan Larson, Rent: The Complete Book and Lyrics of the Broadway Musical

1037.   "Impossible is not a word"— Obert Skye, Leven Thumps and the Gateway to Foo

1038.   "When you're cool for twenty, you get paid for twenty-one."— Miguel Piñero

1039.   "There must be those among whom we can sit down and weep and still be counted as warriors."— Adrienne Rich

1040.   "I'm not in search of sanctity, sacredness, purity; these things are found after this life, not in this life; but in this life I search to be completely human: to feel, to give, to take, to laugh, to get lost, to be found, to dance, to love and to lust, to be so human."— C. JoyBell C.

1041.   "We cannot be sure of having something to live for unless we are willing to die for it."— Ernesto Guevara

1042.   "You don't need anybody to tell you who you are or what you are. You are what you are!"— John Lennon

1043.   "If you can't do great things, do small things in a great way."— Napoleon Hill

1044.   "We should not judge people by their peak of excellence; but by the distance they have traveled from the point where they started."— Henry Ward Beecher

1045.   "Every day People straighten up the hair, why not the heart?"— Ernesto Guevara

1046.   "I think the act of reading imbues the reader with sensitivity toward the outside world that people who don't read can sometimes lack. I know it seems like a contradiction in terms; after all reading is such a solitary, internalizing act that it appears to represent a disengagement from day-to-day life. But reading, and particularly the reading of fiction, encourages us to view the world in new and challenging ways...It allows us to inhabit the consciousness of another which is a precursor to empathy, and empathy is, for me, one of the marks of a decent human being."— John Connolly, The Book of Lost Things

1047.   "I came to the conclusion long ago that all religions were true and that also that all had some error in them, and while I hold by my own religion, I should hold other religions as dear as Hinduism. So we can only pray, if we were Hindus, not that a Christian should become a Hindu; but our innermost prayer should be that a Hindu should become a better Hindu, a Muslim a better Muslim, and a Christian a better Christian."— Mahatma Gandhi

1048.   "For My Dad ~ "I miss you every day. "Lost love is still love, Eddie. It just takes a different form, that's all. You can't hold their hand... You can't tousle their hair... But when those senses weaken another one comes to life... Memory... Memory becomes your partner. You hold it... you dance with it... Life has to end, Eddie... Love doesn't."— Mitch Albom

1049.   "The trick is to enjoy life. Don't wish away your days, waiting for better ones ahead."— Marjorie Pay Hinckley

1050.   "After all, you can't truly be happy if you've never known pain. You can't truly feel joy if you've never felt heartbreak. You can't know what it's like to be filled unless you've been empty."— Kelly Cutrone, If You Have to Cry, Go Outside: And Other Things Your Mother Never Told You

1051.   "The first rule is to keep an untroubled spirit. The second is to look things in the face and know them for what they are."— Marcus Aurelius, Meditations

1052.   "What we love determines what we seek. What we seek determines what we think and do. What we think and do determines who we are — and who we will become."— Dieter F. Uchtdorf

1053.   "As is a tale, so is life: not how long it is, but how good it is, is what matters."— Lucius Annaeus Seneca

1054.   "Prayer is not an old woman's idle amusement. Properly understood and applied, it is the most potent instrument of action."— Mahatma Gandhi

1055.   "That's a misconception, Lennie. The sky is everywhere; it begins at your feet."— Jandy Nelson, The Sky Is Everywhere

1056.   "The greatest accomplishment is not in never falling, but in rising again after you fall."— Vince Lombardi

1057.   "If we tend to the things that are important in life, if we are right with those we love, and behave in line with our faith, our lives will not be cursed with the aching throb of unfulfilled business. Our words will always be sincere, our embraces will be tight. We will never wallow in the agony of 'I could have, I should have'. We can sleep in a storm. And when its time, our goodbyes will be complete."— Mitch Albom

1058.   "Why are you trying so hard to fit in when you were born to stand out?"— Ian Wallace

1059.   "You are not here merely to make a living. You are here in order to enable the world to live more amply, with greater vision, with a finer spirit of hope and achievement. You are here to enrich the world, and you impoverish yourself if you forget the errand."— Woodrow Wilson

1060.   "Life is very short, and there's no time for fussing and fighting my friends"— John Lennon

1061.   "The hardest battle you are ever going to have to fight is the battle to be just you."— Leo Buscaglia

1062.   "It doesn't matter who you are, or where you come from, or how much money you've got in your pocket. You have your own destiny and your own life ahead of you."— Lady Gaga

1063.   "Love me or hate me I promise that it will never make or break me...<3"— Tyra Banks, Tyra's Beauty Inside & Out

1064.   "A man can't soar too high, when he flies with his own wings."— William Blake

1065.   "Boredom can be a lethal thing on a small island."— Christopher Moore, Island of the Sequined Love Nun

1066.   "To read is to empower,To empower is to write,To write is to influence,To influence is to change,To change is to live"."— Jane Evershed

1067.   "The difference we wanna make is number one to let these kids know that they're not alone, that they're actually not that messed up and that they can do whatever they want; they can express themselves however they want, without being persecuted or called a faggot or some kind of racist thing. You know, really just to get people to get over their stuff so they can live."— Gerard Way

1068.   "You have to rise above the squabbling and chaos, and keep believing. You have to always keep your goals in mind." -Hera, goddess of marriage"— Rick Riordan

1069.   "Life's great happiness is to be convinced we are loved."— Victor Hugo, Les Misérables

1070.   "Let us always meet each other with smile, for the smile is the beginning of love."— Mother Teresa

1071.   "Maybe we've lived a thousand lives before this one and in each of them we've found each other... I know I've spent each life before this one searching for you. Not someone like you but you, for your soul and mine must always come together."— Nicholas Sparks, The Notebook

1072.   "To be grateful is to recognize the Love of God in everything He has given us - and He has given us everything. Every breath we draw is a gift of His love, every moment of existence is a grace, for it brings with it immense graces from Him.Gratitude therefore takes nothing for granted, is never unresponsive, is constantly awakening to new wonder and to praise of the goodness of God. For the grateful person knows that God is good, not by hearsay but by experience. And that is what makes all the difference."— Thomas Merton

1073.   "Dare to love yourself as if you were a rainbow with gold at both ends."— Aberjhani, The River of Winged Dreams

1074.   "This is the key to life: To expect everything to be given to you from above, yet to be genuinely surprised and forever grateful, when they are. Expecting all good things to be yours, while not knowing how to take anything for granted. If there may be a key in life, this is the key."— C. JoyBell C.

1075.   "I've had a lot of worries in my life, most of which never happened"— Mark Twain

1076.   "Feet, what do I need you for when I have wings to fly?"— Frida Kahlo

1077.   "If you can't be honest with your friends and colleagues and loved ones, then what is life all about?"— Sophie Kinsella, Can You Keep a Secret?

1078.   "If through a broken heart God can bring His purposes to pass in the world, then thank Him for breaking your heart."— Oswald Chambers

1079.   "For Equilibrium, a Blessing:Like the joy of the sea coming home to shore,May the relief of laughter rinse through your soul.
As the wind loves to call things to dance,May your gravity by lightened by grace.
Like the dignity of moonlight restoring the earth,May your thoughts incline with reverence and respect.
As water takes whatever shape it is in,So free may you be about who you become.
As silence smiles on the other side of what's said,May your sense of irony bring perspective.
As time remains free of all that it frames,May your mind stay clear of all it names.
May your prayer of listening deepen enough
to hear in the depths the laughter of god."— John O'Donohue, To Bless the Space Between Us: A Book of Blessings

1080.   "When we blindly adopt a religion, a political system, a literary dogma, we become automatons."— Anaïs Nin, The Diary of Anaïs Nin, Vol. 4: 1944-1947

1081.　　　　"It's not worth our while to let our imperfections disturb us always."—Henry David Thoreau

1082.　　　　"If you are a dreamer come in"— Shel Silverstein

1083.　　　　"We could never learn to be brave and patient if there were only joy in the world"— Helen Keller

1084.　　　　"I believe that everything that you do bad comes back to you. So everything that I do that's bad, I'm going to suffer from it. But in my mind, I believe what I'm doing is right. So I feel like I'm going to heaven"— Tupac Shakur

1085.　　　　"My hope still is to leave the world a bit better than when I got here."—Jim Henson

1086.　　　　"Great victory requires great risk.-Hera"— Rick Riordan, The Lost Hero

1087.　　　　"You can feel the whole world and still feel lost in it. So many people are in pain-- no matter how smart or accomplished--they cry, they yearn, they hurt. But instead of looking down on things, they look up, which is where I should have been looking, too. Because when the world quiets to the sound of your own breathing, we all want the same things: comfort, love and a peaceful heart."—Mitch Albom

1088.　　　　"Where you stumble and fall, there you will find gold."— Joseph Campbell

1089.　　　　"Silence is argument carried out by other means."— Ernesto Guevara

1090.　　　　"she was glad she had been scarred. She said that whoever loved her now would love her true self, and not her pretty face."— Cassandra Clare, Clockwork Angel

1091.　　　　"However beautiful the strategy, you should occasionally look at the results."— Winston Churchill

1092.　　　　"Love, being in love, isn't a constant thing. It doesn't always flow at the same strength. It's not always like a river in flood. It's more like the sea. It has tides, it ebbs and flows. The thing is, when love is real, whether it's ebbing or flowing, it's always there, it never goes away. And that's the only proof you can have that it is real, and not just a crush or an infatuation or a passing fancy"—Aidan Chambers, This is All: The Pillow Book of Cordelia Kenn

1093.　　　　"Even if you don't have all the things you want, be grateful for the things you don't have that you don't want (Bob Dylan's dad)"— Bob Dylan, Chronicles, Vol. 1

1094.　　　　"I believe in the hands that work, in the brains that think, and in the hearts that love...I believe in sunshine, fresh air, friendship, calm sleep, beautiful thoughts."— Elbert Hubbard

1095.   "Be wary of strong drink, it can make you shoot at the tax collector...and miss."— Robert A. Heinlein, Time Enough for Love

1096.   "When life doesn't meet your expectations, it was important to take it with grace."— Patricia Briggs, When Demons Walk

1097.   "Spend the afternoon, you can't take it with you"— Annie Dillard

1098.   "Sameron adion aso
I shall sing a sweeter song tomorrow"— Theocritus

1099.   "I don't fit into any stereotypes. And I like myself that way."— C. JoyBell C.

1100.   "Perfectly Imperfect
We have all heard that no two snowflakes are alike. Each snowflake takes the perfect form for the maximum efficiency and effectiveness for its journey. And while the universal force of gravity gives them a shared destination, the expansive space in the air gives each snowflake the opportunity to take their own path. They are on the same journey, but each takes a different path.
Along this gravity-driven journey, some snowflakes collide and damage each other, some collide and join together, some are influenced by wind... there are so many transitions and changes that take place along the journey of the snowflake. But, no matter what the transition, the snowflake always finds itself perfectly shaped for its journey.I find parallels in nature to be a beautiful reflection of grand orchestration. One of these parallels is of snowflakes and us. We, too, are all headed in the same direction. We are being driven by a universal force to the same destination. We are all individuals taking different journeys and along our journey, we sometimes bump into each other, we cross paths, we become altered... we take different physical forms. But at all times we too are 100% perfectly imperfect. At every given moment we are absolutely perfect for what is required for our journey. I'm not perfect for your journey and you're not perfect for my journey, but I'm perfect for my journey and you're perfect for your journey. We're heading to the same place, we're taking different routes, but we're both exactly perfect the way we are.Think of what understanding this great orchestration could mean for relationships. Imagine interacting with others knowing that they too each share this parallel with the snowflake. Like you, they are headed to the same place and no matter what they may appear like to you, they have taken the perfect form for their journey. How strong our relationships would be if we could see and respect that we are all perfectly imperfect for our journey."— Steve Maraboli, Life, the Truth, and Being Free

1101.   "Jamie: You know what I figured out today?
Landon: What?
Jamie: Maybe God has a bigger plan for me than I had for myself. Like this journey never ends. Like you were sent to me because I'm sick. To help me through all this. You're my angel."— Nicholas Sparks, A Walk to Remember

1102.   "It's funny how, in this journey of life, even though we may begin at different times and places, our paths cross with others so that we may share our love, compassion, observations, and hope. This is a design of God that I appreciate and cherish."— Steve Maraboli, Unapologetically You: Reflections on Life and the Human Experience

1103.   "How would your life be different if...You stopped worrying about things you can't control and started focusing on the things you can? Let today be the day...You free yourself from fruitless worry, seize the day and take effective action on things you can change."— Steve Maraboli, Life, the Truth, and Being Free

1104.   "You were put on this earth to achieve your greatest self, to live out your purpose, and to do it fearlessly."— Steve Maraboli, Life, the Truth, and Being Free

1105.   "Mr. Franz, I think careers are a 20th century invention and I don't want one."— Jon Krakauer, Into the Wild

1106.   "I believe God is managing affairs and that He doesn't need any advice from me. With God in charge, I believe everything will work out for the best in the end. So what is there to worry about?"— Henry Ford

1107.   "Call him Voldemort, Harry. Always use the proper name for things. Fear of a name increases fear of the thing itself."— J.K. Rowling, Harry Potter and the Sorcerer's Stone

1108.   "Don't try to fix me, I'm not broken..."— Evanescence

1109.   "According to this law [the law of Dharma], you have a unique talent and a unique way of expressing it. There is something that you can do better than anyone else in the whole world--and for every unique talent and unique expression of that talent, there are also unique needs. When these needs are matched with the creative expression of your talent, that is the spark that creates affluence. Expressing your talents to fulfill needs creates unlimited wealth and abundance."— Deepak Chopra

1110.   "Love art in yourself, and not yourself in art."— Constantin Stanislavski, My Life In Art

1111.   "Man is the only creature that consumes without producing. He does not give milk, he does not lay eggs, he is too weak to pull the plough, he cannot run fast enough to catch rabbits. Yet he is lord of all the animals. He sets them to work, he gives back to them the bare minimum that will prevent them from starving, and the rest he keeps for himself."— George Orwell, Animal Farm

1112.   "Listen to your life. See it for the fathomless mystery it is. In the boredom and pain of it, no less than in the excitement and gladness: touch, taste, smell your way to the holy and hidden heart of it, because in the last analysis all moments are key moments, and life itself is grace."— Frederick Buechner, Now and Then: A Memoir of Vocation

1113.   "Because," explained Mary Rommely simply, "the child must have a valuable thing which is called imagination. The child must have a secret world in which live things that never were. It is necessary that she believe. She must start out by believing in things not of this world. Then when the world becomes too ugly for living in, the child can reach back and live in her imagination. I, myself, even in this day and at my age, have great need of recalling the miraculous lives of the Saints and the great miracles that have come to pass on earth. Only by having these things in my mind can I live beyond what I have to live for."— Betty Smith, A Tree Grows in Brooklyn

1114.　　　"Some people try to tell you the things you want in life are out of your grasp, while others lift you up on their shoulders and help you reach them. I may not know a lot, but I prefer to fill my life with people who let me climb on top of their shoulders, not people who try to keep me planted on the ground."— Katie Kacvinsky, Awaken

1115.　　　"When you say "I" and "my" too much, you lose the capacity to understand the "we" and "our"."— Steve Maraboli, Life, the Truth, and Being Free

1116.　　　"We do not remember days, we remember moments."— Cesare Pavese

1117.　　　"How would your life be different if...You approached all relationships with authenticity and honesty? Let today be the day...You dedicate yourself to building relationships on the solid foundation of truth and authenticity."— Steve Maraboli, Life, the Truth, and Being Free

1118.　　　"I close my eyesand I can see a better day.I close my eyesand pray"— Justin Bieber

1119.　　　"One of the pitfalls of childhood is that one doesn't have to understand something to feel it. By the time the mind is able to comprehend what has happened, the wounds of the heart are already too deep."— Carlos Ruiz Zafón, The Shadow of the Wind

1120.　　　"Happiness is a choice that requires effort at times."— Aeschylus

1121.　　　"The greatest challenge of the day is: how to bring about a revolution of the heart, a revolution which has to start with each one of us?"— Dorothy Day

1122.　　　"With our thoughts we make the world."— Gautama Buddha

1123.　　　"be it peace or happiness let it enfold you"— Charles Bukowski

1124.　　　"Dive deep. Drown willingly"— Ted Dekker, White: The Great Pursuit

1125.　　　"No matter who we are, no matter what our circumstances, our feelings and emotions are universal. And music has always been a great way to make people aware of that connection. It can help you open up a part of yourself and express feelings you didn't know you were feeling. It's risky to let that happen. But it's a risk you have to take-because only then will you find you're not alone."— Josh Groban

1126.   "There are only two forces at work in this world- black and white. Only people are grey."— Chris Heimerdinger, Gadiantons and the Silver Sword

1127.   "90% of the game is half mental."— Yogi Berra, The Yogi Book

1128.   "Me with nothing left to lose, plotting my big revenge in the spotlight. Give me violent revenge fantasies as a coping mechanism."— Chuck Palahniuk

1129.   "I believe in God, only I spell it Nature."— Frank Lloyd Wright, Truth Against the World: Frank Lloyd Wright Speaks for an Organic Architecture

1130.   "Try again. Fail again. Fail better."— Samuel Beckett

1131.   "If you live in a past dream, you don't enjoy what is happening right now because you will always wish it to be different than it is. There is no time to miss anyone or anything because you are alive. Not enjoying what is happening right now is living in the past and being only half alive. This leads to self-pity, suffering and tears."— Miguel Ruiz, The Four Agreements: A Practical Guide to Personal Freedom

1132.   "I never loved another person the way I loved myself."— Mae West

1133.   "There is great change to be experienced once you learn the power of letting go. Stop allowing anyone or anything to control, limit, repress, or discourage you from being your true self! Today is YOURS to shape - own it - break free from people and things that poison or dilute your spirit."— Steve Maraboli, Unapologetically You: Reflections on Life and the Human Experience

1134.   "Don't forget your history nor your destiny"— Bob Marley

1135.   "Education is teaching our children to desire the right things."— Plato

1136.   "When forever becomes a place...when forever ceases to be just a word... when it ceases to be just a measurement of time...but instead becomes a place where soul mates can dance to the song in their hearts, that is a reflection of true love."— Steve Maraboli, Life, the Truth, and Being Free

1137.   "The opinion which other people have of you is their problem, not yours."— Elisabeth Kübler-Ross, On Life After Death

1138.   "You must expect great things of yourself before you can do them."— Michael Jordan

1139.   "But there were some things I believed in. Some things I had faith in. And faith isn't about perfect attendance to services, or how much money you put on the little plate. It isn't about going sky clad to the Holy Rites, or meditating each day upon the divine.
Faith is about what you do. It's about aspiring to be better and nobler and kinder than you are. It's about making sacrifices for the good of others - even when there's not going to be anyone telling you what a hero you are."— Jim Butcher, Changes

1140.   "Life is only precious because it ends, kid. Take it from a god. You mortals don't know how lucky you are"— Rick Riordan, The Son of Neptune

1141.   "We forfeit three-fourths of ourselves in order to be like other people."— Arthur Schopenhauer

1142.   "When a man sees you are happy with him but you can be just as happy having nothing to do with him, that's when he won't want to leave your side. When you are happy, you are sexy."— Sherry Argov

1143.   "Do not waste time bothering whether you 'love' your neighbor; act as if you did. As soon as we do this we find one of the great secrets. When you are behaving as if you loved someone, you will presently come to love him."— C.S. Lewis

1144.   "Be so strong that nothing can disturb your peace of mind. Talk health, happiness, and prosperity to every person you meet. Make all your friends feel there is something special in them. Look at the sunny side of everything. Think only the best, be as enthusiastic about the success of others as you are about your own.

1145.   Forget the mistakes of the past and press on to the greater achievements of the future. Give everyone a smile. Spend so much time improving yourself that you have no time left to criticize others. Be too big for worry and too noble for anger."— Norman Vincent Peale

1146.   "Love stories are written in millimeters and milliseconds with a fast, dull pencil whose marks you can barely see, they are written in miles and eons with a chisel on the side of a mountaintop"— Gabrielle Zevin, Memoirs of a Teenage Amnesiac

1147.   "That is the hardest thing of all. It is much harder to judge yourself than to judge others. If you succeed in judging yourself, it's because you're truly a wise man."— Antoine de Saint-Exupéry

1148.   "What I've realized is that life doesn't count for much unless you're willing to do your small part to leave our children — all of our children — a better world. Any fool can have a child. That doesn't make you a father. It's the courage to raise a child that makes you a father."— Barack Obama

1149.   "This is who the f*** I am."— Lady Gaga

1150.   "There is no greater insight into the future than recognizing...when we save our children, we save ourselves"— Margaret Mead

1151.   "You're not alone
Together we stand
I'll be by your side, you know I'll take your hand
When it gets cold
And it feels like the end

There's no place to go
You know I won't give in"— Avril Lavigne

1152.   "Of life's two chief prizes, beauty and truth, I found the first in a loving heart and the second in a laborer's hand."— Kahlil Gibran

1153.   "We're called to be faithful, to take those first difficult steps--and to leave the results up to God."— Alex Harris

1154.   "Lighthouses are more helpful than churches."— Benjamin Franklin

1155.   "This was not a fearie tale. This was not the movies. This was life. It hurt more. It was excruciating. It was excruciatingly beautiful."— Francesca Lia Block, Violet & Claire

1156.   "And I remembered something else that makes us human: faith, the only weapon in our arsenal to battle doubt."— Jodi Picoult, Change of Heart

1157.   "When I pictured myself, it was always like just an outline in a coloring book, with the inside not yet completed."— Sarah Dessen

1158.   "You can't shake hands with a clenched fist."— Indira Gandhi

1159.   "I hope our wisdom will grow with our power, and teach us that the less we use our power the greater it will be."— Thomas Jefferson

1160.   "If I should have a daughter..."Instead of "Mom", she's gonna call me "Point B." Because that way, she knows that no matter what happens, at least she can always find her way to me. And I'm going to paint the solar system on the back of her hands so that she has to learn the entire universe before she can say "Oh, I know that like the back of my hand."
She's gonna learn that this life will hit you, hard, in the face, wait for you to get back up so it can kick you in the stomach. But getting the wind knocked out of you is the only way to remind your lungs how much they like the taste of air. There is hurt, here, that cannot be fixed by Band-Aids or poetry, so the first time she realizes that Wonder-woman isn't coming, I'll make sure she knows she doesn't have to wear the cape all by herself. Because no matter how wide you stretch your fingers, your hands will always be too small to catch all the pain you want to heal. Believe me, I've tried.
And "Baby," I'll tell her "don't keep your nose up in the air like that, I know that trick, you're just smelling for smoke so you can follow the trail back to a burning house so you can find the boy who lost everything in the fire to see if you can save him. Or else, find the boy who lit the fire in the first place to see if you can change him."
But I know that she will anyway, so instead I'll always keep an extra supply of chocolate and rain boots nearby, 'cause there is no heartbreak that chocolate can't fix. Okay, there's a few heartbreaks chocolate can't fix. But that's what the rain boots are for, because rain will wash away everything if you let it.
I want her to see the world through the underside of a glass bottom boat, to look through a magnifying glass at the galaxies that exist on the pin point of a human mind. Because that's how my mom taught me. That there'll be days like this,

"There'll be days like this my momma said" when you open your hands to catch and wind up with only blisters and bruises. When you step out of the phone booth and try to fly and the very people you wanna save are the ones standing on your cape. When your boots will fill with rain and you'll be up to your knees in disappointment and those are the very days you have all the more reason to say "thank you," 'cause there is nothing more beautiful than the way the ocean refuses to stop kissing the shoreline no matter how many times it's sent away. You will put the "wind" in win some lose some, you will put the "star" in starting over and over, and no matter how many land mines erupt in a minute be sure your mind lands on the beauty of this funny place called life. And yes, on a scale from one to over-trusting I am pretty damn naive but I want her to know that this world is made out of sugar. It can crumble so easily but don't be afraid to stick your tongue out and taste it. "Baby," I'll tell her "remember your mama is a worrier but your papa is a warrior and you are the girl with small hands and big eyes who never stops asking for more."
Remember that good things come in threes and so do bad things and always apologize when you've done something wrong but don't you ever apologize for the way your eyes refuse to stop shining. Your voice is small but don't ever stop singing and when they finally hand you heartbreak, slip hatred and war under your doorstep and hand you hand-outs on street corners of cynicism and defeat, you tell them that they really ought to meet your mother." — Sarah Kay

1161.   "I want to live my life in such a way that when I get out of bed in the morning, the devil says, "aw shit, he's up!"— Steve Maraboli, Unapologetically You: Reflections on Life and the Human Experience

1162.   "You are willing to die, you coward, but not to live."— Hermann Hesse, Steppenwolf

1163.   "What is now proved was once only imagined."— William Blake

1164.   "I am always doing what I cannot do yet, in order to learn how to do it."— Vincent van Gogh

1165.   "The right thing at the wrong time is the wrong thing."— Joshua Harris, I Kissed Dating Goodbye: A New Attitude Toward Relationships and Romance

1166.   "When I cannot see words curling like rings of smoke round me I am in darkness—I am nothing."— Virginia Woolf

1167.   "I disapprove of what you say, but I will defend to the death your right to say it."— Evelyn Beatrice Hall, The Friends of Voltaire

1168.   "If you don't love yourself, how in the hell you gonna love somebody else?"— RuPaul

1169.   "I wrote the song 'Down to Earth' a few years ago, and I was really excited to record it for My World album. It's a huge fan favorite. So many people feel where I'm coming from. It doesn't need any spectacular stage effects in the touring show; the best thing I can do is just sing it straight from my heart. I'm not afraid to show my emotions; if you love someone, you should tell them. If you think a girl is beautiful, you should say that. Usher says some songs work best when there's a sob in the singer's voice. You gotta let that deep feeling come through. And that's how I felt about this song. Sometimes the emotion of it is enough to bring tears to my eyes."— Justin Bieber

1170.   "A writer must teach himself that the basest of all things is to be afraid."— William Faulkner

1171.   "I know it is hard for you young mothers to believe that almost before you can turn around the children will be gone and you will be alone with your husband. You had better be sure you are developing the kind of love and friendship that will be delightful and enduring. Let the children learn from your attitude that he is important. Encourage him. Be kind. It is a rough world, and he, like everyone else, is fighting to survive. Be cheerful. Don't be a whiner."— Marjorie Pay Hinckley, Small and Simple Things

1172.   "Doing the best at this moment puts you in the best place for the next moment"— Oprah Winfrey

1173.   "As you walk and eat and travel, be where you are. Otherwise you will miss most of your life."— Gautama Buddha

1174.   "Give me strength, not to be better than my enemies, but to defeat my greatest enemy, the doubts within myself. Give me strength for a straight back and clear eyes, so when life fades, as the setting sun, my spirit may come to you without shame."— P.C. Cast

1175.   "The function of freedom is to free someone else."— Toni Morrison

1176.   "If I am the pawn of the gods, it is because they know me so well, not because they make my mind up for me."— Megan Whalen Turner, The Queen of Attolia

1177.   "In essence, if we want to direct our lives, we must take control of our consistent actions. It's not what we do once in a while that shapes our lives, but what we do consistently."— Anthony Robbins

1178.   "Most people die with their music still locked up inside them."— Benjamin Disraeli

1179.   "It's not whether you got knocked down; it's whether you get back up."— Vince Lombardi

1180.   "When I left Queen's my future seemed to stretch out before me like a straight road. I thought I could see along it for many a milestone. Now there is a bend in it. I don't know what lies around the bend, but I'm going to believe that the best does."— L.M. Montgomery, Anne of Green Gables

1181.   "I like to tell people I have the heart of a small boy, then I tell them it's in a jar on my desk"— Robert Bloch

1182.   "If you surrendered to the air, you could ride it."— Toni Morrison, Song of Solomon

1183.   "Let's start a new tomorrow, today."— Neil Gaiman, Anansi Boys

1184.   "Truth does not become more true by virtue of the fact that the entire world agrees with it, nor less so even if the whole world disagrees with it."— Maimonides, The Guide for the Perplexed

1185.   "Next to trying and winning, the best thing is trying and failing."— L.M. Montgomery

1186.   "But there's always a first time for everything"— Melissa de la Cruz, Blue Bloods

1187.   "the moment you don't feel like praying, get on your knees. And the moment you don't feel like reading your bible, you'd better get that Book open."— Lori Wick, Where the Wild Rose Blooms

1188.   "A truth that no one knows is still the truth."— Sharon Shinn, Jenna Starborn

1189.   "If the world is to be healed through human efforts, I am convinced it will be by ordinary people, people whose love for this life is even greater than their fear."— Joanna R. Macy

1190.   "The beautiful journey of today can only begin when we learn to let go of yesterday."— Steve Maraboli, Unapologetically You: Reflections on Life and the Human Experience

1191.   "The three great essentials to achieve anything worthwhile are, first, hard work; second, stick-to-itiveness; third, common sense."— Thomas A. Edison

1192.   "...even a tiny bit of deceit is dishonorable when it's used for selfish or cowardly reasons.- Mr. Penderwick"— Jeanne Birdsall, The Penderwicks on Gardam Street

1193.   "I don't want to live in the kind of world where we don't look out for each other. Not just the people that are close to us, but anybody who needs a helping hand. I can't change the way anybody else thinks, or what they choose to do, but I can do my bit."— Charles de Lint

1194.   "You have to love dancing to stick to it. It gives you nothing back, no manuscripts to store away, no paintings to show on walls and maybe hang in museums, no poems to be printed and sold, nothing but that single fleeting moment when you feel alive."— Merce Cunningham

1195.   "Ask yourself these three questions, Tatiana Metanova, and you will know who you are. Ask: What do believe in? What do you hope for? What do you love?"— Paullina Simons, The Bronze Horseman

1196.   "The past can't hurt you anymore. Not unless you let it. They made you into a victim, Evey. They made you into a statistic. But, that's not the real you. That's not who you are inside."— Alan Moore, V for Vendetta

1197.   "The value of things is not the time they last, but the intensity with which they occur. That is why there are unforgettable moments and unique people!"— Fernando Pessoa

1198.   "I am the captain of my soul."— Nelson Mandela

1199.   "Passion is a feeling that tells you: this is the right thing to do. Nothing can stand in my way. It doesn't matter what anyone else says. This feeling is so good that it cannot be ignored. I'm going to follow my bliss and act upon this glorious sensation of joy."— Wayne W. Dyer

1200.   "The adventure of life is to learn. The purpose of life is to grow. The nature of life is to change. The challenge of life is to overcome. The essence of life is to care. The opportunity of like is to serve. The secret of life is to dare. The spice of life is to befriend. The beauty of life is to give."— William Arthur Ward

1201.   "It is better for the heart to break, than not to break."— Mary Oliver

1202.   "My name is Salmon, like the fish; first name, Susie. I was fourteen when I was murdered."— Alice Sebold, The Lovely Bones

1203.   "Look not mournfully into the past, it comes not back again. Wisely improve the present, it is thine. Go forth to meet the shadowy future without fear and with a manly heart."— Henry Wadsworth Longfellow

1204.   "Freedom is a heavy load, a great and strange burden for the spirit to undertake. It is not easy. It is not a gift given, but a choice made, and the choice may be a hard one. The road goes upward towards the light; but the laden traveler may never reach the end of it."— Ursula K. Le Guin, The Tombs of Atuan

1205.   "There are several ways to react to being lost. One is to panic: this was usually Valentina's first impulse. Another is to abandon yourself to lostness, to allow the fact that you've misplaced yourself to change the way you experience the world."— Audrey Niffenegger, Her Fearful Symmetry

1206.   "A tiny change today brings a dramatically different tomorrow."— Richard Bach, One

1207.   "No name-calling truly bites deep unless, in some dark part of us, we believe it. If we are confident enough then it is just noise."— Laurell K. Hamilton, A Stroke of Midnight

1208.   "When one door closes, another door opens; but we so often look so long and regretfully upon the closed door, that we do not see the ones which open for us."— Alexander Graham Bell

1209.   "I used to have a sign pinned up on my wall that read: Only to the extent that we expose ourselves over and over to annihilation can that which is indestructible be found in us...It was all about letting go of everything. p.7"— Pema Chödrön, When Things Fall Apart: Heart Advice for Difficult Times

1210.   "Maybe it just means that love can be stronger than fear."— L.J. Smith, The Forbidden Game: Collector's Edition

1211.   "All human beings should try to learn before they die what they are running from, and to, and why."— James Thurber

1212.   "Consider non your superior, whatever their rank or station in life. Treat all fairly or they will seek revenge. Be careful with your money. Hold fast to your belief and others will listen." he continued at a slower pace, " of the affairs of love ... my only advice is to be honest. That's your most powerful too to unlock a heart or gain forgiveness. That is all I have to say"Garrow to Roran p 64"— Christopher Paolini, Eragon

1213.   "God will answer you prayers better than you think. Of course, one will not always get exactly what he has asked for....We all have sorrows and disappointments, but one must never forget that, if commended to God, they will issue in good....His own solution is far better than any we could conceive."— Fanny J. Crosby

1214.   "She could hear, some way off, her brothers calling to each other in the woods behind the house. She hoped desperately that their game wouldn't bring them any closer, that they wouldn't scare the birds away.

1215.   Somehow she knew that you didn't get many moments like this in your life: moments when you knew, without any doubt, that you were alive, when you felt the air in your lungs and the wet grass beneath your feet and the cotton on your skin; moments when you were completely in the present, when neither the past nor the future mattered.
She tried to slow her breathing, hoping somehow to make this moment last forever."— Neil Gaiman, Stardust

1216.   "Wake up, Shake up, Make up and Break up; life is all about moving like ant in search of sugar not sand."— Santosh Kalwar, Quote Me Everyday

1217.   "Now don't you understand man universal law
What you throw out comes back to you, star
Never underestimate those who you scar
Cause karma, karma, karma comes back to you hard"— Lauryn Hill

1218.   "Out, out brief candle, life is but a walking shadow...a tale told by an idiot, full of sound and fury, signifying nothing."— William Shakespeare

1219.   "there is no moment more precious than the exact moment you are living now"— Obert Skye, Leven Thumps and the Gateway to Foo

1220.   "I believe I can fly, I believe I can touch the sky."— R. Kelly

1221. "The most beautiful things in the world cannot be seen or touched, they are felt with the heart."— Antoine de Saint-Exupéry, The Little Prince

1222. "The greatest thing in the world is to know how to belong to oneself."— Michel de Montaigne, The Complete Essays

1223. "For me, I am driven by two main philosophies: know more today about the world than I knew yesterday and lessen the suffering of others. You'd be surprised how far that gets you."— Neil deGrasse Tyson

1224. "Do your best and let God do the rest."— Ben Carson

1225. "Finding one important thing in your life doesn't mean you have to give up all the other important things."— Paulo Coelho, Brida

1226. "What we see depends mainly on what we look for."— John Lubbock

1227. "When obstacles arise, you change your direction to reach your goal; you do not change your decision to get there."— Zig Ziglar

1228. "There was another life that I might have had, but I am having this one."— Kazuo Ishiguro

1229. "Because I trust in the ever-changing climate of the heart. (At least, today I feel that way.) I think it is necessary to have many experiences for the sake of feeling something; for the sake of being challenged, and for the sake of being expressive, to offer something to someone else, to learn what we are capable of."— Jason Mraz

1230. "Nobody made a greater mistake than he who did nothing because he could do only a little."— Edmund Burke

1231. "I'm not going to limit myself just because people won't accept the fact that I can do something else."— Dolly Parton

1232. "It's more fun to think of the future than dwell on the past."— Sara Shepard, Unbelievable

1233. "Accept yourself, your strengths, your weaknesses, your truths, and know what tools you have to fulfill your purpose."— Steve Maraboli, Life, the Truth, and Being Free

1234. "Til shade is gone,til water is gone
Into the shadow with teeth bared
Screaming defiance with the last breath
To spit in Sightblinder's eye on the Last Day."— Robert Jordan, The Dragon Reborn

1235. "Life keeps throwing me lemons because I make the best lemonade..."— King James Gadsden

1236.   "Unhappy memories are persistent. They're specific, and it's the details that refuse to leave us alone. Though a happy memory may stay with you just as long as one that makes you miserable, what you remember softens over time. What you recall is simply that you were happy, not necessarily the individual moments that brought about your joy.
But the memory of something painful does just the opposite. It retains its original shape, all bony fingers and pointy elbows. Every time it returns, you get a quick poke in the eye or jab in the stomach. The memory of being unhappy has the power to hurt us long after the fact. We feel the injury anew each and every time we think of it."— Cameron Dokey, Belle: A Retelling of "Beauty and the Beast"

1237.   "The best discoveries always happened to the people who weren't looking for it. Columbus and America. Pinzon, who stumbled on Brazil while looking for the West Indies. Stanley happening on Victoria Falls. And you. Amy Curry, when I was least expecting her.-Roger Sullivan"— Morgan Matson, Amy and Roger's Epic Detour

1238.   "Jesus said several times, "Come, follow me." His was a program of "do what I do," rather than "do what I say." His innate brilliance would have permitted him to put on a dazzling display, but that would have left his followers far behind. He walked and worked with those he was to serve. His was not a long-distance leadership. He was not afraid of close friendships; he was not afraid that proximity to him would disappoint his followers. The leaven of true leadership cannot lift others unless we are with and serve those to be led."— Spencer W. Kimball

1239.   "We pencil-sketch our previous life so we can contrast it to the Technicolor of the moment."— David Levithan, Boy Meets Boy

1240.   "Live all you can: it's a mistake not to. It doesn't matter what you do in particular, so long as you have had your life. If you haven't had that, what have you had?"— Henry James, The Ambassadors

1241.   "You can't always judge people by the things they done. You got to judge them by what they are doing now."— Kate DiCamillo, Because of Winn-Dixie

1242.   "And I think that's what our world is desperately in need of - lovers, people who are building deep, genuine relationships with fellow strugglers along the way, and who actually know the faces of the people behind the issues they are concerned about."— Shane Claiborne, The Irresistible Revolution: Living as an Ordinary Radical

1243.   "We're miserable because we think that we are mere individuals, alone with our fears and flaws and resentment and mortality."— Elizabeth Gilbert, Eat, Pray, Love

1244.   "I hope we never lose sight of one thing: it was all started by a mouse."— Walt Disney Company

1245.   "Every person has a right to risk their own life for the preservation of it."— Jean-Jacques Rousseau

1246.   "To separate oneself from the burden, the angst, the anguish that we all encounter every day. To say I am alive, I am wonderful, I am. I am. That is something to aspire to."— Garth Stein, The Art of Racing in the Rain

1247.   "Have to? Of course you have to! But only because of you, Harry, won't rest until Voldemort is finished! Think now, for once, if you have never heard of the prophecy! What would you do?"— J.K. Rowling, Harry Potter and the Half-Blood Prince

1248.   "I'd rather die while I'm living than live while I'm dead."— Jimmy Buffett

1249.   "The person in life that you will always be with the most, is yourself. Because even when you are with others, you are still with yourself, too! When you wake up in the morning, you are with yourself, laying in bed at night you are with yourself, walking down the street in the sunlight you are with yourself. What kind of person do you want to walk down the street with? What kind of person do you want to wake up in the morning with? What kind of person do you want to see at the end of the day before you fall asleep? Because that person is yourself, and it's your responsibility to be that person you want to be with. I know I want to spend my life with a person who knows how to let things go, who's not full of hate, who's able to smile and be carefree. So that's who I have to be."— C. JoyBell C.

1250.   "I have learned that you can go anywhere you want to go and do anything you want to do and buy all the things that you want to buy and meet all the people that you want to meet and learn all the things that you desire to learn and if you do all these things but are not madly in love: you have still not begun to live."— C. JoyBell C.

1251.   "In case you never get a second chance: don't be afraid!" "And what if you do get a second chance?" "You take it!"— C. JoyBell C.

1252.   "I am a flawed person. A brook with many stones, a clear blue sky with many blackbirds. I have many shortcomings. A rainbow that's not long enough, a starry night with clouds. But I can only be thankful to the God who loves me just this way, and I can only be grateful to the people in my life who accept the clear blue sky with many blackbirds and who are patient with the rainbow that isn't long enough. And because of this, I am taught love, because of this I love my God, and I love these people."— C. JoyBell C.

1253.   "One mistake does not have to rule a person's entire life."— Joyce Meyer, Any Minute

1254.   "The universe doesn't give you what you ask for with your thoughts - it gives you what you demand with your actions."— Steve Maraboli, Life, the Truth, and Being Free

1255.   "Life before Death.
Strength before Weakness.
Journey before Destination."— Brandon Sanderson, The Way of Kings

1256.   "Make voyages. Attempt them. There's nothing else."— Tennessee
Williams, Camino Real

1257.   "Is there any real purpose in being alive if all we are going to do is get
up every day and live only for ourselves?
Live your life to help others. Give & live selflessly."— Joyce Meyer

1258.   "There is force in the universe, which, if we permit it, will flow through
us and produce miraculous results."— Mahatma Gandhi

1259.   "My dear Watson," said [Sherlock Holmes], "I cannot agree with those
who rank modesty among the virtues. To the logician all things should be seen
exactly as they are, and to underestimate one's self is as much a departure from
truth as to exaggerate one's own powers."— Arthur Conan Doyle, The Adventure
of the Greek Interpreter

1260.   "There are many people who can do big things, but there are very few
people who will do the small things."— Mother Teresa

1261.   "I realized it for the first time in my life: there is nothing but mystery in
the world, how it hides behind the fabric of our poor, browbeat days, shining
brightly, and we don't even know it."— Sue Monk Kidd, The Secret Life of Bees:

1262.   "There are a thousand hacking at the branches of evil to one who is
striking at the root."— Henry David Thoreau, Walden, or Life in the Woods

1263.   "We are what we are, neither a good or as bad as others paint us. And
what we are doesn't change how truly we feel, only how free we are to follow
those feelings."— Melissa Marr, Ink Exchange

1264.   "Love has no limitations. It cannot be measured. It has no boundaries.
Although many have tried, love is indefinable."— Steve Maraboli, Life, the Truth,
and Being Free

1265.   "Happiness comes when your work and words are of benefit to
others."— Gautama Buddha

1266.   "You lose nothing when fighting for a cause ... In my mind the losers
are those who don't have a cause they care about."— Muhammad Ali

1267.   "The library smells like old books — a thousand leather doorways into
other worlds. I hear silence, like the mind of God. I feel a presence in the empty
chair beside me. The librarian watches me suspiciously. But the library is a
sacred place, and I sit with the patron saint of readers. Pulsing goddess light
moves through me for one moment like a glimpse of eternity instantly forgotten.
She is gone. I smell mold, I hear the clock ticking, I see an empty chair. Ask me

now and I'll say this is just a place where you can't play music or eat. She's gone. The library sucks."— Laura Whitcomb, A Certain Slant of Light

1268.   "Stop giving your life away to other people."— Steve Maraboli, Life, the Truth, and Being Free

1269.   "If you feel far from God, guess who moved?"— Robin Jones Gunn, Surprise Endings

1270.   "[T]he race is long - to finish first, first you must finish."— Garth Stein, The Art of Racing in the Rain

1271.   "A successful marriage requires falling in love many times -- always with the same person."— Mignon McLaughlin

1272.   "Onward and Upward! To Narnia and the North!"— C.S. Lewis, The Horse and His Boy

1273.   "Each man should frame life so that at some future hour fact and his dreaming meet."— Victor Hugo

1274.   "It is one of the beautiful compensations of life that no man can sincerely try to help another without helping himself."— Ralph Waldo Emerson

1275.   "We should never negotiate out of fear, but we should never fear to negotiate"— John F. Kennedy

1276.   "Everything that had happened was shockingly beautiful, enough to make you crazy."— Banana Yoshimoto, NP

1277.   "Your mother won a special reward," she told me, "because everyone had a head in her pictures. We all applauded."— Sarah Dessen, Dreamland

1278.   "It is books that are a key to the wide world; if you can't do anything else, read all that you can."— Jane Hamilton

1279.   "Lack of direction, not lack of time, is the problem. We all have twenty-four hour days."— Zig Ziglar

1280.   "Stay hungry. Stay foolish."— Steve Jobs

1281.   "Love those you hate you."— Leo Tolstoy, Anna Karenina

1282.   "What you are is God's gift to you, what you become is your gift to God."— Hans Urs von Balthasar, Prayer

1283.   "Thousands of tired, nerve-shaken, over-civilized people are beginning to find out going to the mountains is going home; that wilderness is a necessity..."— John Muir

1284.   "Your sacred space is where you can find yourself over and over again."— Joseph Campbell

1285.   "You can't find someone who doesn't want to be found."— Isabel Allende, The House of the Spirits

1286.   "My happiness grows in direct proportion to my acceptance, and in inverse proportion to my expectations."— Michael J. Fox

1287.   "Come friends, it's not too late to seek a newer world."— Alfred Tennyson

1288.   "The life given us, by nature is short; but the memory of a well-spent life is eternal."— Marcus Tullius Cicero

1289.   "The absence of the will to live is, alas, not sufficient to make one want to die."— Michel Houellebecq

1290.   "The ground's generosity takes in our compost and grows beauty! Try to be more like the ground."— Rumi

1291.   "A daydreamer is prepared for most things."— Joyce Carol Oates

1292.   "I want a tattoo over my heart that reads TRY HARDER YOU LAZY PARAMEDIC SHITBAG OR I WILL HAUNT YOUR BEDROOM FOREVER"— Warren Ellis

1293.   "You don't have to make something that people call art. Living is an artistic activity, there is an art to getting through the day."— Viggo Mortensen

1294.   "Things will change: you won't feel this way forever. And anyway, sometimes the hardest lessons to learn are the ones your soul needs most."— Kelly Cutrone, If You Have to Cry, Go Outside: And Other Things Your Mother Never Told You

1295.   "Every beginning has an end and every end is a new beginning."— Santosh Kalwar, Quote Me Everyday

1296.   "Happiness depends more on the inward disposition of mind than on outward circumstances."— Benjamin Franklin

1297.   "The dream was always running ahead of me. To catch up, to live for a moment in unison, was the miracle."— Anaïs Nin

1298.   "We have just enough religion to make us hate, but not enough to make us love one another."— Jonathan Swift

1299.   "My young sisters, we have such hope for you. We have such great expectations for you. Don't settle for less than what the Lord wants you to be...Give me a young woman who loves home and family, who reads and ponders the scriptures daily, who has a burning testimony of the Book of Mormon... Give me a young woman who is virtuous and who has maintained her personal purity, who will not settle for less than a temple marriage, and I will give you a young woman who will perform miracles for the Lord now and throughout eternity."— Ezra Taft Benson

1300.   "At times our own light goes out and is rekindled by a spark from another person. Each of us has cause to think with deep gratitude of those who have lighted the flame within us."— Albert Schweitzer

1301.   "You don't win races by wishing, you win them by running faster than everyone else does."— Philip Pullman, Clockwork

1302.   "It is in the knowledge of the genuine conditions of our lives that we must draw our strength to live and our reasons for living."— Simone de Beauvoir

1303.   "I wanted to become the seeker, the aroused and passionate explorer, and it was better to go at it knowing nothing at all, always choosing the unmarked bottle, always choosing your own unproven method, armed with nothing but faith and a belief in astonishment."— Pat Conroy, The Lords of Discipline

1304.   "You're not a human being until you value something more than the life of your body. And the greater the thing you live and die for the greater you are."— Orson Scott Card, The Worthing Chronicle

1305.   "Whoever you are, or whatever it is that you do, when you really want something, it's because that desire originated in the soul of the universe. It's your mission on earth."— Paulo Coelho, The Alchemist

1306.   "We're constantly being told what other people think we are, and that's why it is so important to know yourself."— Sarah McLachlan

1307.   "Is life too short to be taking this shit, or is life too short to be minding it?"— Violet Weingarten

1308.   "There's nothing wrong with you. There's a lot wrong with the world you live in. And definitely get out of high school and make everyone sorry."— Chris Colfer

1309.   "To write well, express yourself like the common people, but think like a wise man."— Aristotle

1310.   "It is not a daily increase, but a daily decrease. Hack away at the inessentials."— Bruce Lee

1311.   "I am seeking, I am striving, I am in it with all my heart."— Vincent van Gogh

1312.   "Let me never fall into the vulgar mistake of dreaming that I am persecuted whenever I am contradicted."— Ralph Waldo Emerson

1313.   "Anxiety is the handmaiden of creativity"— T.S. Eliot

1314.   "A path is only a path, and there is no affront, to oneself or to others, in dropping it if that is what your heart tells you . . . Look at every path closely and deliberately. Try it as many times as you think necessary. Then ask yourself alone, one question . . . Does this path have a heart? If it does, the path is good; if it doesn't it is of no use."— Carlos Castaneda

1315.   "Be ruthless about protecting writing days, i.e., do not cave in to endless requests to have "essential" and "long overdue" meetings on those days. The funny thing is that, although writing has been my actual job for several years now, I still seem to have to fight for time in which to do it. Some people do not seem to grasp that I still have to sit down in peace and write the books, apparently believing that they pop up like mushrooms without my connivance. I must therefore guard the time allotted to writing as a Hungarian Horntail guards its firstborn egg."— J.K. Rowling

1316.   "If you don't have time to do it right, when will you have the time to do it over?"— John Wooden

1317.   "Every problem is a gift - without problems we would not grow."— Anthony Robbins

1318.   "It did not really matter what we expected from life, but rather what life expected from us. We needed to stop asking about the meaning of life, and instead to think of ourselves as those who were being questioned by life—daily and hourly. Our answer must consist, not in talk and meditation, but in right action and in right conduct. Life ultimately means taking the responsibility to find the right answer to its problems and to fulfill the tasks which it constantly sets for each individual."— Viktor E. Frankl, Man's Search for Meaning

1319.   "Ignore all hatred and criticism. Live for what you create, and die protecting it."— Lady Gaga

1320.   "A man may die, nations may rise and fall, but an idea lives on. Ideas have endurance without death."— John F. Kennedy

1321.   "It is said that God has created man in his own image. But it may be that humankind has created God in the image of humankind."— Thích Nhất Hạnh, Going Home: Jesus and Buddha as Brothers

1322.   "Know from whence you came. If you know whence you came, there are absolutely no limitations to where you can go."— James Baldwin

1323.   "Those three things - autonomy, complexity, and a connection between effort and reward - are, most people will agree, the three qualities that work has to have if it is to be satisfying."— Malcolm Gladwell, Outliers: The Story of Success

1324.   "Criticism - however valid or intellectually engaging - tends to get in the way of a writer who has anything personal to say. A tightrope walker may require practice, but if he starts a theory of equilibrium he will lose grace (and probably fall off)."— J.R.R. Tolkien, The Letters of J.R.R. Tolkien

1325.   "If you don't have the time to do something right, where are you going to find the time to fix it?"— Stephen King

1326.   "While we may judge things as good or bad, karma doesn't. It's a simple case of like gets like, the ultimate balancing act, nothing more, nothing less. And if you're determined to fix every situation you deem as bad, or difficult, or somehow unsavory, then you rob the person of their own chance to fix it, learn from it, or even grow from it. Some things, no matter how painful, happen for a reason. A reason you or I may not be able to grasp at first sight, not without knowing a person's entire life story—their cumulative past. And to just barge in and interfere, no matter how well-intentioned, would be akin to robbing them of their journey. Something that's better not done."— Alyson Noel, Shadowland

1327.   "Life is one fool thing after another whereas love is two fool things after each other."— Oscar Wilde, The Happy Prince and Other Tales

1328.   "Happiness in marriage is entirely a matter of chance. If the dispositions of the parties are ever so well known to each other or ever so similar beforehand, it does not advance their felicity in the least. They always continue to grow sufficiently unlike afterwards to have their share of vexation; and it is better to know as little as possible of the defects of the person with whom you are to pass your life."— Jane Austen, Pride And Prejudice

1329.   "You look at yourself and you accept yourself for who you are, and once you accept yourself for who you are you become a better person."— Oprah Winfrey

1330.   "I no longer agree to treat myself with disrespect. Every time a self-critical thought comes to mind, I will forgive the Judge and follow this comment with words of praise, self-acceptance, and love."— Miguel Ruiz

1331.   "feminism is for everybody"— Bell Hooks

1332.   "Do you not then hear this horrible scream all around you that people usually call silence."— Werner Herzog

1333.   "To exist in this vast universe for a speck of time is the great gift of life. Our tiny sliver of time is our gift of life. It is our only life. The universe will go on, indifferent to our brief existence, but while we are here we touch not just part of that vastness, but also the lives around us. Life is the gift each of us has been given. Each life is our own and no one else's. It is precious beyond all counting. It is the greatest value we can have. Cherish it for what it truly is..... Your life is yours alone. Rise up and live it."— Terry Goodkind

1334.   "I challenge every one of you who can hear me to rise to the divinity within you. Do we really realize what it means to be a child of God, to have within us something of the divine nature?"— Gordon B. Hinckley

1335.   "When in a relationship, a real man doesn't make his woman jealous of others, he makes others jealous of his woman."— Steve Maraboli, Unapologetically You: Reflections on Life and the Human Experience

1336.   "Owning our story can be hard but not nearly as difficult as spending our lives running from it. Embracing our vulnerabilities is risky but not nearly as dangerous as giving up on love and belonging and joy—the experiences that make us the most vulnerable. Only when we are brave enough to explore the darkness will we discover the infinite power of our light."— Brené Brown

1337.   "You will never be able to escape from your heart. So it's better to listen to what it has to say."— Paulo Coelho, The Alchemist

1338.   "it is impossible to build one's own happiness on the unhappiness of others. This perspective is at the heart of Buddhist teachings."— Daisaku Ikeda

1339.   "Courage does not always roar. Sometimes courage is the quiet voice at the end of the day saying, 'I will try again tomorrow."— Mary Anne Radmacher

1340.   "The man who thinks he can and the man who thinks he can't are both right. Which one are you?"— Henry Ford

1341.   "Doing nothing for others is the undoing of ourselves."— Horace Mann

1342.   "I am not what I ought to be, I am not what I want to be, I am not what I hope to be in another world; but still I am not what I once used to be, and by the grace of God I am what I am"— John Newton

1343.   "It's funny how one summer can change everything. It must be something about the heat and the smell of chlorine, fresh-cut grass and honeysuckle, asphalt sizzling after late-day thunderstorms, the steam rising while everything drips around it. Something about long, lazy days and whirring air conditioners and bright plastic flip-flops from the drugstore thwacking down the street. Something about fall being so close, another year, another Christmas, another beginning. So much in one summer, stirring up like the storms that crest at the end of each day, blowing out all the heat and dirt to leave everything gasping and cool. Everyone can reach back to one summer and lay a finger to it, finding the exact point when everything changed. That summer was mine."— Sarah Dessen, That Summer

1344.   "Do no harm & leave the world a better place than you found it."— Patricia Cornwell

1345.   "know what you want, work to get it, then value it once you have it."— Nora Roberts, Morrigan's Cross

1346.   "Time to toss the dice"— Robert Jordan

1347.   "He who takes offense when no offense is intended is a fool, and he who takes offense when offense is intended is a greater fool."— Brigham Young

1348.   "What's unnatural is homophobia. Homo sapiens is the only species in all of nature that responds with hate to homosexuality."— Alex Sanchez, The God Box

1349.	"When things go wrong, you'll find they usually go on getting worse for some time; but when things once start going right they often go on getting better and better."— C.S. Lewis, The Horse and His Boy

1350.	"Conquer anger by love, evil by good; conquer the miser with liberality, and the liar with truth."— Gautama Buddha

1351.	"I am Me. In all the world, there is no one else exactly like me. Everything that comes out of me is authentically mine, because I alone chose it -- I own everything about me: my body, my feelings, my mouth, my voice, all my actions, whether they be to others or myself. I own my fantasies, my dreams, my hopes, my fears. I own my triumphs and successes, all my failures and mistakes. Because I own all of me, I can become intimately acquainted with me. By so doing, I can love me and be friendly with all my parts. I know there are aspects about myself that puzzle me, and other aspects that I do not know -- but as long as I am friendly and loving to myself, I can courageously and hopefully look for solutions to the puzzles and ways to find out more about me. However I look and sound, whatever I say and do, and whatever I think and feel at a given moment in time is authentically me. If later some parts of how I looked, sounded, thought, and felt turn out to be unfitting, I can discard that which is unfitting, keep the rest, and invent something new for that which I discarded. I can see, hear, feel, think, say, and do. I have the tools to survive, to be close to others, to be productive, and to make sense and order out of the world of people and things outside of me. I own me, and therefore, I can engineer me. I am me, and I am Okay."— Virginia Satir

1352.	"If one makes a mistake, then an apology is usually sufficient to get things back on an even keel. However-and this is a big 'however'- most people do not ever know why their apology did not seem to have any effect. It is simply that they did not make a mistake; they made a choice...and never understood the difference between the two."— Andy Andrews, The Noticer: Sometimes, All a Person Needs Is a Little Perspective.

1353.	"We join spokes together in a wheel,but it is the center holethat makes the wagon move.
We shape clay into a pot,but it is the emptiness inside
that holds whatever we want.
We hammer wood for a house,but it is the inner space
that makes it livable.
We work with being,but non-being is what we use."— Lao Tzu

1354.	"And by and by Christopher Robin came to the end of things, and he was silent, and he sat there, looking out over the world, just wishing it wouldn't stop."— A.A. Milne, The House at Pooh Corner

1355.	"Tomorrow is a new day; begin it well and serenely and with too high a spirit to be encumbered with your old nonsense."— Ralph Waldo Emerson

1356.	"I believe that God is in me as the sun is in the color and fragrance of a flower - the Light in my darkness, the Voice in my silence."— Helen Keller

1357.   "You don't always have to kiss a lot of frogs to recognize a prince when you find one-Henrietta Barett"— Julia Quinn, Minx

1358.   "There is nothing more important than your eternal salvation."— Kirk Cameron

1359.   "Do not fear the thorns in your path, for they draw only corrupt blood."— Kahlil Gibran

1360.   "Freedom is not having everything we crave, it's being able to go without the things we crave and being OK with it."— Rob Bell

1361.   "I've been doing this a long time, and I've come to learn that predictions don't mean much. Too much lies outside the realm of medical knowledge. A lot of what happens next comes down to you and your specific genetics, your attitude. No, there's nothing we can do to stop the inevitable, but that's not the point. The point is that you should try to make the most of the time you have left."— Nicholas Sparks, The Last Song

1362.   "Keep me up till five because all your stars are out, and for no other reason...Oh dare to do it Buddy! Trust your heart. You're a deserving craftsman. It would never betray you. Good night. I'm feeling very much over-excited now, and a little dramatic, but I think I'd give almost anything on earth to see you writing a something, an anything, a poem, a tree, that was really and truly after your own heart."— J.D. Salinger, Raise High the Roof Beam, Carpenters & Seymour: An Introduction

1363.   "Happiness is not having what you want, it is wanting what you have."— Sheryl Crow

1364.   "You couldn't erase the past. You couldn't even change it. But sometimes life offered you the opportunity to put it right."— Ann Brashares, Girls In Pants: The Third Summer of the Sisterhood

1365.   "Free yourself from the complexities and drama of your life. Simplify. Look within. Within ourselves we all have the gifts and talents we need to fulfill the purpose we've been blessed with."— Steve Maraboli, Life, the Truth, and Being Free

1366.   "Honesty is the best policy."— William Shakespeare

1367.   "Forgive yourself before you die. Then forgive others."— Mitch Albom, Tuesdays With Morrie

1368.   "You can't dwell on what might have been...and it's not fair to condemn him for something he hasn't done.- Grandpa Chet"— Wendelin Van Draanen, Flipped

1369.   "And so I wait. I wait for time to heal the pain and raise me to me feet once again - so that I can start a new path, my own path, the one that will make me whole again."— Jack Canfield, Chicken Soup for the Teenage Soul II

1370.   "Who we are in the present includes who we were in the past."— Fred Rogers, Life's Journeys According to Mister Rogers: Things to Remember Along the Way

1371.   "Great men are like eagles, and build their nest on some lofty solitude"— Arthur Schopenhauer

1372.   "Do not waste the precious moments of this, your present reality, seeking to unveil all of life's secrets. Those secrets are a secret for a reason. Grant your God the benefit of the doubt. Use your NOW moment for the Highest Purpose- the creation and the expression of WHO YOU REALLY ARE. Decide who you are- who you want to be-and then do everything in your power to be that.
It is not nearly so important how well a message is received as how well it is sent. You cannot take responsibility for how well another accepts your truth; you can only ensure how well it is communicated. And by how well, I don't mean merely how clearly; I mean how lovingly, how compassionately, how sensitively, how courageously, and how completely.
If you think your life is about DOINGNESS, you do not understand what you are about. Your soul doesn't care what you do for a living-and when your life is over, neither will you. Your soul cares only about what you're BEING while you're doing whatever you're doing. It is a state of BEINGNESS the soul is after, not a state of doingness."— Neale Donald Walsch

1373.   "For, after all, everyone who wishes to gain true knowledge must climb the Hill Difficulty alone, and since there is no royal road to the summit, I must zigzag it in my own way. I slip back many times, I fall, I stand still, I run against the edge of hidden obstacles, I lose my temper and find it again and keep it better, I trudge on, I gain a little, I feel encouraged, I get more eager and climb higher and begin to see the widening horizon. Every struggle is a victory. One more effort and I reach the luminous cloud, the blue depths of the sky, the uplands of my desire."— Helen Keller, The Story of My Life

1374.   "Each day is God's gift to you. What you do with it is your gift to Him."— T.D. Jakes, Maximize the Moment: God's Action Plan For Your Life

1375.   "Every window in Alcatraz has a view of San Francisco."— Susanna Kaysen, Girl, Interrupted

1376.   "I am not afraid..... I was born to do this."— Joan of Arc

1377.   "Feel your emotions,Live true your passions,Keep still your mind."— Geoffrey M. Gluckman

1378.   "In the end, everything is a gag."— Charles Chaplin

1379.   "You know me better than you think, you know, and you shall know me better yet."— C.S. Lewis, The Magician's Nephew

1380.   "Warriors of light always have a certain gleam in their eyes.
They are of this world, they are part of the lives of others, and they set out on

their journey with no saddlebags and no sandals. They are often cowardly. They do not always make the right decisions.
They suffer over the most trivial things, they have mean thoughts, and sometimes believe that they are incapable of growing. They frequently deem themselves unworthy of any blessing or miracle.
They are not always quite sure what they are doing here. They spend many sleepless nights, believing that their lives have no meaning.
That is why they are warriors of light. Because they make mistakes. Because they ask themselves questions. Because they are looking for a reason - and are sure to find it."— Paulo Coelho

1381.   "But as I have noticed on more than one occasion, life itself is unfair, and there is no complaint department, so we might as well accept things the way they happen, clean up the mess, and move on."— Jeff Lindsay, Dexter in the Dark

1382.   "Every time I plant a seed, he say kill it before it grow, he say kill it before they grow."— Bob Marley

1383.   "Public opinion is a weak tyrant compared with our own private opinion. What a man thinks of himself, that it is which determines, or rather indicates his fate."— Henry David Thoreau

1384.   "Nothing like a nighttime stroll to give you ideas."— J.K. Rowling, Harry Potter and the Goblet of Fire

1385.   "Living never wore one so much as the effort not to live."— Anaïs Nin

1386.   "The creatures that inhabit this earth--be they human beings or animals--are here to contribute, each in its own particular way, to the beauty and prosperity of the world."— Dalai Lama XIV

1387.   "Dead, we are revealed in our true dimensions, and they are surprisingly modest."— Michael Cunningham, The Hours

1388.   "In the mist of Difficulty lies Opportunity."— Oprah Winfrey

1389.   "Man is, that he may have Joy."— The Church of Jesus Christ of Latter-day Saints, The Book of Mormon: Another Testament of Jesus Christ

1390.   "And so even though we face the difficulties of today and tomorrow, I still have a dream. It is a dream deeply rooted in the American dream."— Martin Luther King Jr.

1391.   "Stories are like genies...They can carry us into and though our sorrows. Sometimes they burn, sometimes they dance, sometimes they weep, sometimes they sing. Like genies, everyone has one. Like genies, sometimes we forget that we do.Our stories can set us free...When we set them free."— Francesca Lia Block

1392.   "Don't marry a rich man. Marry a good man. He will spend his life trying to keep you happy. No rich man can buy that!"— Staness Jonekos

1393.   "The less you associate with some people, the more your life will improve. Any time you tolerate mediocrity in others, it increases your mediocrity. An important attribute in successful people is their impatience with negative thinking and negative acting people. As you grow, your associates will change. Some of your friends will not want you to go on. They will want you to stay where they are. Friends that don't help you climb will want you to crawl. Your friends will stretch your vision or choke your dream. Those that don't increase you will eventually decrease you. Consider this: Never receive counsel from unproductive people. Never discuss your problems with someone incapable of contributing to the solution, because those who never succeed themselves are always first to tell you how. Not everyone has a right to speak into your life. You are certain to get the worst of the bargain when you exchange ideas with the wrong person. Don't follow anyone who's not going anywhere. With some people you spend an evening: with others you invest it. Be careful where you stop to inquire for directions along the road of life. Wise is the person who fortifies his life with the right friendships. If you run with wolves, you will learn how to howl. But, if you associate with eagles, you will learn how to soar to great heights. "A mirror reflects a man's face, but what he is really like is shown by the kind of friends he chooses." The simple but true fact of life is that you become like those with whom you closely associate - for the good and the bad. Note: Be not mistaken. This is applicable to family as well as friends. Yes...do love, appreciate and be thankful for your family, for they will always be your family no matter what. Just know that they are human first and though they are family to you, they may be a friend to someone else and will fit somewhere in the criteria above.
"In Prosperity Our Friends Know Us. In Adversity We Know Our friends."
"Never make someone a priority when you are only an option for them."
"If you are going to achieve excellence in big things, you develop the habit in little matters. Excellence is not an exception, it is a prevailing attitude..."...."— Colin Powell

1394.   "The greatest step towards a life of simplicity is to learn to let go."— Steve Maraboli, Life, the Truth, and Being Free

1395.   "She had become accustomed to being lonely. She was used to walking alone and to being considered 'different.' She did not suffer too much."— Betty Smith, A Tree Grows in Brooklyn

1396.   "Everything is determined, the beginning as well as the end, by forces over which we have no control. It is determined for the insect, as well as for the star. Human beings, vegetables, or cosmic dust, we all dance to a mysterious tune, intoned in the distance by an invisible piper."— Albert Einstein

1397.   "Mutual caring relationships require kindness and patience, tolerance, optimism, joy in the other's achievements, confidence in oneself, and the ability to give without undue thought of gain."— Fred Rogers, The World According to Mister Rogers: Important Things To Remember

1398.   "Sometimes I arrive just when God's ready to have someone click the shutter."— Ansel Adams

1399.   "Employ your time in improving yourself by other men's writings so that you shall come easily by what others have labored hard for."— Socrates

1400.   "If you can dream it, you can do it."— Walt Disney Company

1401.   "Do not let another day go by where your dedication to other people's opinions is greater than your dedication to your own emotions!"— Steve Maraboli, Life, the Truth, and Being Free

1402.   "Your own positive future begins in this moment. All you have is right now. Every goal is possible from here."— Lao Tzu

1403.   "Realize deeply that the present moment is all you will ever have."— Eckhart Tolle

1404.   "The aim of every artist is to arrest motion, which is life, by artificial means and hold it fixed so that a hundred years later, when a stranger looks at it, it moves again since it is life."— William Faulkner

1405.   "Music is the literature of the heart; it commences where speech ends."— Alphonse de Lamartine

1406.   "The difference between false memories and true ones is the same as for jewels: it is always the false ones that look the most real, the most brilliant."— Salvador Dalí

1407.   "Real love never fails."— Karen Kingsbury, Forever

1408.   "Christ is not valued at all, unless he is valued above all."— Augustine of Hippo

1409.   "It occurred to me by intuition, and music was the driving force behind that intuition. My discovery was the result of musical perception."— Albert Einstein

1410.   "Life is no brief candle to me. It is a sort of splendid torch which I have got a hold of for the moment, and I want to make it burn as brightly as possible before handing it on to future generations."— George Bernard Shaw

1411.   "I have never felt that anything really mattered but knowing that you stood for the things in which you believed and had done the very best you could."— Eleanor Roosevelt

1412.   "We are not helpless...Many times in our lives we've been powerless, but not this night. Right now we have the power to choose the manner in which we die. If you have been a master of nothing else in all your days, you are now a master of this moment. And I for one am going to give such an answer to this insult that others will dearly regret not being by my side to see it!"— Jeaniene Frost, At Grave's End

1413.   "Great acts are made up of small deeds."— Lao Tzu

1414.   "I was good and bad, but never wicked."— Anne Rice

1415.   "take what you can from your dreams Make them real as anything It takes the work out of the courage"— Dave Matthews Band

1416.   "No other success can compensate for failure in the home."— J. E. McCulloch

1417.   "because he's Will"— Philip Pullman, The Amber Spyglass

1418.   "Most people think happiness is about gaining something, but it's not. It's all about getting rid of the darkness you accumulate."— Carolyn Crane

1419.   "We all know we're going to die; what's important is the kind of men and women we are in the face of this."— Anne Lamott, Bird by Bird: Some Instructions on Writing and Life

1420.   "For God did not give us a spirit of timidity, but of power and of love and of calm and well balanced mind and discipline and self-control."— Anonymous, Holy Bible: King James Version

1421.   "LAW 4 Always Say Less Than Necessary When you are trying to impress people with words, the more you say, the more common you appear, and the less in control. Even if you are saying something banal, it will seem original if you make it vague, open-ended, and sphinxlike. Powerful people impress and intimidate by saying less. The more you say, the more likely you are to say something foolish."— Robert Greene, The 48 Laws of Power

1422.   "Knowing is not enough, we must apply. Willing is not enough, we must do."— Bruce Lee

1423.   "I consider myself a stained-glass window. And this is how I live my life. Closing no doors and covering no windows; I am the multi-colored glass with light filtering through me, in many different shades. Allowing light to shed and fall into many hues. My job is not to direct anything, but only to filter into many colors. My answer is destiny and my guide is joy. And there you have me."— C. JoyBell C.

1424.   "To make real friends you have to put yourself out there. Sometimes people will let you down, but you can't let that stop you. If you get hurt, you just pick yourself up, dust off your feelings, and try again."— Kristin Hannah, Firefly Lane

1425.   "Love me or hate me, I swear it won't make or break me."— Lil Wayne

1426.   "The sky is the limit... for some people aim higher nothing is impossible."— Demi Lovato

1427.   "In the end, just three things matter:How well we have lived How well we have loved How well we have learned to let go"— Jack Kornfield

1428.   "I used to think the world was broken down by tribes,' I said. 'By Black and White. By Indian and White. But I know this isn't true. The world is only broken into two tribes: the people who are assholes and the people who are not."— Sherman Alexie, The Absolutely True Diary of a Part-Time Indian

1429.   "Although time seems to fly, it never travels faster than one day at a time. Each day is a new opportunity to live your life to the fullest. In each waking day, you will find scores of blessings and opportunities for positive change. Do not let your TODAY be stolen by the unchangeable past or the indefinite future! Today is a new day!"— Steve Maraboli, Life, the Truth, and Being Free

1430.   "Every moment of light and dark is a miracle."— Walt Whitman

1431.   "Education is experience, and the essence of experience is self-reliance."— T.H. White, The Once and Future King

1432.   "Your greatest self has been waiting your whole life; don't make it wait any longer."— Steve Maraboli, Life, the Truth, and Being Free

1433.   "If we bear all this suffering and if there are still Jews left, when it is over, then Jews, instead of being doomed, will be held up as an example."— Anne Frank

1434.   "Some people come into our lives and quickly go. Some people move our souls to dance. They awaken us to a new understanding with the passing whisper of their wisdom. Some people make the sky more beautiful to gaze upon. They stay in our lives for a while, leave footprints on our hearts, and we are never, ever the same."— Flavia Weedn

1435.   "There is only one day left, always starting over: It is given to us at dawn and taken away from us at dusk."— Jean-Paul Sartre

1436.   "You would have made a fine warrior, you know that?"
I am one. Death is my enemy."
Yeah, it is, isn't it?" God, it made such sense that he'd bonded with her. She was a fighter... like him. "Your scalpel's your dagger."
Yup."— J.R. Ward, Lover Unbound

1437.   "How are you coming with your home library? Do you need some good ammunition on why it's so important to read? The last time I checked the statistics...I think they indicated that only four percent of the adults in this country have bought a book within the past year. That's dangerous. It's extremely important that we keep ourselves in the top five or six percent.In one of the Monthly Letters from the Royal Bank of Canada it was pointed out that reading good books is not something to be indulged in as a luxury. It is a necessity for anyone who intends to give his life and work a touch of quality. The most real wealth is not what we put into our piggy banks but what we develop in our heads. Books instruct us without anger, threats and harsh discipline. They do not sneer at our ignorance or grumble at our mistakes. They ask only that we spend some time in the company of greatness so that we may absorb some of its attributes. You do not read a book for the book's sake, but for your own.

You may read because in your high-pressure life, studded with problems and emergencies, you need periods of relief and yet recognize that peace of mind does not mean numbness of mind.

You may read because you never had an opportunity to go to college, and books give you a chance to get something you missed. You may read because your job is routine, and books give you a feeling of depth in life.

You may read because you did go to college.

You may read because you see social, economic and philosophical problems which need solution, and you believe that the best thinking of all past ages may be useful in your age, too.

You may read because you are tired of the shallowness of contemporary life, bored by the current conversational commonplaces, and wearied of shop talk and gossip about people.

Whatever your dominant personal reason, you will find that reading gives knowledge, creative power, satisfaction and relaxation. It cultivates your mind by calling its faculties into exercise.

Books are a source of pleasure - the purest and the most lasting. They enhance your sensation of the interestingness of life. Reading them is not a violent pleasure like the gross enjoyment of an uncultivated mind, but a subtle delight. Reading dispels prejudices which hem our minds within narrow spaces. One of the things that will surprise you as you read good books from all over the world and from all times of man is that human nature is much the same today as it has been ever since writing began to tell us about it.

Some people act as if it were demeaning to their manhood to wish to be well-read but you can no more be a healthy person mentally without reading substantial books than you can be a vigorous person physically without eating solid food. Books should be chosen, not for their freedom from evil, but for their possession of good. Dr. Johnson said: "Whilst you stand deliberating which book your son shall read first, another boy has read both."— Earl Nightingale

1438.   "follow your heart! (sppotedleafs motto)"— Erin Hunter, Into the Wild

1439.   "Don't allow yourself to become disheartened when the thread doesn't suit or seems unsightly to you. Wait and watch. Be patient and devoted. As the threads twist and turn, you will begin to understand, and you will see the pattern finally materialize in all its splendor."— Colleen Houck

1440.   "What affects one in a major way, affects all in a minor way."— Martin Luther King Jr.

1441.   "Painful as it may be, a significant emotional event can be the catalyst for choosing a direction that serves us - and those around us - more effectively. Look for the learning."— Louisa May Alcott

1442.   "Approval is overrated...Approval and disapproval alike satisfy those who deliver it more than those who receive it. I don't care for approval, and I don't mind doing without."— Gregory Maguire

1443.   "Just remember: I love you, and love yourselves. 'cause, little monsters, you were born that way baby."— Lady Gaga, Lady Gaga: The Fame

1444.   "Life is 10 percent what happens to you and ninety percent how you respond to it."— Lou Holtz

1445.   "As you walk through forests or the meadows of your mind, Stop and talk to those you fear
Good friendships you may find"— Stephen Cosgrove, Buttermilk Bear

1446.   "It is this belief in a power larger than myself and other than myself which allows me to venture into the unknown and even the unknowable."— Maya Angelou

1447.   "Everyone has a hidden agenda. Except me!"— Michael Crichton

1448.   "In spite of everything I still believe that people are really good at heart. I simply can't build up my hopes on a foundation consisting of confusion, misery and death."— Anne Frank

1449.   "In order to know who you are you need to know God is."— Annette Hoggs-Jackson

1450.   "Growing up means learning what life is. When you're little, you have a set of ideals, standards, criteria, plans, outlooks, and you think that you have to sit around and wait for them to happen to you and then life will work. But life isn't like that, for anybody; you can't fall in love with a standard, you have to fall in love with a person. You can't live in criteria, you have to live your life. You can't wait for your plans to materialize, because they may never materialize the way you think they will. You can't wait to watch your ideals and standards walk up to you, because you can't know what's yours until you have it. I always say, always take the first chance in case you never get a second one, but growing up takes that even one step further, growing up means that you have to hold on to what you have, when you have it, because what you have- that's yours- and all the ideals and criteria you have set in your head, those aren't yours, because those haven't happened to you."— C. JoyBell C.

1451.   "The greatest ideas are the simplest."— William Golding, Lord of the Flies

1452.   "I began to realize how important it was to be an enthusiast in life. He taught me that if you are interested in something, no matter what it is, go at it at full speed ahead. Embrace it with both arms, hug it, love it and above all become passionate about it. Lukewarm is no good. Hot is no good either. White hot and passionate is the only thing to be"— Roald Dahl, My Uncle Oswald

1453.   "You know, the mind is a remarkable thing. Just because you can't see the wound doesn't mean it isn't hurting. It scars all the time, but it heals."— Jodi Picoult, The Pact

1454.   ""What does it mean if I'm afraid? Does it mean something bad is going to happen?" "No, it doesn't mean something bad is going to happen. It just means that you have the chance to be brave."— C. JoyBell C.

1455.   "Awake, arise or be forever fall'n."— John Milton, Paradise Lost

1456.   "We often think of peace as the absence of war, that if powerful countries would reduce their weapon arsenals, we could have peace. But if we look deeply into the weapons, we see our own minds- our own prejudices, fears and ignorance. Even if we transport all the bombs to the moon, the roots of war and the roots of bombs are still there, in our hearts and minds, and sooner or later we will make new bombs. To work for peace is to uproot war from ourselves and from the hearts of men and women. To prepare for war, to give millions of men and women the opportunity to practice killing day and night in their hearts, is to plant millions of seeds of violence, anger, frustration, and fear that will be passed on for generations to come. "— Thích Nhất Hạnh, Living Buddha, Living Christ

1457.   "Give your weakness to one who helps."— Rumi

1458.   "Spoon feeding in the long run teaches us nothing but the shape of the spoon."— E.M. Forster

1459.   "Struggling and suffering are the essence of a life worth living. If you're not pushing yourself beyond the comfort zone, if you're not demanding more from yourself - expanding and learning as you go - you're choosing a numb existence. You're denying yourself an extraordinary trip."— Dean Karnazes, Ultramarathon Man: Confessions of an All-Night Runner

1460.   "We are what we believe we are!"— C.S. Lewis

1461.   "Count your blessings. Once you realize how valuable you are and how much you have going for you, the smiles will return, the sun will break out, the music will play, and you will finally be able to move forward the life that God intended for you with grace, strength, courage, and confidence."— Og Mandino

1462.   "Man cannot possess anything as long as he fears death. But to him who does not fear it, everything belongs. If there was no suffering, man would not know his limits, would not know himself. "— Leo Tolstoy, War and Peace

1463.   "We all have same beginning (BIRTH), and we will have same ending (DEATH). So how different can we be?"— Mitch Albom, Tuesdays With Morrie

1464.   "We all can be only who we are, no more, no less."— Terry Goodkind, Stone of Tears

1465.   "She liked being reminded of butterflies. She remembered being six or seven and crying over the fates of the butterflies in her yard after learning that they lived for only a few days. Her mother had comforted her and told her not to be sad for the butterflies, that just because their lives were short didn't mean they were tragic. Watching them flying in the warm sun among the daisies in their garden, her mother had said to her, see, they have a beautiful life. Alice liked remembering that."— Lisa Genova, Still Alice

1466.   "You cannot bring about prosperity by discouraging thrift.
You cannot strengthen the weak by weakening the strong.
You cannot help the wage earner by pulling down the wage payer.
You cannot further brotherhood of man by encouraging class hatred.
You cannot establish sound security on borrowed money.
You cannot keep out of trouble by spending more than you earn.
You cannot build character and courage by taking away men's initiative and independence.
You cannot help men permanently by doing for them what they could and should do for themselves."— William J.H. Boetcker

1467.   "Do not pray for easy lives. Pray to be stronger men."— John F. Kennedy

1468.   "Nobody gets praised for the right reasons."— Diana Wynne Jones, Castle in the Air

1469.   "You are doing God's work. You are doing it wonderfully well. He is blessing you, and He will bless you, --even--no, -especially--when your days and your nights may be most challenging. Like the woman who anonymously, meekly, perhaps even with hesitation and some embarrassment, fought her way through the crowd just to touch the hem of the Master's garment, so Christ will say to the women who worry and wonder and weep over their responsibility as mothers, `Daughter, be of good comfort; thy faith hath made thee whole.' And it will make your children whole as well."— Jeffrey R. Holland

1470.   "There is no point in keeping vengeance or stubbornness. These things" -he sighed- "these things I so regret in my life. Pride. Vanity. Why do we do the things we do?Morrie Schwartz"— Mitch Albom, Tuesdays With Morrie

1471.   "[Fireheart] mewed, "It's not my place to judge you." Greystripe looked up as Fireheart went on." Greystripe, whatever you decide to do, I will always be your friend."— Erin Hunter, Fire and Ice

1472.   "It is when things are at worst you will get the best."— Santosh Kalwar, You Can

1473.   "living eulogy.
she danced.
she sang. she took.
she gave.
she loved.
she created.

she dissented. she enlivened.
she saw. she grew. she sweated.
she changed.
she learned. she laughed.
she shed her skin.
she bled on the pages of her days,she walked through walls,she lived with
intention."— Mary Anne Radmacher

1474.   "Then said Almitra, Speak to us of Love.
And he raised his head and looked upon the people, and there fell a stillness
upon them. And with a great voice he said:When love beckons to you, follow
him,Though his ways are hard and steep.
And when his wings enfold you yield to him,Though the sword hidden among his
pinions may wound you."— Kahlil Gibran, The Prophet

1475.   "You will make all kinds of mistakes; but as long as you are generous
and true and also fierce you cannot hurt the world or even seriously distress her.
She was meant to be wooed and won by youth."— Winston Churchill, My Early
Life, 1874-1904

1476.   "You are stronger than you know."— Lori Osterman

1477.   "He was talking about the sign that said 'THE COMPLICATED
FUTILITY OF IGNORANCE.'
'All knew was that I didn't want my daughter or anybody's child to see a message
that negative every time she comes into the library,' he said. 'And then I found
out it was you who was responsible for it.'
'What's so negative about it?' I said.
'What could be a more negative word than "futility"?' he said.
'"Ignorance,"' I said."— Kurt Vonnegut, Hocus Pocus

1478.   "That's what you want to do? Then nothing beats a trial but a failure.
Give it everything you've got. I've told you many times, 'Cant do is like Dont
Care.' Neither of them have a home."— Maya Angelou

1479.   "you cannot find happiness, outside the plan of happiness!"— John
Bytheway

1480.   "We can't choose our fate, but we can choose others. Be careful in
knowing that."— J.K. Rowling, Harry Potter and the Order of the Phoenix

1481.   "A beautiful thing happens when we start paying attention to each
other. It is by participating more in your relationship that you breathe life into it."—
Steve Maraboli, Unapologetically You: Reflections on Life and the Human
Experience

1482.   "It is during our darkest moments that we must focus to see the
light."— Aristotle

1483.   "What we achieve inwardly will change outer reality."— Plutarch

1484.   "Re-examine all you have been told. Dismiss what insults your soul."—Walt Whitman

1485.   "Believe in yourself and all that you are. Know that there is something inside you that is greater than any obstacle."— Christian D. Larson

1486.   "Do you have to make me feel like there's nothing left of me? You can take everything I have, you can break everything I am, like I am made of glass, like I am made of paper. Go on and try to tear me down I will be rising from the ground like a Skyscraper..."— Demi Lovato

1487.   "Here is a rule to remember in future, when anything tempts you to feel bitter: not "This is misfortune," but "To bear this worthily is good fortune."—Marcus Aurelius, Meditations

1488.   "The most powerful relationship you will ever have is the relationship with yourself."— Steve Maraboli, Life, the Truth, and Being Free

1489.   "If you do what you've always done, you'll get what you've always gotten."— Anthony Robbins

1490.   "A man, though wise, should never be ashamed of learning more, and must unbend his mind."— Sophocles, Antigone

1491.   "The main thing is the YOU beneath the clothes and skin--the ability to do, the will to conquer, the determination to understand and know this great, wonderful, curious world."— W.E.B. Du Bois

1492.   "And people who don't dream, who don't have any kind of imaginative life, they must… they must go nuts. I can't imagine that."— Stephen King

1493.   "Life is ours to be spent, not to be saved."— D.H. Lawrence

1494.   "I was halfway across America, at the dividing line between the East of my youth and the West of my future."— Jack Kerouac, On the Road

1495.   "Man made God in his own image..."— Eckhart Tolle, A New Earth: Awakening to Your Life's Purpose

1496.   "Work is love made visible. And if you can't work with love, but only with distaste, it is better that you should leave your work and sit at the gate of the temple and take alms of the people who work with joy"— Kahlil Gibran

1497.   "Differences are not intended to separate, to alienate. We are different precisely in order to realize our need of one another."— Desmond Tutu

1498.   "The one place where a man ought to get a square deal is in a courtroom, be he any color of the rainbow, but people have a way of carrying their resentments right into a jury box. As you grow older, you'll see white men cheat black men every day of your life, but let me tell you something and don't you forget it - whenever a white man does that to a black man, no matter who he is, how rich he is, or how fine a family he comes from, that white man is trash. ~Atticus Finch"— Harper Lee, To Kill a Mockingbird

1499.   "Dance like you're stamping on a human face forever, love like you've been in a serious car crash that minced the front of your brain, stab like no one can arrest you, and live like there's no such thing as God."— Warren Ellis

1500.   "Be compassionate ... and take responsibility for each other. If we only learned those lessons, this world would be a better place."— Mitch Albom, Tuesdays With Morrie

1501.   "In the name of the best within you, do not sacrifice this world to those who are at its worst. In the name of the values that keep you alive, do not let your vision of people be distorted by the ugly, the cowardly, the mindless in those who have never achieved integrity. Do not lose your knowledge that our proper estate is an upright posture,an intransigent mind and a step that travels unlimited roads. Do not let your fire go out, spark by irreplaceable spark, in the hopeless swamps of the approximate, the not-quite, the not-yet, the not-at-all. Do not let the hero in your soul perish, in lonely frustration for the life you deserved, but have never been able to reach. Check your road and the nature of your battle. The world you desired can be won, it exists, it is real, it's yours."— Ayn Rand

1502.   "A woman could be as beautiful as she felt herself to be."— Laura Lee Guhrke, Guilty Pleasures

1503.   "Every individual has a place to fill in the world and is important in some respect, whether he chooses to be so or not."— Nathaniel Hawthorne

1504.   "Too many people realize at the end of their lives that they've taken for granted those who really love them."— Lesley M.M. Blume, Cornelia and the Audacious Escapades of the Somerset Sisters

1505.   "Somehow difficulties are easier to endure when you know your dream is waiting for you at the end."— Lisa Mangum, The Golden Spiral

1506.   "What you do matters — but not much. What you are matters tremendously."— Catherine de Hueck Doherty

1507.   "If you don't feel as close to God today as you did yesterday, who moved?"— Chris Heimerdinger, Feathered Serpent, Part 1

1508.   "I think that the best thing we can do for our children is to allow them to do things for themselves, allow them to be strong, allow them to experience life on their own terms, allow them to take the subway...let them be better people, let them believe more in themselves."— C. JoyBell C.

1509.   "To love means loving the unlovable. To forgive means pardoning the unpardonable. Faith means believing the unbelievable. Hope means hoping when everything seems hopeless."— G.K. Chesterton

1510.   "Success is determined not by whether or not you face obstacles, but by your reaction to them. And if you look at these obstacles as a containing fence, they become your excuse for failure. If you look at them as a hurdle, each one strengthens you for the next."— Ben Carson, Gifted Hands: The Ben Carson Story

1511.   "Destiny is real. And she's not mild-mannered. She will come around and hit you in the face and knock you over and before you know what hit you, you're naked- stripped of everything you thought you knew and everything you thought you didn't know- and there you are! A bloody nose, bruises all over you, and naked. And it's the most beautiful thing."— C. JoyBell C.

1512.   "Maybe you think you'll be entitled to more happiness later by forgoing all of it now, but it doesn't work that way. Happiness takes as much practice as unhappiness does. It's by living that you live more. By waiting you wait more. Every waiting day makes your life a little less. Every lonely day makes you a little smaller. Every day you put off your life makes you less capable of living it."— Ann Brashares, Sisterhood Everlasting

1513.   "She's a woman, you're a dude. You're not supposed to understand her. That's not what she's after.... She doesn't want you to understand her. She knows that's impossible. She just wants you to understand yourself. Everything else is negotiable."— Neal Stephenson, Snow Crash

1514.   "A respectable appearance is sufficient to make people more interested in your soul"— Karl Lagerfeld

1515.   "I do not know what I may appear to the world, but to myself I seem to have been only like a boy playing on the sea-shore, and diverting myself in now and then finding a smoother pebble or a prettier shell than ordinary, whilst the great ocean of truth lay all undiscovered before me."

1516.   — Isaac Newton

1517.   "It doesn't matter what you do...so long as you change something from the way it was before you touched it into something that's like you after you take your hands away."— Ray Bradbury, Fahrenheit 451

1518.   "If you believe you can, you might. If you know you can, you will."— Steve Maraboli, Life, the Truth, and Being Free

1519.   "Myth is much more important and true than history. History is just journalism and you know how reliable that is."— Joseph Campbell

1520.   "You shouldn't judge someone until you've walk a mile through an underground tunnel in her uncomfortable shoes"— Ally Carter, I'd Tell You I Love You, But Then I'd Have to Kill You

1521.   "Me plus you. (Imma tell you one time) Me plus you. (Imma tell you one time)
Me plus you. (Imma tell you one time)

One time.When I met ya girl my heart when knock (knock knock)Now them butterflies in my stomach won't stop (stop stop)Even love is a struggle and it's all we got.So we gun keep climbing to the mountain top.'Cause your world, is my world, and my breath is your breath, and my heart is yours..."— Justin Bieber

1522.　　　"When those you love die, the best you can do is honor their spirit for as long as you live. You make a commitment that you're going to take whatever lesson that person or animal was trying to teach you, and you make it true in your own life... it's a positive way to keep their spirit alive in the world, by keeping it alive in yourself."— Patrick Swayze, The Time of My Life

1523.　　　"Many people say I'm the best women's soccer player in the world. I don't think so. And because of that, someday I just might be."— Mia Hamm

1524.　　　"The morning wind spreads its fresh smell. We must get up and take that in, that wind that lets us live. Breathe before it's gone."— Rumi

1525.　　　"I will be generous with my love today. I will sprinkle compliments and uplifting words everywhere I go. I will do this knowing that my words are like seeds and when they fall on fertile soil, a reflection of those seeds will grow into something greater."— Steve Maraboli, Life, the Truth, and Being Free

1526.　　　"You only get one life. Live it to the fullest. All your miseries will be forgiven when you will be dead."— Santosh Kalwar

1527.　　　"Sometimes you can learn, even from a bad experience. By coping you become stronger. The pain does not go away, but it becomes manageable."— Somaly Mam, The Road of Lost Innocence: The True Story of a Cambodian Heroine

1528.　　　"The two of you, there's something uncanny about the way you two are with each other. I mean everything--the way you look at each other, the way she relaxes when you put your hand on her back, the way you both seem to know what the other is always thinking, it's always struck me as extraordinary. That's another reason I keep putting marriage off. I know I want something like what you two share, and I'm not sure I've found it yet. I'm not sure I ever will. And with love like that, they say anything's possible, right?"— Nicholas Sparks, The Choice

1529.　　　"Elend: "Each moment you fight is a gift to those in this cavern. Each second we fight is a second longer that thousands of people can draw breath. Each stroke of the sword, each koloss felled, each breath earned is another victory! It is a person protected for a moment longer, a life extended, an enemy frustrated!"
There was a brief pause.
"In the end they shall kill us. But first they shall fear us!"— Brandon Sanderson, The Hero of Ages

1530.　　　"She might be pointing to a doorway, or a person, or the sky. But such things were so common to my eyes, so undistinguished; that they would register as "nothing" I walked in a gray world of nothing."— Jerry Spinelli, Stargirl

1531.   "Don't let what you cannot do interfere with what you can do."— John R. Wooden

1532.   "With time and perspective we recognize that such problems in life do come for a purpose, if only to allow the one who faces such despair to be convinced that he really does need divine strength beyond himself, that she really does need the offer of heaven's hand. Those who feel no need for mercy usually never seek it and almost never bestow it. Those who have never had a heartache or a weakness or felt lonely or forsaken never have had to cry unto heaven for relief of such personal pain. Surely it is better to find the goodness of God and the grace of Christ, even at the price of despair, than to risk living our lives in a moral or material complacency that has never felt any need for faith or forgiveness, any need for redemption or relief."— Jeffery R. Holland

1533.   "America is too great for small dreams."— Ronald Reagan

1534.   "Men take care not to make women weep, for God counts their tears."— Thomas S. Monson

1535.   "And then, despite everything, I smiled and looked at the note and knew that spring would come —it always does. so I stared out that cold window, watching my breath collect on the glass, trying not to think about my life after the thaw."— Ally Carter, Don't Judge a Girl by Her Cover

1536.   "We have all forgotten what we really are. All that we call common sense and rationality and practicality and positivism only means that for certain dead levels of our life we forget that we have forgotten. All that we call spirit and art and ecstasy only means that for one awful instant we remember that we forget."— G.K. Chesterton

1537.   "Though my work may be menial, though my contribution may be small, I can perform it with dignity and offer it with unselfishness. My talents may not be great, but I can use them to bless the lives of others.... The goodness of the world in which we live is the accumulated goodness of many small and seemingly inconsequential acts."— Gordon B. Hinckley

1538.   "To accomplish great things, we must not only act but also dream, not only plan, but also believe!"— Anatole France

1539.   "It's up to you today to start making healthy choices. Not choices that are just healthy for your body, but healthy for your mind."— Steve Maraboli, Unapologetically You: Reflections on Life and the Human Experience

1540.   "you don't have to worry about burning bridges, if you're building your own"— Kerry E. Wagner

1541.   "My experiences have taught me that things rarely improve with a simple change of scenery."— Pittacus Lore, The Power of Six

1542.   "A photographer is like a cod, which produces a million eggs in order that one may reach maturity."— George Bernard Shaw

1543.   "We may have all come on different ships, but we're in the same boat now."— Martin Luther King Jr.

1544.   "All shall be done, but it may be harder than you think."— C.S. Lewis, The Lion, the Witch, and the Wardrobe

1545.   "Nobody steals books but your friends."— Roger Zelazny, The Guns of Avalon

1546.   "People aren't born good or bad. Maybe they're born with tendencies either way, but it's the way you live your life that matters. And the people you know. Valentine was Hodge's friend, and I don't think Hodge really had anyone else in his life to challenge him or make him be a better person. If I'd had that life, I don't know how I would have turned out. But I didn't. I have my family. And I have you."— Cassandra Clare, City of Glass

1547.   "When I begin to doubt my ability to work the word, I simply read another writer and know I have nothing to worry about. My contest is only with myself, to do it right, with power, and force, and delight, and gamble."— Charles Bukowski

1548.   "It cannot be emphasized too strongly or too often that this great nation was founded, not by religionists, but by Christians, not on religions, but on the gospel of Jesus Christ!"— Patrick Henry

1549.   "It is impossible to be both selfish and happy"— Joyce Meyer, Any Minute

1550.   "Try to remember it always," he said once Gogol had reached him, leading him slowly back across the breakwater, to where his mother and Sonia stood waiting. "Remember that you and I made this journey together to a place where there was nowhere left to go."— Jhumpa Lahiri, The Namesake

1551.   "I have met some highly intelligent believers, but history has no record to say that [s]he knew or understood the mind of god. Yet this is precisely the qualification which the godly must claim—so modestly and so humbly—to possess. It is time to withdraw our 'respect' from such fantastic claims, all of them aimed at the exertion of power over other humans in the real and material world."— Christopher Hitchens, The Portable Atheist: Essential Readings for the Nonbeliever

1552.   "I will not die an unlived life.
I will not live in fear
of falling or catching fire.
I choose to inhabit my days,
to allow my living to open me,
to make me less afraid,
more accessible;
to loosen my heart
until it becomes a wing,a torch, a promise.
I choose to risk my significance,to live so that which came to me as seed

goes to the next as blossom,
and that which came to me as blossom,
goes on as fruit."— Dawna Markova, I Will Not Die an Unlived Life: Reclaiming
Purpose and Passion

1553.   "The night is just a part of the day"— Paulo Coelho, Brida

1554.   "Believe me, It would be better if we didn't meet again. Go back to
school. Go back to your life. And next time they ask you, say no. Killing is for
grown-ups and you're still a child."— Anthony Horowitz, Stormbreaker

1555.   "If you want to be a writer, you have to write every day... You don't go
to a well once but daily. You don't skip a child's breakfast or forget to wake up in
the morning..."— Walter Mosley

1556.   "I want to Live! Not Die, Not Hide, LIVE!"— Margaret Peterson Haddix,
Among the Hidden

1557.   "God, send me anywhere, only go with me. Lay any burden on me,
only sustain me. And sever any tie in my heart except the tie that binds my heart
to Yours."— David Livingstone

1558.   "I liked things better when I didn't understand them."— Bill Watterson

1559.   "For he that diligently seeketh shall find; and the mysteries of God shall
be unfolded unto them, by the power of the Holy Ghost, as well in these times as
in times of old as in times to come; wherefore, the course of the Lord is one
eternal round" - 1 Nephi 10:19"— Joseph Smith Jr., The Book of Mormon:
Another Testament of Jesus Christ

1560.   "Respect for self is the beginning of cultivating virtue in men and
women."— Gordon B. Hinckley

1561.   "God made the world round so we would never be able to see too far
down the road."— Karen Blixen

1562.   "The purpose of life is to discover your gift. The meaning of life is to
give your gift away."— David Viscott

1563.   "Every Generation Needs a New Revolution"— Thomas Jefferson,
Quotations of Thomas Jefferson

1564.   "Survivors can't always choose their methods."— Patricia Briggs,
Dragon Blood

1565.   "A sail boat that sails backwards can never see the sun rise."— Bill
Cosby

1566.   "Advice to friends. Advice to fellow mothers in the same boat. "How do
you do it all?" Crack a joke. Make it seem easy. Make everything seem easy.
Make life seem easy and parenthood and marriage and freelancing for pennies,

writing a novel and smiling after a rejection, keeping the faith after two, reminding oneself that four years of work counted for a lot, counted for everything. Make the bed. Make it nice. Make the people laugh when you sit down to write and if you can't make them laugh make them cry. Make them want to hug you or hold you or punch you in the face. Make them want to kill you or fuck you or be your friend. Make them change. Make them happy. Make the baby smile. Make him laugh. Make him dinner. Make him proud.

Hold the phone, someone is on the other line. She says it's important. People are dying. Children. Friends. Press mute because there is nothing you can say. Press off because you're running out of minutes. Running out of time. Soon he'll be grown up and you'll regret the time you spent pushing him away for one more paragraph in the manuscript no one will ever read. Put down the book, the computer, the ideas. Remember who you are now. Wait. Remember who you were. Wait. Remember what's important. Make a list. Ten things, no twenty. Twenty thousand things you want to do before you die but what if tomorrow never comes? No one will remember. No one will know. No one will laugh or cry or make the bed. No one will have a clue which songs to sing to the baby. No one will be there for the children. No one will finish the first draft of the novel. No one will publish the one that's been finished for months. No one will remember the thought you had last night, that great idea you forgot to write down."— Rebecca Woolf

1567.   "The best way to prepare for death is to live life to its fullest."— John Bytheway

1568.   "Real courage is when you know you're licked before you begin, but you begin anyway and see it through no matter what."— Harper Lee, To Kill a Mockingbird

1569.   "I don't understand dating... and the other things that people do... all I know is that you ought to find the one you recognize. The one who gives you four arms, four legs, four eyes, and has the other half of your heart. There's only one of those, so what are all the other things for? Like dating?"— C. JoyBell C.

1570.   "It was the moment I realized what music can do to people, how it can make you hurt and feel so good all at once."— Nina LaCour, Hold Still

1571.   "Be happy with who you are and what you do, and you can do anything you want."— Steve Maraboli, Life, the Truth, and Being Free

1572.   "Life is painful. It has thorns, like the stem of a rose. Culture and art are the roses that bloom on the stem. The flower is yourself, your humanity. Art is the liberation of the humanity inside yourself."— Daisaku Ikeda

1573.   "Before I go," he said, and paused -- "I may kiss her?"

1574.   It was remembered afterwards that when he bent down and touched her face with his lips, he murmured some words. The child, who was nearest to him, told them afterwards, and told her grandchildren when she was a handsome old lady, that she heard him say, "A life you love."— Charles Dickens, A Tale of Two Cities

1575. "Listen to what you know instead of what you fear."— Richard Bach

1576. "Do the kind of things that come from the heart, when you do, you won't be dissatisfied, you won't be envious, you won't be longing for somebody else's things. On the contrary, you'll be overwhelmed with what comes back"— Morrie Schwartz

1577. "Happiness cannot be pursued; it must ensue."— Viktor E. Frankl, Man's Search for Meaning

1578. "If a bullet should enter my brain, let that bullet destroy every closet door."— Harvey Milk

1579. "Never compromise your values."— Steve Maraboli, Life, the Truth, and Being Free

1580. "It is harder to crack prejudice than an atom."— Albert Einstein

1581. "Storms make trees take deeper roots."— Dolly Parton

1582. "When you lost sight of your path, listen for the destination in your heart (Allen Walker, D-gray Man)"— Katsura Hoshino

1583. "It is a very natural human trait to destroy that which frightens us."— Laurell K. Hamilton, Guilty Pleasures

1584. "Small is the number of them that see with their own eyes and feel with their own hearts."— Albert Einstein

1585. "Faster, Faster, until the thrill of speed overcomes the fear of death."— Hunter S. Thompson

1586. "When I try, I fail. When I trust, He succeeds."— Corrie ten Boom

1587. "Do not allow yourselves to be made to feel inadequate or frustrated because you cannot do everything others seem to be accomplishing. Only you and your Father in Heaven know your needs, strengths, and desires. Around this knowledge your personal course must be charted and your choices made."— Marvin. J. Ashton

1588. "If you have the guts to be yourself, other people'll pay your price."— John Updike, Rabbit, Run

1589. "I want you to learn the lesson of the lotus. This flower springs forth from muddy waters. It raises its delicate petals to the sun and perfumes the world while, at the same time, its roots cling to the elemental muck, the very essence of the mortal experience. Without that soil, the flower would wither and die."— Colleen Houck

1590. "Read. Read 1000 pages for every 1 page that you write."— Sherman Alexie

1591.   "We can never know what might have been but what is to come is another matter entirely"— C.S. Lewis

1592.   "Only when we give joyfully, without hesitation or thought of gain, can we truly know what love means."— Leo Buscaglia

1593.   "Buy or borrow self-improvement books, but don't read them. Stack them around your bedroom and use them as places to rest bowls of cookies. Watch exercise shows on television, but don't do the exercises. Practice believing that the benefit lies in imagining yourself doing the exercises. Don't power walk. Saunter slowly in the sun, eating chocolate, and carry a blanket so you can take a nap."— S.A.R.K.

1594.   "Cynicism is what passes for insight when courage is lacking"— Anita Roddick

1595.   "You can surrender without a prayer, but never really pray without surrender. You can fight without ever winning, but never ever win without a fight."— Neil Peart

1596.   "I am overwhelmed by the grace and persistence of my people."— Maya Angelou

1597.   "The moment you stop worrying about success is when success will happen."— Glenn Beck

1598.   "Gossip is just a tool to distract people who have nothing better to do from feeling jealous of those few of us still remaining with noble hearts."— Anna Godbersen, Splendor

1599.   "People have only as much liberty as they have the intelligence to want and the courage to take."— Emma Goldman

1600.   "Never let the future disturb you. You will meet it, if you have to, with the same weapons of reason which today arm you against the present."— Marcus Aurelius, Meditations

1601.   "Be not angry that you cannot make others as you wish them to be, since you cannot make yourself as you wish to be."— Thomas à Kempis

1602.   "Don't look to the approval of others for your mental stability"— Karl Lagerfeld

1603.   "If you want the best the world has to offer, offer the world your best."— Neale Donald Walsch

1604.   "I give hope to men. I keep none for myself."— J.R.R. Tolkien

1605.   "But the effect of her being on those around her was incalculably diffusive: for the growing good of the world is partly dependent on unhistoric acts; and that things are not so ill with you and me as they might have been, is half owing to the number who lived faithfully a hidden life, and rest in unvisited tombs."— George Eliot, Middlemarch

1606.   "The universe is made of stories, not of atoms."— Muriel Rukeyser

1607.   "Don't give in to fear. Be strong, like I know you are. An never give up, d'you understand, never. No matter what happens. I stare at him.I won't, I says. I ain't no quitter, Pa.That's my girl."— Moira Young, Blood Red Road

1608.   "It's funny. I met a man once who did a lot of mountain climbing. I asked him which was harder, ascending or descending? He said without a doubt descending, because ascending you were so focused on reaching the top, you avoided mistakes. The backside of a mountain is a fight against human nature," he said. "You have to care as much about yourself on the way down as you did on the way up."— Mitch Albom, For One More Day

1609.   "Live authentically. Why would you continue to compromise something that's beautiful to create something that is fake?"— Steve Maraboli, Life, the Truth, and Being Free

1610.   "The question is not how to get cured, but how to live."— Joseph Conrad

1611.   "Real courage is doing the right thing when nobody's looking. Doing the unpopular thing because it's what you believe, and the heck with everybody."— Justin Cronin, The Summer Guest

1612.   "Realize that true happiness lies within you. Waste no time and effort searching for peace and contentment and joy in the world outside. Remember that there is no happiness in having or in getting, but only in giving. Reach out. Share. Smile. Hug. Happiness is a perfume you cannot pour on others without getting a few drops on yourself."— Og Mandino

1613.   "A child fish asks mother fish, 'Mother, why cannot we live on the Earth?' Mother fish replied, 'Dear... it is not the place for fish, it is the place for selfish"— Santosh Kalwar

1614.   "The question is very understandable, but no one has found a satisfactory answer to it so far. Yes, why do they make still more gigantic planes, still heavier bombs and, at the same time, prefabricated houses for reconstruction? Why should millions be spent daily on the war and yet there's not a penny available for medical services, artists, or for poor people?Why do some people have to starve, while there are surpluses rotting in other parts of the world? Oh, why are people so crazy?"— Anne Frank

1615.   "He who speaks without an attentive ear is mute."— Stephen King, The Dark Tower

1616.   "Here lies one whose name was writ on water."— John Keats

1617.   "Love means never having to be apart"— James Patterson, Sundays at Tiffany's

1618.   "Adversity is a natural part of being human. It is the height of arrogance to prescribe a moral code or health regime or spiritual practice as an amulet to keep things from falling apart. Things do fall apart. It is in their nature to do so. When we try to protect ourselves from the inevitability of change, we are not listening to the soul. We are listening to our fear of life and death, our lack of faith, our smaller ego's will to prevail. To listen to your soul is to stop fighting with life--to stop fighting when things fall apart; when they don't go our away, when we get sick, when we are betrayed or mistreated or misunderstood. To listen to the soul is to slow down, to feel deeply, to see ourselves clearly, to surrender to discomfort and uncertainty and to wait."— Elizabeth Lesser

1619.   "Everyone's greatest fantasy is to walk away from the life (they think) you lead"— Pete Wentz

1620.   "Love so joyfully and freely given can never be taken away. It is never truly gone."— Cameron Dokey, Before Midnight: A Retelling of "Cinderella"

1621.   "I think one of the sweetest lessons taught by the Prophet, and yet one of the saddest, occurred close to the time of his death. He was required to leave his plan and vision of the Rocky Mountains and give himself up to face a court of supposed justice.
These are his words: 'I am going like a lamb to the slaughter; but I am calm as a summer's morning; I have a conscience void of offense towards God, and towards all men' (D&C 135:4). That statement of the Prophet teaches us obedience to law and the importance of having a clear conscience toward God and toward our fellowmen. The Prophet Joseph Smith taught these principles--by example.
There was to be one great final lesson before his mortal life ended. He was incarcerated in Carthage Jail with his brother Hyrum, with John Taylor, and with Willard Richards. The angry mob stormed the jail; they came up the stairway, blasphemous in their cursing, heavily armed, and began to fire at will. Hyrum was hit and died. John Taylor took several balls of fire within his bosom. The Prophet Joseph, with his pistol in hand, was attempting to defend his life and that of his brethren, and yet he could tell from the pounding on the door that this mob would storm that door and would kill John Taylor and Willard Richards in an attempt to kill him.
And so his last great act here upon the earth was to leave the door and lead Willard Richards to safety, throw the gun on the floor, and go to the window, that they might see him, that the attention of this ruthless mob might be focused upon him rather than the others. Joseph Smith gave his life. Willard Richards was spared, and John Taylor recovered from his wounds.
'Greater love hath no man than this, that a man lay down his life for his friends' (John 15:13). The Prophet Joseph Smith taught us love--by example."— Thomas S. Monson

1622.   "Music, my rampart and my only one."— Edna St. Vincent Millay

1623. "Republicans are for both the man and the dollar, but in case of conflict the man before the dollar."— Abraham Lincoln

1624. "I want all my senses engaged. Let me absorb the world's variety and uniqueness."— Maya Angelou

1625. "Every search begins with beginner's luck. And every search ends with the victor's being severely tested."— Paulo Coelho

1626. "Life is a journey, not a destination; there are no mistakes, just chances we've taken."— India.Arie

1627. "Letting go means to come to the realization that some people are a part of your history, but not a part of your destiny."— Steve Maraboli

1628. "I do not believe in taking the right decision, I take a decision and make it right."— Muhammad Ali Jinnah

1629. "I find it odd- the greed of mankind. People only like you for as long as they perceive they can get what they want from you. Or for as long as they perceive you are who they want you to be. But I like people for all of their changing surprises, the thoughts in their heads, the warmth that changes to cold and the cold that changes to warmth... for being human. The rawness of being human delights me."— C. JoyBell C.

1630. "This above all: to thine own self be true."— William Shakespeare, Hamlet

1631. "Sit in a room and read--and read and read. And read the right books by the right people. Your mind is brought onto that level, and you have a nice, mild, slow-burning rapture all the time."— Joseph Campbell, The Power of Myth

1632. "The Arc of the Moral Universe Is Long, but It Bends Toward Justice"— Martin Luther King Jr.

1633. "Life has no victims. There are no victims in this life. No one has the right to point fingers at his/her past and blame it for what he/she is today. We do not have the right to point our finger at someone else and blame that person for how we treat others, today. Don't hide in the corner, pointing fingers at your past. Don't sit under the table, talking about someone who has hurt you. Instead, stand up and face your past! Face your fears! Face your pain! And stomach it all! You may have to do so kicking and screaming and throwing fits and crying- but by all means- face it! This life makes no room for cowards."— C. JoyBell C., The Sun Is Snowing: Poetry & Prose by C. Joybell C

1634. "In this sad world of ours sorrow comes to all and it often comes with bitter agony. Perfect relief is not possible except with time. You cannot now believe that you will ever feel better. But this is not true. You are sure to be happy again. Knowing this, truly believing it will make you less miserable now. I have had enough experience to make this statement."— Abraham Lincoln

1635.   "It is only with true love and compassion that we can begin to mend what is broken in the world. It is these two blessed things that can begin to heal all broken hearts."— Steve Maraboli, Life, the Truth, and Being Free

1636.   "Your work is going to fill a large part of your life, and the only way to be truly satisfied is to do what you believe is great work. And the only way to do great work is to love what you do. If you haven't found it yet, keep looking. Don't settle."— Steve Jobs

1637.   "People live their lives bound by what they accept as correct and true. That's how they define Reality. But what does it mean to be "correct" or "true"? Merely vague concepts… Their Reality may all be a mirage. Can we consider them to simply be living in their own world, shaped by their beliefs?"— Masashi Kishimoto

1638.   "The heights by great men reached and kept were not attained in sudden flight but, they while their companions slept, they were toiling upwards in the night."— Henry Wadsworth Longfellow, Good Poems for Hard Times

1639.   "But we never get back our youth… The pulse of joy that beats in us at twenty becomes sluggish. Our limbs fail, our senses rot. We degenerate into hideous puppets, haunted by the memory of the passions of which we were too much afraid, and the exquisite temptations that we had not the courage to yield to."— Oscar Wilde, The Picture of Dorian Gray

1640.   "Something amazing happens when you're in love and don't give a damn about what day it is anymore."— Chad Sugg

1641.   "A lot of people have gone further than they thought they could because someone else thought they could"— Zig Ziglar

1642.   "If the stars should appear but one night every thousand years how man would marvel and adore."— Ralph Waldo Emerson

1643.   "Life is beautiful, terms and conditions applied"— S. Nirmal

1644.   "Be not afraid of life. Believe that life is worth living, and your belief will help create the fact."— William James, The Will to Believe and Other Essays in Popular Philosophy

1645.   "Go placidly amid the noise and the haste, and remember what peace there may be in silence. As far as possible without surrender be on good terms with all persons. Speak your truth quietly and clearly; and listen to others, even to the dull and the ignorant, they too have their story. Avoid loud and aggressive persons, they are vexations to the spirit.
If you compare yourself with others, you may become vain or bitter; for always there will be greater and lesser persons than yourself. Enjoy your achievements as well as your plans. Keep interested in your own career, however humble; it is a real possession in the changing fortunes of time.
Exercise caution in your business affairs, for the world is full of trickery. But let not this blind you to what virtue there is; many persons strive for high ideals, and

everywhere life is full of heroism. Be yourself. Especially do not feign affection. Neither be cynical about love; for in the face of all aridity and disenchantment it is as perennial as the grass. Take kindly the counsel of the years, gracefully surrendering the things of youth.

Nurture strength of spirit to shield you in sudden misfortune. But do not distress yourself with dark imaginings. Many fears are born of fatigue and loneliness. Beyond a wholesome discipline, be gentle with yourself. You are a child of the universe, no less than the trees and the stars; you have a right to be here. And whether or not it is clear to you, no doubt the universe is unfolding as it should. Therefore, be at peace with God, whatever you conceive Him to be. And whatever your labors and aspirations in the noisy confusion of life, keep peace in your soul. With all its sham, drudgery and broken dreams; it is still a beautiful world. Be cheerful.

Strive to be happy."— Max Ehrmann, Desiderata: A Poem for a Way of Life

1646.   "Four things to learn in life: To think clearly without hurry or confusion; To love everybody sincerely; To act in everything with the highest motives; To trust God unhesitatingly."— Helen Keller

1647.   "To accomplish great things, we must dream as well as act."— Anatole France

1648.   "I ask you right here please to agree with me that a scar is never ugly. That is what the scar makers want us to think. But you and I, we must make an agreement to defy them. We must see all scars as beauty. Okay? This will be our secret. Because take it from me, a scar does not form on the dying. A scar means, I survived."— Chris Cleave, Little Bee

1649.   "The day is ending. It's time for something that was beautiful to turn into something else that is beautiful. Now, Let go."— Elizabeth Gilbert, Eat, Pray, Love

1650.   "Child, you have to learn to see things in the right proportions. Learn to see great things great and small things small."— Corrie ten Boom

1651.   "What a wonderful life I've had! I only wish I'd realized it sooner."— Colette

1652.   "There is nothing frightening in the dark if you just face it."— L.J. Smith, The Secret Circle: The Captive Part II and The Power

1653.   "Feel the fear and do it anyway!"— Susan Jeffers, Feel the Fear and Do It Anyway

1654.   "I will keep the law given by God; sanctioned by man. Laws and principles are not for the times when there is no temptation: they are for such moments as this, when body and soul rise in mutiny against their rigor; stringent are they; inviolate they shall be. If at my individual convenience I might break them, what would be their worth?"— Charlotte Brontë, Jane Eyre

1655.   "All men are created equal. It is what you do from there that makes the difference. We are all free agents in life. We make our own decisions. We control our own destiny."— Glenn Beck

1656.   "You can tempt me, desert me, or cause me great pain; you can create a dark world that my cause me to fear; you can rule your world with blood and terror, that's true. But you can't win. And I know that. Weak as I am, with my imperfections and sins, even with all of my failing, I am stronger than you. I will soon have a body. And I have my agency now. I will increase in my faith and knowledge and power. I am not perfect, but I will be, and there's not a thing you can do! I will become like the Father if I follow the Son. You are powerless to stop me. You can threaten and tempt and whisper lies in my ear, but you can't stop me, Satan; I see that so clearly now! I can stop myself, yes, but only if I follow you. And I reject you temptations. I reject your whispered lies. I reject you, Lucifer, and your entire plan. You have no power to control me. I am in control of myself. And try as you might, you won't control me on earth. We will defeat you in heaven, and we will defeat you on earth. Here, or the earth, it doesn't matter; I am always stronger than you."— Chris Stewart

1657.   "In times of stress, the best thing we can do for each other is to listen with our ears and our hearts and to be assured that our questions are just as important as our answers."— Fred Rogers, The World According to Mister Rogers: Important Things To Remember

1658.   "Deciding whether or not to trust a person is like deciding whether or not to climb a tree because you might get a wonderful view from the highest branch or you might simply get covered in sap and for this reason many people choose to spend their time alone and indoors where it is harder to get a splinter."— Lemony Snicket, The Penultimate Peril

1659.   "Run when you can, walk if you have to, crawl if you must; just never give up."— Dean Karnazes

1660.   "Some people could look at a mud puddle and see an ocean with ships."— Zora Neale Hurston, Their Eyes Were Watching God

1661.   "Sometimes I go to God and say, "God, if Thou dost never answer another prayer while I live on this earth, I will still worship Thee as long as I live and in the ages to come for what Thou hast done already. God's already put me so far in debt that if I were to live one million millenniums I couldn't pay Him for what He's done for me."— A.W. Tozer

1662.   "A complete stranger has the capacity to alter the life of another irrevocably. This domino effect has the capacity to change the course of an entire world. That is what life is; a chain reaction of individuals colliding with others and influencing their lives without realizing it. A decision that seems miniscule to you, may be monumental to the fate of the world."— J.D. Stroube, Caged by Damnation

1663. "When you were born you were crying and everyone else was smiling. Live your life so at the end, you're the one who is smiling and everyone else is crying."— Ralph Waldo Emerson

1664. "Why are you being so mean?"
"Friends tell friends the truth."
"yeah, but not to hurt, to help."—Laurie Halse Anderson, Wintergirls

1665. "Of course, a sign doesn't mean anything unless you know how to interpret it."— Arthur Golden, Memoirs of a Geisha

1666. "Before a dream is realized, the Soul of the World tests everything that was learned along the way. It does this not because it is evil, but so that we can, in addition to realizing our dreams, master the lessons we've learned as we've moved toward that dream. That's the point at which most people give up. It's the point at which, as we say in the language of the desert, one 'dies of thirst just when the palm trees have appeared on the horizon."— Paulo Coelho, The Alchemist

1667. "To every problem, there is a most simple solution."— Agatha Christie, The Clocks

1668. "There are three people in yourself: Who people think you are, who you think you are, and who you really are."— William Shakespeare

1669. "Nite Owl II: But the country's disintegrating. What's happened to America? What's happened to the American dream?

1670. The Comedian: It came true. You're lookin' at it."— Alan Moore, Watchmen

1671. "I have already settled it for myself so flattery and criticism go down the same drain and I am quite free."— Georgia O'Keeffe

1672. "There had been times when he knew, somewhere in him, that he would get used to it, whatever it was, because he had learnt that some hard things became softer after a very little while."— Nick Hornby, About a Boy

1673. "By 20, you should be smart. By 30, you should be strong. By 40, you should be rich. By 50, you should be wise. But if you are smart, strong, rich and wise, you don't need any age limits."— Santosh Kalwar, Quote Me Everyday

1674. "We hold these truths to be self-evident, that all men are created equal."— Thomas Jefferson, The Declaration of Independence

1675. "Sometimes the best of god's gifts arrive by the shattering of all the window panes."— Paulo Coelho, Brida

1676. "If they give you ruled paper, write the other way."— Juan Ramón Jiménez

1677.   "I was taught to strive not because there were any guarantees of success but because the act of striving is in itself the only way to keep faith with life."— Madeleine Albright, Madam Secretary: A Memoir

1678.   "You must learn to take a step back and visualize the whole piece. If you focus only on the thread given to you, you lose sight of what it can become."— Colleen Houck

1679.   "If we constantly focus only on the stones in our mortal path, we will almost surely miss the beautiful flower or cool stream provided by the loving Father who outlined our journey. Each day can bring more joy than sorrow when our mortal and spiritual eyes are open to God's goodness. Joy in the gospel is not something that begins only in the next life. It is our privilege now, this very day. We must never allow our burdens to obscure our blessings. There will always be more blessings than burdens--even if some days it doesn't seem so. Jesus said, "I am come that they might have life, and that they might have it more abundantly." Enjoy those blessings right now. They are yours and always will be."— Jeffrey R. Holland

1680.   "Deep down, I don't believe it takes any special talent for a person to lift himself off the ground and hover in the air. We all have it in us—every man, woman, and child—and with enough hard work and concentration, every human being is capable of...the feat....You must learn to stop being yourself. That's where it begins, and everything else follows from that. You must let yourself evaporate. Let your muscles go limp, breathe until you feel your soul pouring out of you, and then shut your eyes. That's how it's done. The emptiness inside your body grows lighter than the air around you. Little by little, you begin to weigh less than nothing. You shut your eyes; you spread your arms; you let yourself evaporate. And then, little by little, you lift yourself off the ground. Like so."— Paul Auster, Mr. Vertigo

1681.   "The reward of a thing well done is having done it."— Ralph Waldo Emerson

1682.   "You don't have to be stupid to be a Christian ... but it probably helps."— Ambrose Bierce

1683.   "I would rather have 30 minutes of "wonderful" than a lifetime of nothing special."— Julia Roberts

1684.   "Of course we're Christian. The very name of the church declares that. The more people see us and come to know us, the more I believe they will come to realize that we are trying to exemplify in our lives and in our living the great ideals which (Jesus Christ) taught."— Gordon B. Hinckley

1685.   "When you've found another soul who sees in to your own...take good care of each other. And remember to be kind..."— Jackson Browne

1686.   "Even if it's absurd to think you can change things, it's even more absurd to believe that it is foolish and unimportant to try."— Peter C. Newman, Here Be Dragons: Telling Tales Of People, Passion and Power

1687.   "Islam and Christianity promise eternal paradise to the faithful. And that is a powerful opiate, certainly, the hope of a better life to come. But there's a Sufi story that challenges the notion that people believe only because they need an opiate. Rabe'a al-Adiwiyah, a great woman saint of Sufism, was seem running through the streets of her hometown, Basra, carrying a torch in one hand and a bucket of water in the other. When someone asked her what she was doing, she answered, 'I am going to take this bucket of water and pour it on the flames of hell, and then I am going to use this torch to burn down the gates of paradise so that people will not love God for want of heaven of fear of hell, but because He is God.'"— John Green, Looking for Alaska

1688.   "As the smoke clears,I awaken,And untangle you from me.
Would it make you feel better
To watch me, while I bleed?
All my windows still are broken,But I'm standing on my feet."— Demi Lovato

1689.   "My Creed
I do not choose to be a common man,It is my right to be uncommon … if I can,I seek opportunity … not security.
I do not wish to be a kept citizen.
Humbled and dulled by having the State look after me.
I want to take the calculated risk;To dream and to build.
To fail and to succeed.
I refuse to barter incentive for a dole;I prefer the challenges of life
To the guaranteed existence;The thrill of fulfillment
To the stale calm of Utopia.
I will not trade freedom for beneficence
Nor my dignity for a handout
I will never cower before any master
Nor bend to any threat.
It is my heritage to stand erect.
Proud and unafraid;To think and act for myself,To enjoy the benefit of my creations
And to face the world boldly and say:This, with God's help, I have done
All this is what it means
To be an Entrepreneur."— Dean Alfange

1690.   "Many people pray to be kept out of unexpected problems.Some people pray to be able to confront and overcome them."— Toba Beta, Betelgeuse Incident

1691.   "To be kind, honest and have positive thoughts; to forgive those who harm us and treat everyone as a friend; to help those who are suffering and never to consider ourselves superior to anyone else: even if this advice seems rather simplistic, make the effort of seeing whether by following it you can find greater happiness."— Dalai Lama XIV

1692.   "Write while the heat is in you. The writer who postpones the recording of his thoughts uses an iron which has cooled to burn a hole with. He cannot inflame the minds of his audience."— Henry David Thoreau

1693.   "How satisfying it is to leave a mark on a blank surface. To make a map of my movement - no matter how temporary."— Craig Thompson, Blankets

1694.   "You can't just wish change; you have to live the change in order for it to become a reality."— Steve Maraboli, Life, the Truth, and Being Free

1695.   "There is a road from the eye to the heart that does not go through the intellect."— G.K. Chesterton

1696.   "You can only be afraid of what you think you know."— Jiddu Krishnamurti

1697.   "It had never occurred to me that our lives, which had been so closely interwoven, could unravel with such speed."— Kazuo Ishiguro

1698.   "Nobody can go back and start a new beginning, but anyone can start today and make a new ending."— Maria Robinson

1699.   "That's chess!" snapped Ron. "You've got to make some sacrifices!"— J.K. Rowling, Harry Potter and the Sorcerer's Stone

1700.   "I never did give them hell. I just told the truth, and they thought it was hell."— Harry S. Truman

1701.   "Most people fail at whatever they attempt because of an undecided heart. Should I? Should I not? Go forward? Go back? Success requires the emotional balance of a committed heart. When confronted with a challenge, the committed heart will search for a solution. The undecided heart searches for an escape.A committed heart does not wait for conditions to be exactly right. Why? Because conditions are never exactly right. Indecision limits the Almighty and His ability to perform miracles in your life. He has put the vision in you -- proceed. To wait, to wonder, to doubt, to be indecisive is to disobey God. -Andy Andrews, The Traveler's Gift"— Andy Andrews

1702.   "Tell all the Truth but tell it slant--
Success in Cirrcuit lies
Too bright for our infirm Delight
The Truth's superb surprise
As Lightening to the Children eased
With explanation kind
The Truth must dazzle gradually
Or every man be blind--"— Emily Dickinson

1703.   "Don't be afraid of the shadows that only mean there's a light nearby."— Evanescence

1704.   "a dog is not considered a good dog because he is a good barker. a man is not considered a good man because he is a good talker."— Gautama Buddha

1705.   "All of the great empires of the future will be empires of the mind."— Winston Churchill

1706.   "Taking no chances means wasting your dreams."— Ellen Hopkins, Glass

1707.   "Actually, you can be bad at something...but if you love doing it that will be enough. - August Boatwright"— Sue Monk Kidd, The Secret Life of Bees

1708.   "Temptation is the feeling we get when encountered by an opportunity to do what we innately know we shouldn't."— Steve Maraboli

1709.   "Faith, n. Belief without evidence in what is told by one who speaks without knowledge, of things without parallel."— Ambrose Bierce, The Devil's Dictionary [Facsimile Edition]

1710.   "I wanted change and excitement and to shoot off in all directions myself, like the colored arrows from a Fourth of July rocket."— Sylvia Plath

1711.   "Religious people fear hell -- Spiritual people have walked thru it."— Frank Warren, PostSecret: Confessions on Life, Death, and God

1712.   "We could all do with a bit more joy in our lives couldn't we? The wonderful thing is that when we start spreading joy, we begin to actually experience more joy in our lives too!"— Steve Goodier

1713.   "The future belongs to God, and it is only he who reveals it, under extraordinary circumstances. How do I guess at the future? Based on the omens of the present. The secret is here in the present. If you pay attention to the present, you can improve upon it. And, if you improve on the present, what comes later will also be better. Forget about the future, and live ach day according to the teachings, confident that God loves his children. Each day, in itself, brings with it an eternity."— Paulo Coelho

1714.   "[The decay of Logic results from an] untroubled assumption that the particular is real and the universal is not."— C.S. Lewis

1715.   "Be in this world as if you were a stranger or a wayfarer."— Prophet Muhammad, salallahu alayhi wasallam

1716.   "Just an observation: it is impossible to be both grateful and depressed. Those with a grateful mindset tend to see the message in the mess. And even though life may knock them down, the grateful find reasons, if even small ones, to get up."— Steve Maraboli, Life, the Truth, and Being Free

1717.   "Difficulties strengthen the mind, as labor does the body."— Lucius Annaeus Seneca

1718.   "I always cheer up immensely if an attack is particularly wounding because I think, well, if they attack one personally, it means they have not a single political argument left."— Margaret Thatcher

1719.	"Trees that are slow to grow bear the best fruit."— Molière

1720.	"Most lives are not distinguished by great achievements. They are measured by an infinite number of small ones. Each time you do a kindness for someone or bring a smile to his face, it gives your life meaning. Never doubt your value, little friend. The world would be a dismal place without you in it. (tweaked version of a passage from Scandal in Spring)"— Lisa Kleypas, Scandal in Spring

1721.	"Protect your enthusiasm from the negativity and fear of others. Never decide to do nothing just because you can only do little. Do what you can. You would be surprised at what "little" acts have done for our world."— Steve Maraboli, Unapologetically You: Reflections on Life and the Human Experience

1722.	"As soon as you honor the present moment, all unhappiness and struggle dissolve, and life begins to flow with joy and ease. When you act out the present-moment awareness, whatever you do becomes imbued with a sense of quality, care, and love - even the most simple action."— Eckhart Tolle, The Power of Now: A Guide to Spiritual Enlightenment

1723.	"We're so engaged in doing things to achieve purposes of outer value that we forget the inner value, the rapture that is associated with being alive, is what it is all about."— Joseph Campbell

1724.	"Sometimes letting go is simply changing the labels you place on an event. Looking at the same event with fresh eyes."— Steve Maraboli, Unapologetically You: Reflections on Life and the Human Experience

1725.	"Love, and do what you will. If you keep silence, do it out of love. If you cry out, do it out of love. If you refrain from punishing, do it out of love."— Augustine of Hippo

1726.	"Only when I fall do I get up again."— Vincent van Gogh

1727.	"Loneliness and the feeling of being unwanted is the most terrible."— Mother Teresa

1728.	"A lot of the conflict you have in your life exists simply because you're not living in alignment; you're not be being true to yourself."— Steve Maraboli, Unapologetically You: Reflections on Life and the Human Experience

1729.	"Yet he who reigns within himself, and rules Passions, desires, and fears, is more a king."— John Milton, Paradise Regained

1730.	"The earth will never be the same again
Rock, water, tree, iron, share this grief
As distant stars participate in the pain.
A candle snuffed, a falling star or leaf,
A dolphin death, O this particular loss
A Heaven-mourned; for if no angel cried
If this small one was tossed away as dross,
The very galaxies would have lied.

How shall we sing our love's song now
In this strange land where all are born to die?
Each tree and leaf and star shows how
The universe is part of this one cry, Every life is noted and is cherished, and
nothing loved is ever lost or perished."— Madeleine L'Engle, A Ring of Endless
Light

1731.   "Do not be afraid. Do not be satisfied with mediocrity. Put out into the
deep and let down your nets for a catch."— John Paul II

1732.   "A sailor chooses the wind that takes the ship from a safe port. Ah,
yes, but once you're abroad, as you have seen, winds have a mind of their own.
Be careful, Charlotte, careful of the wind you choose."— Avi, The True
Confessions of Charlotte Doyle

1733.   "When you get up in the morning, you have two choices - either to be
happy or to be unhappy. Just choose to be happy"— Norman Vincent Peale

1734.   "I would not sit waiting for some vague tomorrow, nor for something to
happen. One could wait a lifetime, and find nothing at the end of the waiting. I
would begin here, I would make something happen."— Louis L'Amour, Sacketts
Land

1735.   "Nothing is impossible to a determined woman."— Louisa May Alcott,
Behind a Mask: The Unknown Thrillers Of Louisa May Alcott

1736.   "We live out our lives as we are meant to live them-with some choice,
with some chance, but mostly as a result of the persons we are."— Terry Brooks,
The Druid of Shannara

1737.   "...you must always be yourself, and do things at your own pace.
Someday, you'll catch up."— Natsuki Takaya

1738.   "Some luck lies in not getting what you thought you wanted but getting
what you have, which once you have it you may be smart enough to see is what
you would have wanted had you known. "— Garrison Keillor, Lake Wobegon
U.S.A.

1739.   "Life is All About How you Handle Plan B
Plan A is always my first choice.
You know, the one where
Everything works out to be
Happily ever-after.
But more often than not,I find myself dealing with
The upside-down, inside-out version --
Where nothing goes as it should.
It's at this point that the real
Test of my character comes in...
Do I sink, or do I swim?
Do I wallow in self-pity and play the victim,Or simply shift gears
And make the best of the situation?

The choice is all mine...
Life is all about how you handle Plan B."— Suzy Toronto, The Sacred Sisterhood Of Wonderful Wacky Women

1740.   "Even the smallest person can change the course of the future"— Galadriel (Lord of the Rings)

1741.   "Lean forward into your life...catch the best bits and the finest wind. Just tip your feathers in flight a wee bit and see how dramatically that small lean can change your life."— Mary Anne Radmacher, Lean Forward Into Your Life: Begin Each Day as If It Were on Purpose

1742.   "I'd like you to know that I have forgiven him. Again and again. Once done, course, back comes the Enemy to persecute and persecute, and I must ante up to God and forgive yet again."— Jan Karon, Home to Holly Springs

1743.   "I suppose we'll never know what really happened in that room, though he did tell police, "I did it because I'm a dirty dog." This is not a very convincing alibi. He may as well have said, "I got 99 problems, but a bitch ain't one."— Chuck Klosterman, Killing Yourself to Live: 85% of a True Story

1744.   "In school we learn that mistakes are bad, and we are punished for making them. Yet, if you look at the way humans are designed to learn, we learn by making mistakes. We learn to walk by falling down. If we never fell down, we would never walk."— Robert T. Kiyosaki, Rich Dad, Poor Dad

1745.   "Mad, adj. Affected with a high degree of intellectual independence."— Ambrose Bierce, The Unabridged Devil's Dictionary

1746.   "Security is mostly a superstition. It does not exist in nature, nor do the children of men as a whole experience it. Avoiding danger is no safer in the long run than outright exposure. Life is either a daring adventure, or nothing."— Helen Keller, The Open Door

1747.   "Truly powerful people have great humility. They do not try to impress, they do not try to be influential. They simply are. People are magnetically drawn to them. They are most often very silent and focused, aware of their core selves. ... They never persuade, nor do they use manipulation or aggressiveness to get their way. They listen. If there is anything they can offer to assist you, they offer it; if not, they are silent."— Sanaya Roman, Living with Joy: Keys to Personal Power and Spiritual Transformation

1748.   "What would you attempt to do if you knew you could not fail?"— Robert H. Schuller

1749.   "There are no traffic jams on the extra mile."— Zig Ziglar

1750.   "People would rather believe than know."— Edward O. Wilson

1751.   "We make patterns, we share moments. Sometimes, I think I'm the only one to see it."— Jenny Downham, Before I Die

1752.   "People who lack the clarity, courage, or determination to follow their own dreams will often find ways to discourage yours. Live your truth and don't EVER stop!"— Steve Maraboli, Life, the Truth, and Being Free

1753.   "So, have we solved the secret of happiness?
"I believe so," he said
Are you going to tell me?
"Yes.Ready?"
Ready.
"Be satisfied."
That's it?
"Be grateful."
That's it?
"For what you have. For the love you receive. And for what God has given you."
That's it?
He looked me in the eye. Then he sighed deeply.
"That's it."— Mitch Albom, Have a Little Faith: a True Story

1754.   "In this country we have no place for hyphenated Americans."— Theodore Roosevelt

1755.   "Don't turn over the rocks if you don't want to see the pale creatures who live under them."— Janet Fitch, White Oleander

1756.   "Reading the Bible will help you get to know the word, but it's when you put it down and live your life that you get to know the author."— Steve Maraboli, Life, the Truth, and Being Free

1757.   "Miracles don't happen. You make them happen. They're not wishes or dreams or candles on a cake. They're not impossible. Reality is real. It's totally and completely under my control."— Julie Anne Peters, Far from Xanadu

1758.   "Don't try to steer the boat.Don't open shop for yourself. Listen. Keep silent.You are not God's mouthpiece. Try to be an ear,And if you do speak, ask for explanations."— Rumi, The Essential Rumi

1759.   "A man, to be greatly good, must imagine intensely and comprehensively; he must put himself in the place of another and many others; the pains and pleasures of his species must become his own. The great instrument of moral good is the imagination."— Percy Bysshe Shelley, A Defence of Poetry and Other Essays

1760.   "Nothing great will ever be achieved without great men, and men are great only if they are determined to be so."— Charles de Gaulle

1761.   "Nobody's perfect. I'm perfectly flawed."— Evanescence

1762.   "What'll you do if you can't find a way to cure him?" Seth asked.

1763.   Dale paused. "I'll never know that day has come, because I'll never stop trying."— Brandon Mull, Fablehaven

1764.   "Crowded classrooms and half-day sessions are a tragic waste of our greatest national resource - the minds of our children."— Walt Disney Company

1765.   "To be cheerful when others are in despair, to keep the faith when others falter, to be true even when we feel forsaken—all of these are deeply desired outcomes during the deliberate, divine tutorials which God gives to us—because He loves us. These learning experiences must not be misread as divine indifference. Instead, such tutorials are a part of the divine unfolding."— Neal A. Maxwell

1766.   "Our Age of Anxiety is, in great part, the result of trying to do today's jobs with yesterday's tools!"— Marshall McLuhan

1767.   "Friends are like bras, attached near your heart for support. Foes are like panties, deported, every now and then, when they get dirty."— Santosh Kalwar, Quote Me Everyday

1768.   "It doesn't matter who you are, where you come from. The ability to triumph begins with you - always."— Oprah Winfrey

1769.   "When the voice of your friend or the page of your book sinks into democratic equality with the pattern of the wallpaper, the feel of your clothes, your memory of last night, and the noises from the road, you are falling asleep. The highly selective consciousness enjoyed by fully alert men, with all its builded sentiments and consecrated ideals, has as much to be called real as the drowsy chaos, and more."— C.S. Lewis

1770.   "It's the heart that really matters in the end."— Rob Thomas

1771.   "If bringing down the wall would require you to fly, you must believe you can fly. Otherwise, when the decisive moment comes, you will surely discover you have no wings."— Patrick Carman, The Dark Hills Divide

1772.   "If you could only sense how important you are to the lives of those you meet; how important you can be to the people you may never dream of. There is something of yourself that you leave at every meeting with another person."— Roderick Evans

1773.   "And life is what we make it. Always has been, always will be."— Grandma Moses

1774.   ""Today's dirty hands are tomorrow's muddy water"— Danielle Hylton-Outland

1775.   "One must still have chaos in oneself to be able to give birth to a dancing star."— Friedrich Nietzsche

1776.   "There comes a time when we realize that our parents cannot save themselves or save us, that everyone who wades through time eventually gets dragged out to sea by the undertow- that, in short, we are all going."— John Green, Looking for Alaska

1777.　　　"I don't know why people are afraid of lust. Then I can imagine that they are very afraid of me, for I have a great lust for everything. A lust for life, a lust for how the summer-heated street feels beneath my feet, a lust for the touch of another's skin on my skin...a lust for everything. I even lust after cake. Yes, I am very lusty and very scary."— C. JoyBell C.

1778.　　　"Accepting oneself does not preclude an attempt to become better."— Flannery O'Connor

1779.　　　"The most exquisite paradox... as soon as you give it all up, you can have it all. As long as you want power, you can't have it. The minute you don't want power, you'll have more than you ever dreamed possible."— Ram Dass

1780.　　　"Help" is a prayer that is always answered. It doesn't matter how you pray--with your head bowed in silence, or crying out in grief, or dancing. Churches are good for prayer, but so are garages and cars and mountains and showers and dance floors. Years ago I wrote an essay that began, "Some people think that God is in the details, but I have come to believe that God is in the bathroom."— Anne Lamott, Plan B: Further Thoughts on Faith

1781.　　　"Those who have the ability to be grateful are the ones who have the ability to achieve greatness."— Steve Maraboli, Life, the Truth, and Being Free

1782.　　　"I don't know, I don't want to talk as much. (...) It's nicer to think dear, pretty thoughts and keep them in one's heart, like treasures. I don't like to have them laughed at or wondered over."— L.M. Montgomery, Anne of Green Gables

1783.　　　"Fear can only grow in darkness. Once you face fear with light, you win."— Steve Maraboli, Life, the Truth, and Being Free

1784.　　　"Obstacles are those frightening things you see when you take your eyes off your goal."— Henry James

1785.　　　"One day we will learn that the heart can never be totally right when the head is totally wrong"— Martin Luther King Jr., Strength to Love

1786.　　　"This world is your best teacher. There is a lesson in everything. There is a lesson in each experience. Learn it and become wise. Every failure is a stepping stone to success. Every difficulty or disappointment is a trial of your faith. Every unpleasant incident or temptation is a test of your inner strength. Therefore nil desperandum. March forward hero!"— Sivananda Saraswati

1787.　　　"Where your treasure is, there will your heart be also"— J.K. Rowling, Harry Potter and the Deathly Hallows

1788.　　　"A very small percentage of the people in this world will actually experience and live today. So many people will be stuck on another day, another time that traumatized them and caused them to spiritually stutter so they miss out on this day."— Steve Maraboli, Unapologetically You: Reflections on Life and the Human Experience

1789.   "You will write if you will write without thinking of the result in terms of a result, but think of the writing in terms of discovery, which is to say that creation must take place between the pen and the paper, not before in a thought or afterwards in a recasting...It will come if it is there and if you will let it come."— Gertrude Stein

1790.   "Don't be disheartened by the forces of evil. Nothing can happen that God hasn't allowed. Even resistance is all part of grand orchestration. The devil always has you right were God wants you."— Steve Maraboli, Life, the Truth, and Being Free

1791.   "We are faced with the fact, my friends, that tomorrow is today. Procrastination is still the thief of time. Over the bleached bones and jumbled residues of numerous civilizations are written the pathetic words 'Too Late'."— Martin Luther King Jr.

1792.   "We're not alone--at least, we're alone only if we choose to be alone. We're alone only if we choose to go through life relying solely on our own strength rather than learning to draw upon the power of God. "— Sheri L. Dew, If Life Were Easy, It Wouldn't Be Hard: And Other Reassuring Truths

1793.   "Good days, they come around the oddest corners."— Colum McCann, Let the Great World Spin

1794.   "Buy a pup and your money will buy Love unflinching that cannot lie."— Rudyard Kipling

1795.   "When we make our own misery we sometimes cling to it even when we want so bad to change, because misery is something we know. The misery is comfortable."— Dean Koontz, One Door Away from Heaven

1796.   "In every journey comes a moment... one like no other. And in that moment, you must decide between who you are... and who you want to be."— J.C. Marino, Dante's Journey

1797.   "Nothing remains forever, only thing that remain forever is romantically stupid word forever."— Santosh Kalwar, Quote Me Everyday

1798.   "Forget yourself and go to work."— Bryant S. Hinckley

1799.   "I change the world, the world changes me."— Libba Bray

1800.   "Our great human adventure is the evolution of consciousness. We are in this life to enlarge the soul, liberate the spirit, and light up the brain."— Tom Robbins, Wild Ducks Flying Backward

1801.   "The thinnest slice would be teeming with memories of a love so strong it turned you inside out and left you gasping, and would be an identical match to a slice stored in the heart of a soul mate."— Jodi Picoult

1802.   "God loves us. He's watching us, he wants us to succeed, and we'll know someday that he has not left one thing undone for the eternal welfare of each of us. If we only knew it, there are heavenly hosts pulling for us -- friends in heaven that we can't remember now, who yearn for our victory."— Ezra Taft Benson

1803.   "...What you fear will not go away; it will take you into yourself and bless you and keep you. That's the world, and we all live there."— William Stafford

1804.   "Pray to God, but row towards shore."— Lee Ezell

1805.   "Self-respect is the root of discipline: The sense of dignity grows with the ability to say no to oneself."— Abraham Joshua Heschel

1806.   "We ask ourselves, who am I to be brilliant, gorgeous, handsome, talented and fabulous? Actually, who are you not to be?"— Nelson Mandela

1807.   "Skies are crying, I am watching, Catching teardrops in my hands.
Only silence, as it's ending, Like we never had a chance.
Do you have to make me feel
Like there's nothing left of me?"— Demi Lovato

1808.   "There are two things we should always be 1. raw and 2. ready. When you are raw, you are always ready and when you are ready you usually realize that you are raw. Waiting for perfection is not an answer, one cannot say "I will be ready when I am perfect" because then you will never be ready, rather one must say "I am raw and I am ready just like this right now, how and who I am."— C. JoyBell C.

1809.   "There is no reality except in action."— Jean-Paul Sartre, Existentialism is a Humanism

1810.   "Success is a lousy teacher. It seduces smart people into thinking they can't lose."— Bill Gates

1811.   "I'm often asked what I think about as I run. Usually the people who ask this have never run long distances themselves. I always ponder the question. What exactly do I think about when I'm running? I don't have a clue."— Haruki Murakami, What I Talk About When I Talk About Running

1812.   "Tolerance of intolerance is cowardice."— Ayaan Hirsi Ali

1813.   "You enter the forest
at the darkest point, where there is no path.
Where there is a way or path, it is someone else's path.
You are not on your own path.
If you follow someone else's way, you are not going to realize
your potential."— Joseph Campbell, The Hero's Journey: Joseph Campbell on His Life & Work

1814.   "The temptation of the age is to look good without being good."—
Brennan Manning, The Ragamuffin Gospel: Good News for the Bedraggled,
Beat-Up, and Burnt Out

1815.   "Action springs not from thought, but from a readiness for
responsibility."— Dietrich Bonhoeffer

1816.   "Difficulties increase the nearer we get to the goal."— Johann
Wolfgang von Goethe

1817.   "A great human revolution in just a single individual will help achieve a
change in the destiny of a nation and, further, can even enable a change in the
destiny of all humankind."— Daisaku Ikeda, The Human Revolution

1818.   "Associate yourself with people of good quality, for it is better to be
alone than to be in bad company"— Booker T. Washington

1819.   "No matter what your history has been, your destiny is what you create
today. What are you going to create?"— Steve Maraboli, Life, the Truth, and
Being Free

1820.   "Life is like a play: it's not the length, but the excellence of the acting
that matters."— Lucius Annaeus Seneca

1821.   "The major work of the world is not done by geniuses. It is done by
ordinary people, with balance in their lives, who have learned to work in an
extraordinary manner."— Gordon B. Hinckley

1822.   "Didn't anyone ever tell you that the mouth is the front gate of all
misfortune?"— Andrew Davidson, The Gargoyle

1823.   "I know that you cannot live on hope alone, but without it, life is not
worth living. And you...And you...And you...Gotta give em hope."— Harvey Milk,
The Harvey Milk Interviews: In His Own Words

1824.   "...You find a way, somehow to get through the most horrible things;
things you think would kill you. You find a way and you move through the days,
one by one, in shock, in despair, but you move. The days pass, one after the
other, and you go along with them - occasionally stunned, and not entirely
relieved, to find that you are still alive."— Michelle Richmond, The Year of Fog

1825.   "Love and compassion are the mother and father of a smile. We need
to create more smiles in our world today. Smiles, after all, pave the way to a
happy world."— Steve Maraboli, Life, the Truth, and Being Free

1826.   "Harry, despite your privileged insight into Voldemort's world (which,
incidentally, is a gift any Death Eater would kill to have), you have never been
seduced by the Dark Arts, never, even for a second, shown the slightest desire to
become one of Voldemort's followers!"
"Of course I haven't!" said Harry indignantly. "He killed my mum and dad!"

"You are protected, in short, by your ability to love!" said Dumbledore loudly."— J.K. Rowling, Harry Potter and the Half-Blood Prince

1827.	"The first thing you have to know about writing is that it is something you must do every day. There are two reasons for this rule: Getting the work done and connecting with your unconscious mind."— Walter Mosley

1828.	"The meaning I picked, the one that changed my life: Overcome fear, behold wonder."— Richard Bach

1829.	"What we can do, we must do: we must use what we are given, and we must use it the best we can, however much or little help we have for the task. What you have been given is a hard thing--a very hard thing... But my darling, what if there were no one who could do the difficult things?"— Robin McKinley, Sunshine

1830.	"And thus we see that by small means the Lord can bring about great things" - 1 Nephi 16:29"— Joseph Smith Jr.

1831.	"You are better than you think. A-one, a-two a-three."— Kurt Vonnegut

1832.	"People need not fear the unknown if they are capable of achieving what they need and want."— Paulo Coelho, The Alchemist

1833.	"Truly, my dear young friends, you are a chosen generation. I hope you will never forget it. I hope you will never take it for granted. I hope there will grow in your hearts an overpowering sense of gratitude to God, who has made it possible for you to come upon the earth in this marvelous season of the world's history."— Gordon B. Hinckley

1834.	"My past has not defined me, destroyed me, deterred me, or defeated me; it has only strengthened me."— Steve Maraboli, Unapologetically You: Reflections on Life and the Human Experience

1835.	"I have learned that the person I have to ask for forgiveness from the most is: myself. You must love yourself. You have to forgive yourself, every day, whenever you remember a shortcoming, a flaw, you have to tell yourself "That's just fine". You have to forgive yourself so much, until you don't even see those things anymore. Because that's what love is like."— C. JoyBell C.

1836.	"Make today worth remembering."— Zig Ziglar

1837.	"Judging is preventing us from understanding a new truth. Free yourself from the rules of old judgments and create the space for new understanding."— Steve Maraboli, Life, the Truth, and Being Free

1838.	"I have frequently seen people become neurotic when they content themselves with inadequate or wrong answers to the questions of life. They seek position, marriage, reputation, outward success of money, and remain unhappy and neurotic even when they have attained what they were seeking. Such people are usually confined within too narrow a spiritual horizon. Their life has not sufficient content, sufficient meaning. If they are enabled to develop into more spacious personalities, the neurosis generally disappears."— C.G. Jung

1839.   "Heaven is comfort, but it's still not living."— Alice Sebold, The Lovely Bones

1840.   "It does not matter how long you live, but how well you do it."— Martin Luther King Jr.

1841.   "There are some things that it is better to begin than to refuse, even though the end may be dark."— J.R.R. Tolkien, The Two Towers

1842.   "Your life is a print-out of your thoughts."— Steve Maraboli, Life, the Truth, and Being Free

1843.   "Life is difficult for everyone. We all have stress and we all need someone in our lives that we can lean on. Never think that you cannot talk to someone because they have problems to or that your friend or loved one would be better off without you or your problems. You'll soon find out that they need you just as much as you need them."— Joshua Hartzell

1844.   "Love is the only thing that we can carry with us when we go, and it makes the end so easy."— Louisa May Alcott, Little Women Book Two Book: Good Wives

1845.   "Look beyond yourself..."— Michael Jackson

1846.   "If there never was a night or day and memories could fade away, then we'd be nothing left but the dreams we made"— Selena Gomez

1847.   "I have the nerve to walk my own way, however hard, in my search for reality, rather than climb upon the rattling wagon of wishful illusions."— Zora Neale Hurston

1848.   "When it rains it pours. Maybe the art of life is to convert tough times to great experiences: we can choose to hate the rain or dance in it."— Joan Marques

1849.   "My life has been full of terrible misfortunes, most of which never happened."— Michel de Montaigne

1850.   "Watch for the thing that will show itself to you. Because that thing, when you find it, will be your future."— Arthur Golden, Memoirs of a Geisha

1851.   "Sometimes we know in our bones what we really need to do, but we're afraid to do it. Taking a chance and stepping beyond the safety of the world we've always known is the only way to grow, though and without risk there is no reward."— Wil Wheaton, Just a Geek: Unflinchingly honest tales of the search for life, love, and fulfillment beyond the Starship Enterprise

1852.	"Faith is like radar that sees through the fog -- the reality of things at a distance that the human eye cannot see."— Corrie ten Boom

1853.	"Some people like me, some don't. I don't understand where the difference comes from. My heart like them all. For a simple childish reason. We all are created equal, we all are humans."— Santosh Kalwar, A Very First Book Of Poems: Heartbreak

1854.	"You can wake up every day looking forward to new adventures with hope smiling brightly before you because you have a Savior. You are baptized in His Church.... You just need to stay in, pressing forward with a brightness of hope to your heavenly home."— Julie B. Beck

1855.	"Pain and suffering are the soil of strength and courage."— Lurlene McDaniel, Someone Dies, Someone Lives

1856.	"I've made mistakes. More than my share. Hopefully, I've learned from them, but can't guarantee anything. There's only one thing I can promise. I'm taking this to the end."-Bobby Pendragon"— D.J. MacHale

1857.	"Nothing is so hard that it can't be found by searching."— Kim Harrison, White Witch, Black Curse

1858.	"If we had no winter, the spring would not be so pleasant: if we did not sometimes taste of adversity, prosperity would not be so welcome."— Anne Bradstreet

1859.	"just because you refuse to acknowledge something, refuse to look at it or think about it, doesn't mean it's not there, that it doesn't affect you and the choices you make in your life."— Rachel Gibson, Tangled Up In You

1860.	"Gradually the healing took place, seeming as it always does that it wasn't taking place."— Ursula K. Le Guin

1861.	"That's the scary thing about hope," she said. "If you let it go too long it turns into faith."— Christopher Moore, Coyote Blue

1862.	"Hold yourself to a higher standard than anyone else expects of you. Never excuse yourself."— Henry Ward Beecher

1863.	"The greatest thing about tomorrow is, I will be better than I am today. And that's how I look at my life. I will be a better golfer, I will be a better person, I will be a better father, I will be a better husband, I will be a better friend. That's the beauty of tomorrow."— Tiger Woods

1864.	"Before, I wanted to say: "I found love!" But now, I want to say: "I found a person. And he belongs to me and I belong to him."— C. JoyBell C.

1865.	"When I was little and running on the race track at school, I always stopped and waited for all the other kids so we could run together even though I knew (and everybody else knew) that I could run much faster than all of them! I pretended to read slowly so I could "wait" for everyone else who couldn't read as fast as I could! When my friends were short I pretended that I was short too and if my friend was sad I pretended to be unhappy. I could go on and on about all the ways I have limited myself, my whole life, by "waiting" for people. And the only thing that I've ever received in return is people thinking that they are faster than me, people thinking that they can make me feel bad about myself just because I let them and people thinking that I have to do whatever they say I should do. My mother used to teach me "Cinderella is a perfect example to be" but I have learned that Cinderella can go fuck herself, I'm not waiting for anybody, anymore! I'm going to run as fast as I can, fly as high as I can, I am going to soar and if you want you can come with me! But I'm not waiting for you anymore."— C. JoyBell C.

1866.   "The man that decided to change on the 12th hours died at the 11th."— Hlovate, Contengan Jalanan

1867.   "I believe in going with the flow. I don't believe in fighting against the flow. You ride on your river and you go with the tides and the flow. But it has to be your river, not someone else's. Everyone has their own river, and you don't need to swim, float, sail on their's, but you need to be in your own river and you need to go with it. And I don't believe in fighting the wind. You go and you fly with your wind. Let everyone else catch their own gusts of wind and let them fly with their own gusts of wind, and you go and you fly with yours."— C. JoyBell C.

1868.   "I am fallen, flawed and imperfect. Yet drenched in the grace and mercy that is found in Jesus Christ, there is strength"— Adam Young

1869.   "... In love, everyone does things that hurt the other person, so there really is no "Right" and "Wrong". You just have to decide what you're willing to forgive"— Yvonne Wood, Dead Beautiful

1870.   "If you want to write a fantasy story with Norse gods, sentient robots, and telepathic dinosaurs, you can do just that. Want to throw in a vampire and a lesbian unicorn while you're at it? Go ahead. Nothing's off limits. But the endless possibility of the genre is a trap. It's easy to get distracted by the glittering props available to you and forget what you're supposed to be doing: telling a good story. Don't get me wrong, magic is cool. But a nervous mother singing to her child at night while something moves quietly through the dark outside her house? That's a story. Handled properly, it's more dramatic than any apocalypse or goblin army could ever be."— Patrick Rothfuss

1871.   "The truth was a mirror in the hands of God. It fell, and broke into pieces. Everybody took a piece of it, and they looked at it and thought they had the truth."— Rumi

1872.   "Have you ever felt the longing for someone you could admire? For something, not to look down at, but up to?"— Ayn Rand

1873.   "Most people overestimate what they can do in one year and underestimate what they can do in ten years."— Bill Gates

1874.   "To ugly ducklings everywhere,Don't worry about those fluffy yellow morons:They'll never get to be swans"— Zoë Marriott, The Swan Kingdom

1875.   "Live simply so that others may simply live."— Mahatma Gandhi

1876.   "It's okay to be a loser, it just depends on how good you are at being one."— Billie Joe Armstrong

1877.   "My friends say I'm a fool to think that you're the one for me, I guess I'm just a sucker for love. (love love) 'Cause honestly the truth is that you know I'm never leaving, 'cause you're my angel sent from above. (bove bove) Me and you can do no wrong. My money is yours give you a lil more 'cause I love ya, love ya. With me girl is where you belong...-Love Me"— Justin Bieber

1878.   "Stop thinking about life and choose to live it"— Paulo Coelho, The Fifth Mountain

1879.   "Sometimes it's the same moments that take your breath away that breathe purpose and love back into your life."— Steve Maraboli, Unapologetically You: Reflections on Life and the Human Experience

1880.   "I firmly believe that any man's finest hour, the greatest fulfillment of all that he holds dear, is that moment when he has worked his heart out in a good cause and lies exhausted on the field of battle - victorious." "— Vince Lombardi

1881.   "Every moment in life is an act of faith"— Paulo Coelho, Brida

1882.   "I prefer you to make mistakes in kindness than work miracles in unkindness."— Mother Teresa

1883.   "Faith is deliberate confidence in the character of God whose ways you may not understand at the time."— Oswald Chambers

1884.   "Change is not always growth, but growth is often rooted in change. Drizzt Do'Urden"— R.A. Salvatore

1885.   "Baby you're a firework, c'mon show 'em what you're worth..." ~Firework"— Katy Perry

1886.   "A student to teacher: "I am so alone; I don't know what to do?" Teacher: "Do not worry about being alone, we always come alone and go alone. In a very sweet accident, we meet others who are alone and start to be part of them in various forms of relationships such as friends, husband, wife, mother, father, sister and so on. So, life is about sharing a moment together, not thinking as if you are alone."— Santosh Kalwar, Quote Me Everyday

1887.   "You kick ass Sam. And don't forget it"— Pittacus Lore, The Power of Six

1888.   "Sugar, it's no parade but you'll get down the street one way or another, so you'd just as well throw your shoulders back and pick up the pace."— Barbara Kingsolver, The Poisonwood Bible

1889.   "The personal life deeply lived always expands into truths beyond itself."— Anaïs Nin

1890.   "Scholars, theologians, and even poets have yet to be able to truly describe and touch upon the beauty, romance, and magic of a relationship built on 100% authenticity"— Steve Maraboli, Life, the Truth, and Being Free

1891.   "There's only one racing strategy that matters. It's the one I run by:Get in the lead and don't let anyone pass you."— Megan McCafferty, Sloppy Firsts

1892.   "Plus there's the fact," he went on, making it clear he didn't need me to reply anyway, "that music is a total constant. That's why we have such a strong visceral connection to it, you know? Because a song can take you back instantly to a moment, or a place, or even a person. No matter what else has changed in you or the world, that one song stays the same, just like that moment. Which is pretty amazing, when you actually think about it."— Sarah Dessen, Just Listen

1893.   "It's not about what you've done; it's how you've experienced whatever has happened to you. Matt Lawrence in The Overachievers"— Alexandra Robbins

1894.   "HOW do you define a word without concrete meaning? To each his own, the saying goes, so
WHY push to attain an ideal state of being that no two random people will agree is
WHERE you want to be? Faultless. Finished. Incomparable. People can never be these, and anyway,
WHEN did creating a flawless facade become a more vital goal than learning to love the person
WHO lives inside your skin? The outside belongs to others. Only you should decide for you -
WHAT is perfect."— Ellen Hopkins, Perfect

1895.   "Learn everything you can, anytime you can, from anyone you can, there will always come a time when you will be grateful you did."— Sarah Caldwell

1896.   "If you hear how wonderful you are often enough, you begin to believe it, no matter how you try to resist it."— Ben Carson

1897.   "I think that I shall never see
A poem lovely as a tree.
A tree whose hungry mouth is pressed
Against the earth's sweet flowing breast;
A tree that looks at God all day
And lifts her leafy arms to pray;
A tree that may in summer wear

A nest of robins in her hair;
Upon whose bosom snow has lain;
Who intimately lives with rain.
Poems are made by fools like me,But only God can make a tree."— Joyce
Kilmer, Trees & Other Poems

1898.　　　"In our world," said Eustace, "a star is a huge ball of flaming gas." Even
in your world, my son, that is not what a star is, but only what it is made of."—
C.S. Lewis, The Voyage of the Dawn Treader

1899.　　　"People will always have opinions about your decision because they're
not courageous enough to take action on their opinion."— Steve Maraboli

1900.　　　"Until justice rolls down like water and righteousness like a mighty
stream."— Martin Luther King Jr.

1901.　　　"I understood what he was doing, that he had spent four years fulfilling
the absurd and tedious duty of graduating from college and now he was
emancipated from that world of abstraction, false security, parents, and material
excess."— Jon Krakauer, Into the Wild

1902.　　　"Books have a way of finding their way into our lives, usually, right
when we need them the most."— Christian Marotti

1903.　　　"We spend money that we do not have, on things we do not need, to
impress people who do not care."— Will Smith

1904.　　　"Understanding is the reward of faith. Therefore, seek not to
understand that you may believe, but believe that you may understand."—
Augustine of Hippo

1905.　　　"All young people, regardless of sexual orientation or identity, deserve
a safe and supportive environment in which to achieve their full potential."—
Harvey Milk

1906.　　　"Now I'm told this is life, and pain's just a simple compromise."—
Hayley Williams

1907.　　　"We are constantly invited to be who we are."— Henry David Thoreau

1908.　　　"Sometimes it falls upon a generation to be great, you can be that
generation"— Nelson Mandela

1909.　　　"I saw Eternity the other night,
Like a great ring of pure and endless light,
All calm, as it was bright,
And round beneath it, Time, in hours, days, years,
Driven by the spheres,
Like a vast shadow moved, in which the world
And all her train were hurled."— Madeleine L'Engle, A Ring of Endless Light

1910. "Evil exists in us all, Torak. Some fight it. Some feed it. That's how it's always been."— Michelle Paver

1911. "Don't let your habits become handcuffs"— Elizabeth Berg, The Year of Pleasures

1912. "Change isn't easy. Changing the way you live means changing the way you think, means changing what you believe about life. That's hard."— Dean Koontz, One Door Away from Heaven

1913. "What's right isn't always popular, and what's popular isn't always right."— Sharon M. Draper

1914. "Earth is sad, Moon is shy, Sun is happy but wait a moment, I just forgot to tell you that I am the child of open sky."— Santosh Kalwar

1915. "My faith is big enough to accept all of God's wonders."— Kirsten Miller, The Eternal Ones

1916. "It is not given to us to know what difference we can make, and perhaps we can make no difference at all. But that is no reason not to make the attempt," said Saliman quietly. "The Light shines more brightly in the darkness."— Alison Croggon, The Crow

1917. "To talk to each other is but a more animated and an audible thinking."— Charlotte Brontë, Jane Eyre

1918. "If you can control your behavior when everything around you is out of control, you can model for your children a valuable lesson in patience and understanding...and snatch an opportunity to shape character."— Jane Clayson Johnson, I Am a Mother

1919. "Bending beats breaking."— Betty Greene

1920. "I've never quite believed that one chance is all I get"— Anne Tyler

1921. "Heaven help the roses if the bombs begin to fall"— Stevie Wonder

1922. "The kind of beauty I want most is the hard-to-get kind that comes from within - strength, courage, dignity."— Ruby Dee

1923. "Who would bring light must endure burning."— David Zindell, The Wild

1924. "The greatest day in your life and mine is when we take total responsibility for our attitudes. That's the day we truly grow up."— John C. Maxwell

1925. "There is no failure except in no longer trying."— Elbert Hubbard

1926. "How would your life be different if...You stopped validating your victim mentality? Let today be the day...You shake off your self-defeating drama and embrace your innate ability to recover and achieve."— Steve Maraboli, Life, the Truth, and Being Free

1927. "The dictionary is the only place that success comes before work. work is the key to success, and hard work can help you accomplish anything."— Vince Lombardi

1928. "At every given moment we are absolutely perfect for what is required for our journey."— Steve Maraboli, Life, the Truth, and Being Free

1929. "Hang in there. It is astonishing how short a time it can take for very wonderful things to happen."— Frances Hodgson Burnett

1930. "Are you going to allow the world around you to change while you remain stagnant? Make this the time you throw away old habits that have hindered your happiness and success and finally allow your greatest self to flourish."— Steve Maraboli, Life, the Truth, and Being Free

1931. "At the moment of commitment the entire universe conspires to assist you."— Johann Wolfgang von Goethe

1932. "Accept whatever comes to you woven in the pattern of your destiny, for what could more aptly fit your needs?"— Marcus Aurelius, Meditations

1933. "The personal, as everyone's so fucking fond of saying, is political. So if some idiot politician, some power player, tries to execute policies that harm you or those you care about, take it personally. Get angry. The Machinery of Justice will not serve you here – it is slow and cold, and it is theirs, hardware and soft-. Only the little people suffer at the hands of Justice; the creatures of power slide from under it with a wink and a grin. If you want justice, you will have to claw it from them. Make it personal. Do as much damage as you can. Get your message across. That way, you stand a better chance of being taken seriously next time. Of being considered dangerous. And make no mistake about this: being taken seriously, being considered dangerous marks the difference - the only difference in their eyes - between players and little people. Players they will make deals with. Little people they liquidate. And time and again they cream your liquidation, your displacement, your torture and brutal execution with the ultimate insult that it's just business, its politics, it's the way of the world, it's a tough life and that it's nothing personal. Well, fuck them. Make it personal."— Richard K. Morgan, Altered Carbon

1934. "Holding a grudge & harboring anger/resentment is poison to the soul. Get even with people...but not those who have hurt us, forget them, instead get even with those who have helped us."— Steve Maraboli, Unapologetically You: Reflections on Life and the Human Experience

1935. "How would your life be different if...You didn't allow yourself to be defined by your past? Let today be the day...You stop letting your history interfere with your destiny and awaken to the opportunity to release your greatest self."— Steve Maraboli, Life, the Truth, and Being Free

1936.   "You start by writing to live. You end by writing so as not to die."—
Carlos Fuentes

1937.   "Peace demands the most heroic labor and the most difficult sacrifice.
It demands greater heroism than war. It demands greater fidelity to the truth and
a much more perfect purity of conscience."— Thomas Merton

1938.   "Everything ends, and Everything matters.Everything matters not in
spite of the end of you and all that you love, but because of it. Everything is all
you've got…and after Everything is nothing. So you were wise to welcome
Everything, the good and the bad alike, and cling to it all. Gather it in. Seek the
meaning in sorrow and don't ever turn away, not once, from here until the end.
Because it is all the same, it is all unfathomable, and it is all infinitely preferable
to the one dreadful alternative."— Ron Currie Jr., Everything Matters!

1939.   "you don't have to be great to get started, but you have to get started to
be great."— Les Brown

1940.   "Other men look up and down, left and right; but men like us are
different. We are visionaries."— Eoin Colfer, Airman

1941.   "You've been given the innate power to shape your life…but you cannot
just speak change, you have to LIVE change. Intent paired with action builds the
bridge to success. You can't just want it; you have to do it, live it…BE it! Success
isn't something you have, it's something you DO!"— Steve Maraboli

1942.   "The summit of happiness is reached when a person is ready to be
what he is."— Desiderius Erasmus Roterodamus

1943.   "Noble and great. Courageous and determined. Faithful and fearless.
That is who you are and who you have always been. And understanding it can
change your life, because this knowledge carries a confidence that cannot be
duplicated any other way."— Sheri L. Dew

1944.   "YOU are the big drop of dew under the lotus leaf, I am the smaller one
on its upper side, 'said the dewdrop to the lake."— Rabindranath Tagore

1945.   "My friends, if we tend to the things that are important in life, if we are
right with those we love and behave in line with our faith, our lives will not be
cursed with the aching throb of unfulfilled business. Our words will always be
sincere, our embraces tight. We will never wallow in agony of 'I could have, I
should have.' We can sleep in a storm. "And when it's time, our good-byes will be
complete."— Mitch Albom, Have a Little Faith: a True Story

1946.   "See? See what you can do? Never mind you can't tell one letter from
another, never mind you born a slave, never mind you lose your name, never
mind your daddy dead, never mind nothing. Here, this here, is what a man can
do if he puts his mind to it and his back in it. Stop sniveling,' [the land] said. 'Stop
picking around the edges of the world. Take advantage, and if you can't take
advantage, take disadvantage. We live here. On this planet, in this nation, in this
county right here. Nowhere else! We got a home in this rock, don't you see!

Nobody starving in my home; nobody crying in my home, and if I got a home you got one too! Grab it. Grab this land! Take it, hold it, my brothers, make it, my brothers, shake it, squeeze it, turn it, twist it, beat it, kick it, kiss it, whip it, stomp it, dig it, plow it, seed it, reap it, rent it, buy it, sell it, own it, build it, multiply it, and pass it on – can you hear me? Pass it on!"— Toni Morrison, Song of Solomon

1947.   "Dead yesterdays and unborn tomorrows, why fret about it, if today be sweet."— Omar Khayyám

1948.   "It is a sad day when one looks back and sees that his largest regrets have become some of the most integral elements of his dreams."— John Knowles

1949.   "Money can't buy happiness, but it certainly is a stress reliever."— Besa Kosova

1950.   "Life is about becoming more of who you really are...."— Oprah Winfrey

1951.   "Boggle with sex addicts is up there with go-kart racing with junkies."— Russell Brand, My Booky Wook

1952.   "Women's philanthropic leadership is fundamental to their advancement in society."— Kay Ballard

1953.   "Lord, be my rock of safety, the stronghold that saves me. For the honor of your name lead me and guide me."— Anonymous, Holy Bible: King James Version

1954.   "If people reach perfection they vanish, you know."— T.H. White, The Once and Future King

1955.   "Everyone you have ever loved in your life becomes a part of your soul. They never leave. They're always inside you, and you can bring them out whenever you want."— Nate Kenyon, Sparrow Rock

1956.   "How much time he gains who does not look to see what his neighbor says or does or thinks, but only at what he does himself, to make it just and holy."— Marcus Aurelius, Meditations

1957.   "Love does not cost anything. Kind words and deeds do not cost anything. The real beauty of the world is equal for everyone to see. It was given by God equally to all, without restrictions. Everyone was given a beautiful vehicle in which to express love to others. Feelings are free to express and give to ourselves and each other through our willingness to give and care. What is complicated about this...? Why have we made others feel they have to climb mountains and swim oceans in order to make a difference. All we need to understand my friends is that human life was given equally to us all, not partially but in totality. The sun was given to all. It does not shine on the few. So, just has nature is indifferent to our station or situation, we need to know that we are all equal. We need to focus on the things that are constant and not place our values on things that can be blown away with the next, great, wind. Value life in whatever house it dwells. For when it comes time that we are all stripped to bare bones before the divine and facing eternity, we will understand that the only law we were meant to follow, was to love ourselves and each other. Nothing more...nothing less."— Carla Jo Masterson

1958.   "We have to pray with our eyes on God, not on the difficulties."— Oswald Chambers

1959.   "Because if you don't stand up for the stuff you don't like, when they come for the stuff you do like, you've already lost."— Neil Gaiman

1960.   "Peace is present right here and now, in ourselves and in everything we do and see. Every breath we take, every step we take, can be filled with peace, joy, and serenity. The question is whether or not we are in touch with it. We need only to be awake, alive in the present moment."— Thích Nhất Hạnh, Peace Is Every Step: The Path of Mindfulness in Everyday Life

1961.   "Love is what carries you, for it is always there, even in the dark, or most in the dark, but shining out at times like gold stitches in a piece of embroidery. "— Wendell Berry, Hannah Coulter

1962.   "The greatest blessing granted to mankind come by way of madness, which is a divine gift."— Socrates

1963.   "Think of the patience God has had for you and let it resonate to others. If you want more patient world, let patience be your motto"— Steve Maraboli, Unapologetically You: Reflections on Life and the Human Experience

1964.   "You do not have to sit outside in the dark. If, however, you want to look at the stars, you will find that darkness is necessary. But the stars neither require nor demand it."— Annie Dillard, Teaching a Stone to Talk: Expeditions and Encounters

1965.   "What I stand for is what I stand on."— Wendell Berry

1966.   "Faith activates God - Fear activates the Enemy."— Joel Osteen

1967.   "The atheist staring from his attic window is often nearer to God than the believer caught up in his own false image of God."— Martin Buber

1968.   "Creativity comes from trust. Trust your instincts."— Rita Mae Brown

1969.   "I always secretly looked forward to nothing going as planned. That way, I wasn't limited by my imagination. That way, anything can, and always did, happen."— CrimethInc.

1970.   "You have forgotten the One
who doesn't care about ownership, who doesn't try to turn a profit
from every human exchange."— Rumi, The Essential Rumi

1971.   "How would your life be different if…You stopped focusing on what you didn't want and started focusing on what you do want? Let today be the day…You establish a clear intent, make a plan, and take actions towards your intent."— Steve Maraboli, Life, the Truth, and Being Free

1972.   "We never know the quality of someone else's life, though we seldom resist the temptation to assume and pass judgment."— Tami Hoag, Dark Horse

1973.   "Only those are fit to live who do not fear to die; and none are fit to die who have shrunk from the joy of life and the duty of life. Both life and death are parts of the same Great Adventure."— Theodore Roosevelt

1974.   "Forget the place you're trying to get to and see the beauty in right now…"— Evanescence

1975.   "True intimacy with God always brings humility."— Beth Moore

1976.   "Small mistakes tend to lead to large ones. Ours is a lifetime appointment, and all you have is your reputation. Once it's gone, it doesn't comeback."— David Baldacci, The Simple Truth

1977.   "I think . . . I said things to Silas. He'll be angry.'
'If he didn't care about you, you couldn't upset him,' was all she said."— Neil Gaiman, The Graveyard Book

1978.   "Empowerment is the ability to refine, improve, and enhance your life without co-dependency."— Steve Maraboli, Life, the Truth, and Being Free

1979.   "The journey of a thousand miles begins with a single step. Watch your step."— Thomas S. Monson

1980.   "Trust men and they will be true to you; treat them greatly and they will show themselves great."— Ralph Waldo Emerson

1981.   "First you find out what you have, Dad would say. Then you figure out how to make it work for what you need, 'cause you don't get what you want. You get just what you have and no more. "— Lilith Saintcrow, Betrayals

1982.   "If Harvey had not been taken from us 30 years ago, I think he would want me to say to all the gay and lesbian kids out there tonight who have been told they are less than by the churches, by the government, by their families, that you are beautiful, wonderful creatures of value, and that no matter what anyone tells you, God does love you and that very soon, I promise you, you will have equal rights, federally, across this great nation of ours."— Dustin Lance Black

1983.   "Jealousy is the lock that closes your heart, understanding is the key that opens it."— Ken Petti

1984.   "Don't only practice your art, but force your way into its secrets, for it and knowledge can raise men to the divine."— Ludwig van Beethoven

1985.   "Go for it, while you can. I know you have it in you. And I can't promise you'll get everything you want, but I can promise nothing will change if you don't try."— J.M. Darhower, Sempre

1986.   "Politeness is okay, but it gets old and boring. You want to attack life with a passion, not a politeness, you want people to think about you and remember you and say "she is so passionate" you don't want people to think about you and remember you and say "she is so polite," because, who cares about polite?"— C. JoyBell C.

1987.   "And will you succeed?
Yes! You will, indeed!
(98 and 3/4 percent guaranteed.)
KID, YOU'LL MOVE MOUNTAINS!
So...
be your name Buxbaum or Bixby or Bray
or Mordecai Ali Van Allen O'Shea,you're off to Great Places!
Today is your day!
Your mountain is waiting.
So...get on your way!"— Dr. Seuss, Oh, the Places You'll Go!

1988.   "I wonder," he said, "whether the stars are set alight in heaven so that one day each one of us may find his own again..."— Antoine de Saint-Exupéry, The Little Prince

1989.   "I run because if I didn't, I'd be sluggish and glum and spend too much time on the couch. I run to breathe the fresh air. I run to explore. I run to escape the ordinary. I run...to savor the trip along the way. Life becomes a little more vibrant, a little more intense. I like that."— Dean Karnazes, Ultramarathon Man: Confessions of an All-Night Runner

1990.   "There is no such thing as a child who hates to read; there are only children who have not found the right book."— Frank Serafini

1991.   "The road to enlightenment is long and difficult, and you should try not to forget snacks and magazines."— Anne Lamott, Traveling Mercies: Some Thoughts on Faith

1992.   "It's the things you fight for and struggle with before earning that have the greatest worth."— Sarah Dessen, Along for the Ride

1993.   "You told me once of the plants that lie dormant through the drought, that wait, half-dead, deep in the earth. The plants that wait for the rain. You said they'd wait for years, if they had to; that they'd almost kill themselves before they grew again. But as soon as those first drops of water fall, those plants begin to stretch and spread their roots. They travel up through the soil and sand to reach the surface. There's a chance for them again."— Lucy Christopher, Stolen: A Letter to My Captor

1994.	"Begin doing what you want to do now. We are not living in eternity. We have only this moment, sparkling like a star in our hand--and melting like a snowflake..."— Francis Bacon

1995.	"That which makes you different is what makes you strong. Whether you're gay, straight, purple, orange, dinosaur; I don't care."— Darren Criss

1996.	"In my deepest wound I saw your glory, and it dazzled me."— Augustine of Hippo

1997.	"God not only loves the obedient - He enlightens them."— Henry B. Eyring

1998.	"In all debates, let truth be thy aim, not victory, or an unjust interest."— William Penn

1999.	"Sacrifice," the captain said. "You made one. I made one. We all made them. But you were angry over yours. You kept thinking about what you lost. You didn't get it. Sacrifice is a part of life. It's supposed to be. It's not something to regret. It's something to aspire to."— Mitch Albom, The Five People You Meet in Heaven

2000.	"I've learned one thing: you can only really get to know a person after a row. Only then can you judge their true character!"— Anne Frank, The Diary of a Young Girl

2001.	"Tough times never last. Tough people do"— Robert H. Schuller

2002.	"Remember, whatever you focus upon, increases...When you focus on the things you need, you'll find those needs increasing. If you concentrate your thoughts on what you don't have, you will soon be concentrating on other things that you had forgotten you don't have-and feel worse! If you set your mind on loss, you are more likely to lose...But a grateful perspective brings happiness and abundance into a person's life."— Andy Andrews, The Noticer: Sometimes, All a Person Needs Is a Little Perspective.

2003.	"Advice is like snow; the softer it falls, the longer it dwells upon, and the deeper it sinks into the mind."— Samuel Taylor Coleridge

2004.	"Success is never final. Failure is never fatal. It's courage that counts."— Vince Lombardi

2005.	"When you stop existing and you start truly living, each moment of the day comes alive with the wonder and synchronicity."— Steve Maraboli, Life, the Truth, and Being Free

2006.	"There are heroisms all round us waiting to be done."— Arthur Conan Doyle

2007.	"...A scar signifies past pain, a wound that did not heal as it ought. But it testifies, too, to survival... (Here be Dragons)"— Sharon Kay Penman

2008.   "Music is the only language in which you cannot say a mean or sarcastic thing."— John Erskine

2009.   "It's what you learn after you know it all that counts."— John Wooden

2010.   "It's not about who you sleep with, or whether you know about sports or tools or have a pearl-wearing wife or whether commercials make you cry. [...] it's about whether you step up. When something hard comes along. A man steps up. He doesn't dodge it or run away from it or try to push it onto someone else. He steps up. Even if it isn't his responsibility. And that's why there are so many guys and so few men. Because stepping up is hard."— Ben Monopoli, The Painting of Porcupine City

2011.   "Behold the turtle. He makes progress only when he sticks his neck out."— James Bryant Conant

2012.   "Sometimes it takes falling apart to ever have a chance of being fully whole."— Amanda Rose

2013.   "There is nothing more rare, nor more beautiful, than a woman being unapologetically herself; comfortable in her perfect imperfection. To me, that is the true essence of beauty."— Steve Maraboli, Unapologetically You: Reflections on Life and the Human Experience

2014.   "You are not a victim. No matter what you have been through, you're still here. You may have been challenged, hurt, betrayed, beaten, and discouraged, but nothing has defeated you. You are still here! You have been delayed but not denied. You are not a victim, you are a victor. You have a history of victory."— Steve Maraboli, Unapologetically You: Reflections on Life and the Human Experience

2015.   "Smile at strangers and you just might change a life."— Steve Maraboli

2016.   "There are powers far beyond us, plans far beyond what we could have ever thought of, visions far more vast than what we can ever see on our own with our own eyes, there are horizons long gone beyond our own horizons. This is courage- to throw away what is our own that is limited and to thrust ourselves into the hands of these higher powers- God and Destiny. To do this is to abide in the realm of the eternal, to walk in the path of the everlasting to follow in the footprints of God and demi-gods. The hardest part for man is the letting go. For some reason, he thinks himself big enough to know and to see what's good for him. But in the letting go........is found freedom. In the letting go........ is found the flight!"— C. JoyBell C.

2017.   "Quietly endure, silently suffer and patiently wait."— Martin Luther King Jr., Why We Can't Wait

2018.   "Be a light unto the world, and hurt it not. Seek to build not destroy. Bring My people home.How?By your shining example. Seek only Godliness. Speak only in truthfulness. Act only in love.
Live the Law of Love now and forever more. Give everything require nothing.

Avoid the mundane.Do not accept the unacceptable.Teach all who seek to learn of Me.Make every moment of your life an outpouring of love.Use every moment to think the highest thought, say the highest word, do the highest deed. In this, glorify your Holy Self, and thus too, glorify Me.Bring peace to the Earth by bringing peace to all those whose lives you touch. Be peace. Feel and express in every moment your Divine Connection with the All, and with every person, place, and thing.Embrace every circumstance, own every fault, share every joy, contemplate every mystery, walk in every man's shoes, forgive every offense (including your own), heal every heart, honor every person's truth, adore every person's God, protect every person's rights, preserve every person's dignity, promote every person's interests, provide every person's needs, presume every person's holiness, present every person's greatest gifts, produce every person's blessing, pronounce every person's future secure in the assured love of God.Be a living, breathing example of the Highest Truth that resides within you. Speak humbly of yourself, lest someone mistake your Highest Truth for boast. Speak softly, lest someone think you are merely calling for attention. Speak gently, that all might know of Love. Speak openly, lest someone think you have something to hide. Speak candidly, so you cannot be mistaken. Speak often, so that your word may truly go forth. Speak respectfully, that no one be dishonored. Speak lovingly, that every syllable may heal. Speak of Me with every utterance. Make of your life a gift. Remember always, you are the gift!Be a gift to everyone who enters your life, and to everyone whose life you enter. Be careful not to enter another's life if you cannot be a gift. (You can always be a gift, because you always are the gift—yet sometimes you don't let yourself know that.) When someone enters your life unexpectedly, look for the gift that person has come to receive from you…I HAVE SENT YOU NOTHING BUT ANGELS."— Neale Donald Walsch, Conversations With God: An Uncommon Dialogue, Vol. 2

2019.   "Yes, terrible things happen, but sometimes those terrible things- they save you."— Chuck Palahniuk, Haunted

2020.   "I realized then that even though I was a tiny speck in an infinite cosmos, a blip on the timeline of eternity, I was not without purpose."— R.J. Anderson, Ultraviolet

2021.   "You're only poor if you give up. The most important thing is that you did something. Most people only talk and dream of getting rich. You've done something."— Robert T. Kiyosaki, Rich Dad, Poor Dad

2022.   "I want you to have big dreams, big goals. I want you to strive to achieve them. But I don't want to see you beating yourself up every time you make a mistake."— Kelley Armstrong, The Gathering

2023.   "For those who know the value of and exquisite taste of solitary freedom (for one is only free when alone), the act of leaving is the bravest and most beautiful of all."— Isabelle Eberhardt, The Nomad: The Diaries of Isabelle Eberhardt

2024.   "The meaning of life is that it is to be lived, and it is not to be traded and conceptualized and squeezed into a patter of systems."— Bruce Lee, Striking Thoughts: Bruce Lee's Wisdom for Daily Living

2025.   "Now you people have names. That's because you don't know who you are. We know who we are, so we don't need names."— Neil Gaiman, Coraline

2026.   "Make every effort to change things you do not like. If you cannot make a change, change the way you have been thinking. You might find a new solution."— Maya Angelou, Letter to My Daughter

2027.   "If you remember nothing else, remember this: Inspiration from outside one's self is like the heat in an oven. It makes passable Bath buns. But inspiration from within is like a volcano: It changes the face of the world."— Alan Bradley, The Weed That Strings the Hangman's Bag

2028.   "We can choose to throw stones, to stumble on them, to climb over them, or to build with them."— William Arthur Ward

2029.   "Why choose to fail when success is an option?"— Jillian Michaels

2030.   "You have been blessed with immeasurable power to make positive changes in your life."— Steve Maraboli, Life, the Truth, and Being Free

2031.   "Life did not stop, and one had to live."— Leo Tolstoy, War and Peace

2032.   "Everybody in this life has their challenges and difficulties. That is part of our mortal test. The reason for some of these trials cannot be readily understood except on the basis of faith and hope because there is often a larger purpose which we do not always understand. Peace comes through hope."— James E. Faust

2033.   "Once you start recognizing the truth of your story, finish the story. It happened but you're still here, you're still capable, powerful, you're not your circumstance. It happened and you made it through. You're still fully equipped with every single tool you need to fulfill your purpose."— Steve Maraboli

2034.   "Write to please just one person. If you open a window and make love to the world, so to speak, your story will get pneumonia."— Kurt Vonnegut, Bagombo Snuff Box

2035.   "Mistakes are the portals of discovery."— Cecelia Ahern

2036.   "So much for endings. Beginnings are always more fun. True connoisseurs, however, are known to favor the stretch in between, since it's the hardest to do anything with. That's about all that can be said for plots, which anyway are just one thing after another, a what and a what and a what."— Margaret Atwood

2037.   "Courage doesn't always roar. Sometimes courage is the quiet voice at the end of the day saying, "I will try again tomorrow."— Mary Anne Radmacher

2038.   "But what he didn't understand was that this dreamland was preferable, walking through this life half-sleeping, everything at arm's length or farther away. I understood those mermaids. I didn't care if they sang to me.All I wanted was to block out all the human voices as they called me name again and again, pulling me upward into light, to drown."— Sarah Dessen, Dreamland

2039.	"That which we persist in doing becomes easier to do, not that the nature of the thing has changed, but our power to do so is increased."— Heber J. Grant

2040.	"You must understand that love never keeps a man from pursuing his Personal Legend. If he abandons that pursuit, it's because it wasn't a true love... the love that speaks the language of the world."— Paulo Coelho

2041.	"You will find, that when you have someone to love, that the face is less important than the brain, and the body is less important than the heart."— Adrian Tan

2042.	"The strength of a woman is not measured by the impact that all her hardships in life have had on her; but the strength of a woman is measured by the extent of her refusal to allow those hardships to dictate her and who she becomes."— C. JoyBell C.

2043.	"I advise you to stop sharing your dreams with people who try to hold you back, even if they're your parents. Because, if you're the kind of person who senses there's something out there for you beyond whatever it is you're expected to do - if you want to be EXTRA-ordinary- you will not get there by hanging around a bunch of people who tell you you're not extraordinary. Instead, you will probably become as ordinary as they expect you to be."— Kelly Cutrone, If You Have to Cry, Go Outside: And Other Things Your Mother Never Told You

2044.	"God turns you from one feeling to another and teaches by means of opposites so that you will have two wings to fly, not one"— Rumi, Essential Rumi

2045.	"The best love in the world is the love of a man. The love of a man who came from your womb, the love of your son! I don't have a daughter, but maybe the love of a daughter is the best, too. I am first and foremost me, but right after that, I am a mother. The best thing that I can ever be is me. But the best gift that I will ever have is being a mother."— C. JoyBell C.

2046.	"I don't paint dreams or nightmares, I paint my own reality."— Frida Kahlo

2047.	"You are beautiful. Know this. Anyone who tells you otherwise is simply lying. You are beautiful."— Steve Maraboli, Unapologetically You: Reflections on Life and the Human Experience

2048.	"Let us try to teach generosity and altruism, because we are born selfish. Let us understand what our own selfish genes are up to, because we may then at least have the chance to upset their designs, something that no other species has ever aspired to do."— Richard Dawkins, The Selfish Gene

2049.	"The romantics would call this a love story, the cynics would call it a tragedy. In my mind it's a little bit of both, and no matter how you choose to view it in the end, it does not change the fact that it involves a great deal of my life and the path I've chosen to follow."— Nicholas Sparks, The Notebook

2050. "Every adversity, every failure, every heartache carries with it the seed of an equal or greater benefit."— Napoleon Hill

2051. "Freedom is indivisible; the chains on any one of my people were the chains on all of them, the chains on all of my people were the chains on me."— Nelson Mandela, Long Walk to Freedom: The Autobiography of Nelson Mandela with Connections

2052. "Don't let anyone take care of you. Can you maybe leave that for me to do? I mean, take care of you? Feel free to take care of me in return... because I think I'll need you to do that."— Melina Marchetta, The Piper's Son

2053. "Only mystery makes us live. Only mystery."— Federico García Lorca, Le Poète À New York

2054. "Again and again I will suffer; again and again I will get back on my feet. I will not be defeated. I won't let my spirit be destroyed."— Banana Yoshimoto, Kitchen

2055. "You get in life what you have the courage to ask for."— Nancy D. Solomon

2056. "Everybody wants to be on the mountaintop, but if you'll remember, mountaintops are rocky and cold. There is no growth on the top of a mountain. Sure, the view is great, but what's a view for? A view just gives us a glimpse of our next destination-our next target. But to hit that target, we must come off the mountain, go through the valley, and begin to climb the next slope. It is in the valley that we slog through the lush grass and rich soil, learning and becoming what enables us to summit life's next peak."— Andy Andrews, The Noticer: Sometimes, All a Person Needs Is a Little Perspective.

2057. "In the end, it is important to remember that we cannot become what we need to be, by remaining what we are."— Max DePree, Leadership Is an Art

2058. "Bean finds the best apple in our tree and hands it up to me."You know what this tastes like when you first bite into it?" she asks."No, what?""Blue sky.""You're zoomed.""You ever eat blue sky?" "No," I admit."Try it sometime," she says. "It's apple-flavored."— Rodman Philbrick, The Last Book in the Universe

2059. "Thus, when we plead for the gift of charity, we aren't asking for lovely feelings toward someone who bugs us or someone who has injured or wounded us. We are actually pleading for our very natures to be changed, for our character and disposition to become more and more like the Savior's, so that we literally feel as He would feel and thus do what He would do."— Sheri L. Dew, If Life Were Easy, It Wouldn't Be Hard: And Other Reassuring Truths

2060.   "She was so intelligent that she could think herself into beauty. Intelligence...they don't talk about it much, the poets, but when a woman is intelligent and passionate and good..."— Eva Ibbotson, A Company of Swans

2061.   "So that the new generation that will be born can enjoy happiness.To pay the cost we will have to shoulder corpses and cross a river of blood(Riza Hawkeye -- Fullmetal Alchemist)"— Hiromu Arakawa

2062.   "People in general would rather die than forgive. It's THAT hard. If God said in plain language. "I'm giving you a choice, forgive or die," a lot of people would go ahead and order their coffin."— Sue Monk Kidd

2063.   "Don't live down to expectations. Go out there and do something remarkable."— Wendy Wasserstein

2064.   "I was always looking outside myself for strength and confidence, but it comes from within. It is there all the time."— Anna Freud

2065.   "The Jewish sages also tell us that God dances when His children defeat Him in argument, when they stand on their feet and use their minds. So questions like Anne's are worth asking. To ask them is a very fine kind of human behavior. If we keep demanding that God yield up His answers, perhaps someday we will understand them. And then we will be something more than clever apes, and we shall dance with God."— Mary Doria Russell, The Sparrow

2066.   "I wished the dream were real, and this reality a dream. But that wasn't the case. And that was why, whenever I woke up, I'd be crying. It wasn't because I was sad. When you return from a happy dream to sad reality, there's a chasm you have to step across, and you can't cross it without shedding tears. It doesn't matter how many times you do it."— Kyōichi Katayama

2067.   "...the monstrous thing is not that men have created roses out of this dung heap, but that, for some reason or other, they should want roses. For some reason or other man looks for the miracle, and to accomplish it he will wade through blood. He will debauch himself with ideas, he will reduce himself to a shadow if for only one second of his life he can close his eyes to the hideousness of reality. Everything is endured- disgrace, humiliation, poverty, war, crime, ennui- in the belief that overnight something will occur, a miracle, which will render life tolerable. And all the while a meter is running inside and there is no hand that can reach in there and shut it off."— Henry Miller, Tropic of Cancer

2068.   "I will not know that day has come because I will not stop trying."— Brandon Mull, Rise of the Evening Star

2069.   "I never thought of it like that. I always thought of you as a part of me, like my own eyes or my own hands. You don't go around thinking 'I love my eyes, I love my hands', do you? But think what it would be like to live without your eyes or your hands. To be mad, or to be blind. I can't talk about it. It's how I feel."— Elizabeth Marie Pope, The Perilous Gard

2070.		"don't you think between here and now we will see each other once or twice?"— Richard Bach

2071.		"For everything in this journey of life we are on, there is a right wing and a left wing: for the wing of love there is anger; for the wing of destiny there is fear; for the wing of pain there is healing; for the wing of hurt there is forgiveness; for the wing of pride there is humility; for the wing of giving there is taking; for the wing of tears there is joy; for the wing of rejection there is acceptance; for the wing of judgment there is grace; for the wing of honor there is shame; for the wing of letting go there is the wing of keeping. We can only fly with two wings and two wings can only stay in the air if there is a balance. Two beautiful wings is perfection. There is a generation of people who idealize perfection as the existence of only one of these wings every time. But I see that a bird with one wing is imperfect. An angel with one wing is imperfect. A butterfly with one wing is dead. So this generation of people strive to always cut off the other wing in the hopes of embodying their ideal of perfection, and in doing so, have created a crippled race."— C. JoyBell C.

2072.		"Travel is never a matter of money but of courage"— Paulo Coelho, Aleph

2073.		"Hate looks like everybody else until it smiles"— Tahereh Mafi

2074.		"I want to continue being crazy; living my life the way I dream it, and not the way the other people want it to be."— Paulo Coelho, Veronika Decides to Die

2075.		"Leave behind the passive dreaming of a rose-tinted future. The energy of happiness exists in living today with roots sunk firmly in reality's soil."— Daisaku Ikeda

2076.		"...Despite the mayhem that followed, Bruno found that he was still holding Shmuel's hand in his own and nothing in the world would have persuaded him to let go."— John Boyne, The Boy in the Striped Pajamas

2077.		"The only thing that will ever make me fall in love is: if I fall in love."— C. JoyBell C.

2078.		"I cannot trust a man to control others who cannot control himself."— Robert E. Lee

2079.		"Christmas is not as much about opening our presents as opening our hearts."— Janice Maeditere

2080.		"The beauty of this idea is that my decision to keep Peeta alive at the expense of my own life is itself an act of defiance. A refusal to play the Hunger Games by the Capitol's rules. My private agenda dovetails completely with my public one. And if I really could save Peeta... in terms of a revolution, this would be ideal. Because I will be more valuable dead. They can turn me into some kind of martyr for the cause and paint my face on banners, and it will do more to rally people than anything I could do if I was living. But Peeta would be more valuable alive, and tragic, because he will be able to turn his pain into words that will transform people."— Suzanne Collins, Catching Fire

2081.		"Once your mindset changes, everything on the outside will change along with it."— Steve Maraboli, Life, the Truth, and Being Free

2082.		"My sun sets to rise again."— Robert Browning

2083.		"Souls are like athletes, that need opponents worthy of them, if they are to be tried and extended and pushed to the full use of their powers, and rewarded according to their capacity."— Thomas Merton, The Seven Storey Mountain

2084.		"I've always wanted to be a cat. Warm and domesticated when you want to be, wild when you don't."— Jenny Downham, Before I Die

2085.		"Every single desire can lead to dream and every single dream has possibility to become reality."— Santosh Kalwar, Quote Me Everyday

2086.		"When you find yourself in need of spiritual nourishment, it is in the opportunities to serve others that you will find the abundance you seek."— Steve Maraboli, Life, the Truth, and Being Free

2087.		"Man is born broken. He lives by mending. The grace of God is glue."— Eugene O'Neill

2088.		"With an eye made quiet by the power of harmony, and the deep power of joy, we see into the life of things."— William Wordsworth

2089.		"Never let yourself be persuaded that any one Great Man, any one leader, is necessary to the salvation of America. When America consists of one leader and 158 million followers, it will no longer be America."— Dwight D. Eisenhower

2090.		"If you're not happy in life then you need to change, calibrate, readjust...flush your negative energy and fill it with positive energy; How do we do that you might ask? Well I would start by making others happy, diseases are not the only thing that spreads easy. We are all connected in some form of unseen energy... think how those around you will impact you and make you feel if they were happy?"— Al Munoz

2091.		"Nothing is more practical than finding God, That is, than falling in a love in a quite absolute, final way. What you are in love with, what seizes your imagination will affect everything. It will decide what will get you out of bed in the mornings, What you will do with your evenings, How you spend your weekends, What you read, Who you know, What breaks your heart, And what amazes you with joy and gratitude. Fall in love, stay in love, and it will decide everything."— Pedro Arrupe

2092.		"Why is it the songs all end with the good people winning, but in life they don't?"

They don't make songs when the good lose," I muttered. "They make war chants against the bad. So there won't be any songs for us."— Sherwood Smith, Crown Duel

2093.   "Regardless of Sunshine or Rain, Be Thankful for another GREAT day...and treat Life as the ULTIMATE Gift.... Because IT IS :)"— Pablo

2094.   "Spending time looking for what is missing in your life is futile; if you fail to look within yourself. When we challenge everything we believe we are, we reveal that which we never knew about our own selves."— Nicolas G. Janovsky, Gay: A New Path Forward

2095.   "Nothing but good times ahead."— Jennifer Crusie, Welcome to Temptation

2096.   "Everything changes except the love."— Santosh Kalwar

2097.   "Many of us are returning from a long journey during which we were forced to search for things that were of no interest to us. Now we realize that they were false. But this return cannot be made without pain, because we have been away for a long time and feel that we are strangers in our own land. It will take some time to find the friends who also left, and the places where our roots and treasures lie. But this will happen."— Paulo Coelho, The Witch Of Portobello

2098.   "It's not as bad as you sometimes think it is. It ALL works out. Don't worry. I say that to myself every morning. It will all work out. If you do your best, it all works out. Put your trust in God and move forward, with faith and confidence in the future. The lord will not forsake us... If we put our trust in him, if we will pray to him, if we will live worthy of his blessings, He will hear our prayers."— Gordon B. Hinckley

2099.   "No law can be sacred to me but that of my nature. Good and bad are but names very readily transferable to that or this; the only right is what is after my constitution; the only wrong is what is against it."— Ralph Waldo Emerson

2100.   "Be confident small immortals. You are not the only voice that all things utter, nor is there eternal silence in the places where you cannot come."— C.S. Lewis, Perelandra

2101.   "When defeat comes, accept it as a signal that your plans are not sound, rebuild those plans, and set sail once more toward your coveted goal."— Napoleon Hill, Think and Grow Rich

2102.   "Anyone who knows me should learn to know me again; for I am like the Moon, you will see me with new face every day."— Rumi

2103.   "If you really want to do something, you'll find a way. If you don't, you'll find an excuse."— Jim Rohn

2104.   "You can have many great ideas in your head, but what makes the difference is the action. Without action upon an idea, there will be no manifestation, no results, and no reward"— Miguel Ruiz, The Four Agreements: A Practical Guide to Personal Freedom

2105.   "God has given us more than fourteen billion cells and connections in our brain. Why would God give us such a complex organ system unless he expects us to use it?"— Ben Carson

2106.   "Anger is an essential part of being human. People are taught to deny themselves anger, and in this, they are actually opening themselves up to hate. The more you deny yourself the freedom to be angry, the more you will hate. Let yourself be angry, and hate will disintegrate, and when hate disintegrates, forgiveness prevails! The more you deny that you are angry, in attempts to be "holy" the more inhuman you will become, and the more inhuman you will become, the harder it will be to forgive."— C. JoyBell C.

2107.   "If you give up what you want most for what you think you should want more, you'll end up miserable."— Brandon Sanderson, The Hero of Ages

2108.   "Thou shalt not be a victim, thou shalt not be a perpetrator, but, above all, thou shalt not be a bystander."— Yehuda Bauer

2109.   "Books. They are lined up on shelves or stacked on a table. There they are wrapped up in their jackets, lines of neat print on nicely bound pages. They look like such orderly, static things. Then you, the reader come along. You open the book jacket, and it can be like opening the gates to an unknown city, or opening the lid of a treasure chest. You read the first word and you're off on a journey of exploration and discovery."— David Almond

2110.   "Even a happy life cannot be without a measure of darkness, and the word happy would lose its meaning if it were not balanced by sadness. It is far better take things as they come along with patience and equanimity."— C.G. Jung

2111.   "A good plan violently executed now is better than a perfect plan executed at some indefinite time in the future."— George S. Patton Jr.

2112.   "Finding happiness should not be seen as finding a needle in a haystack. Happiness is within. Each day is a blessing that brings an abundance of happiness. Therefore, finding happiness should be like finding a gift in a stack of gifts."— Steve Maraboli, Life, the Truth, and Being Free

2113.   "Time cannot be packaged and ribboned and left under trees for Christmas morning. Time can't be given. But it can be shared"— Cecelia Ahern, The Gift

2114.   "The story of my recent life.' I like that phrase. It makes more sense than 'the story of my life', because we get so many lives between birth and death. A life to be a child. A life to come of age. A life to wander, to settle, to fall in love, to parent, to test our promise, to realize our mortality- and in some lucky cases, to do something after that realization."— Mitch Albom, Have a Little Faith: a True Story

2115.	"We are not called by God to do extraordinary things, but to do ordinary things with extraordinary love."— Jean Vanier

2116.	"In imagination she sailed over storied seas that wash the distant shining shores of "faëry lands forlorn," where lost Atlantis and Elysium lie, with the evening star for pilot, to the land of Heart's Desire. And she was richer in those dreams than in realities; for things seen pass away, but the things that are unseen are eternal."— L.M. Montgomery, Anne of the Island

2117.	"Dancing in all its forms cannot be excluded from the curriculum of all noble education; dancing with the feet, with ideas, with words, and, need I add that one must also be able to dance with the pen?"— Friedrich Nietzsche

2118.	"To me, all creativity is magic. Ideas start out in the empty void of your head - and they end up as a material thing, like a book you can hold in your hand. That is the magical process. It's an alchemical thing. Yes, we do get the gold out of it but that's not the most important thing. It's the work itself."— Alan Moore

2119.	"You cannot stay on the summit forever; you have to come down again. So why bother in the first place? Just this: What is above knows what is below, but what is below does not know what is above. One climbs, one sees. One descends, one sees no longer, but one has seen. There is an art of conducting oneself in the lower regions by the memory of what one saw higher up. When one can no longer see, one can at least still know."— René Daumal

2120.	"They who forgive most shall be most forgiven."— Anonymous, Holy Bible: King James Version

2121.	"...most of the time, all you have is the moment, and the imperfect love of the people around you."— Anne Lamott, Traveling Mercies: Some Thoughts on Faith

2122.	"She smiled. She knew she was dying. But it did not matter any longer. She had known something which no human words could ever tell and she knew it now. She had been awaiting it and she felt it, as if it had been, as if she had lived it. Life had been, if only because she had known it could be, and she felt it now as a hymn without sound, deep under the little whole that dripped red drops into the snow, deeper than that from which the red drops came. A moment or an eternity- did it matter? Life, undefeated, existed and could exist. She smiled, her last smile, to so much that had been possible."— Ayn Rand, We the Living

2123.	"No one invites you to the top - you have to claw your way up. When you get there, you will sit with the others who were also uninvited - giggling. "— Staness Jonekos

2124.	"The only true gift is a portion of thyself."— Ralph Waldo Emerson

2125.	"The recipe for great art has always been misery and a good bowel movement."— Don Roff

2126.   "A somebody was once a nobody who wanted to and did."— John Burroughs

2127.   "It is time to browse through the precious books that have meant the most to you that you may rediscover illuminating phrases and sentences to light your pathway to the future..."— Wilferd Peterson

2128.   "The more one pleases generally, the less one pleases profoundly."— Krister Stendahl

2129.   "But it seems to me that once you begin a gesture it's fatal not to go through with it."— John Updike, A&P: Lust in the Aisles

2130.   "Millions saw the apple fall, Newton was the only one who asked why?"— Bernard M. Baruch

2131.   "to write is human, to edit is divine"— Stephen King, On Writing

2132.   "I had no epiphany, no singular revelation, no moment of truth, but a steady accumulation of a thousand slights, a thousand indignities and a thousand unremembered moments produced in me an anger, a rebelliousness, a desire to fight the system that imprisoned my people. There was no particular day on which I said, henceforth I will devote myself to the liberation of my people; instead, I simply found myself doing so, and could not do otherwise."— Nelson Mandela, Long Walk to Freedom

2133.   "If you think your boss is stupid, remember: you wouldn't have a job if he was any smarter."— John M. Gottman

2134.   "If I look at the mass I will never act."— Mother Teresa

2135.   "The man who has begun to live more seriously within begins to live more simply without"— Ernest Hemingway

2136.   "Tragedy and adversary are the stones we sharpen our swords against so we can fight new battles."— Sherrilyn Kenyon, Infinity

2137.   "The terrible thing, the almost impossible thing, is to hand over your whole self--all your wishes and precautions--to Christ. But it is far easier than what we are all trying to do instead. For what we are trying to do is to remain what we call "ourselves," to keep personal happiness as our great aim in life, and yet at the same time be "good."— C.S. Lewis, Mere Christianity

2138.   "What destroys us most effectively is not a malign fate but our own capacity for self-deception and for degrading our own best self."— George Eliot, Adam Bede

2139.   "The moment you become miserly you are closed to the basic phenomenon of life: expansion, sharing. The moment you start clinging to things, you have missed the target--you have missed. Because things are not the target, you, your innermost being, is the target--not a beautiful house, but a beautiful you; not much money, but a rich you; not many things, but an open being, available to millions of things."— Osho

2140.   "Being defeated is often a temporary condition. Giving up is what makes it permanent."— Marilyn Vos Savant

2141.   "And isn't the whole world yours? For how often you set it on fire with your love and saw it blaze and burn up and secretly replaced it with another world while everyone slept. You felt in such complete harmony with God, when every morning you asked him for a new earth, so that all the ones he had made could have their turn. You thought it would be shabby to save them and repair them; you used them up and held out your hands, again and again, for more world. For your love was equal to everything."— Rainer Maria Rilke, The Notebooks of Malte Laurids Brigge

2142.   "All Earthquakes and Disasters are warnings; there's too much corruption in the world"— Aristotle

2143.   "No lake so still but it has its wave.
No circle so perfect but that it has its blur.
I would change things for you if I could; As I can't you must take them as they are."— Confucius

2144.   "Be creative, be useful, be practical, be generous and finish big"— Lisa Genova

2145.   "But you only get so many do-overs in this life, so many chances to, if not change your past, alter your future."— Sarah Dessen, Just Listen

2146.   "Despite popular belief to the contrary, there is absolutely no power in intention. The seagull may intend to fly away, may decide to do so, may talk with the other seagulls about how wonderful it is to fly, but until the seagull flaps his wings and takes to the air, he is still on the dock. There's no difference between that gull and all the others. Likewise, there is no difference in the person who intends to do things differently and the one who never thinks about it in the first place. Have you ever considered how often we judge ourselves by our intentions while we judge others by their actions? Yet intention without action is an insult to those who expect the best from you."— Andy Andrews, The Noticer: Sometimes, All a Person Needs Is a Little Perspective.

2147.   "Sometimes you just have to jump out the window and grow wings on the way down."— Ray Bradbury

2148.   "Think Positive."— Deepak Chopra

2149.   "Partings are the beginnings of new meetings. Beginnings happen because there are endings."— Natsuki Takaya, Fruits Basket, Vol. 22

2150.   "Live it well and this life can be grand."— Amelia Atwater-Rhodes, Hawksong

2151.   "Age considers; youth ventures."— Rabindranath Tagore

2152.   "Relish love in your old age! Aged love is like aged wine; it becomes more satisfying, more refreshing, more valuable, more appreciated and more intoxicating!"— Leo Buscaglia

2153.   "Of all the idiots I have met in my life, and the Lord knows they have not been few or little, I think that I have been the biggest."— Karen Blixen

2154.   "It is possible for the human spirit to win after all."— Jack Kerouac

2155.   "What you are or where you came from is not important. It is who you are and the choices you make, that determine who you will become. If you can look inward and be satisfied, the opinions of others should melt away."— J.D. Stroube, Caged in Darkness

2156.   "All we do is read the stupid textbook," said Ron."— J.K. Rowling, Harry Potter and the Order of the Phoenix

2157.   "I ended my first book with the words 'no answer.' I know now, Lord, why you utter no answer. You are yourself the answer. Before your face questions die away. What other answer would suffice? Only words, words; to be led out to battle against other words."— C.S. Lewis

2158.   "He said something interesting: he said that he thinks there is only free will when you are in time, in the present. He says in the past we can only do what we did, and we can only be there if we were there."— Audrey Niffenegger

2159.   "If you kin see de light at daybreak, you don't keer if you die at dusk. It's so many people never seen de light at all."— Zora Neale Hurston, Their Eyes Were Watching God

2160.   "The greatest act of faith some days is to simply get up and face another day."— Amy Gatliff

2161.   "My view is that if your philosophy is not unsettled daily then you are blind to all the universe has to offer."— Neil deGrasse Tyson

2162.   "I think the reason we sometimes have the false sense that God is so far away is because that is where we have put him. We have kept him at a distance, and then when we are in need and call on him in prayer, we wonder where he is. He is exactly where we left him."— Ravi Zacharias, Has Christianity Failed You?

2163.   "Trust in someone means that we no longer have to protect ourselves. We believe we will not be hurt or harmed by the other, at least not deliberately. We trust his or her good intentions, though we know we might be hurt by the way circumstances play out between us. We might say that hurt happens; it's a given of life. Harm is inflicted; it's a choice some people make."— David Richo

2164.   "Everything you'll ever need to know is within you; the secrets of the universe are imprinted on the cells of your body."— Dan Millman, Way of the Peaceful Warrior: A Book That Changes Lives

2165.   "The pessimist resembles a man who observes with fear and sadness that his wall calendar, from which he daily tears a sheet, grows thinner with each passing day. On the other hand, the person who attacks the problems of life actively is like a man who removes each successive leaf from his calendar and files it neatly and carefully away with its predecessors, after first having jotted down a few diary notes on the back. He can reflect with pride and joy on all the richness set down in these notes, on all the life he has already lived to the fullest. What will it matter to him if he notices that he is growing old? Has he any reason to envy the young people whom he sees, or wax nostalgic over his own lost youth? What reasons has he to envy a young person? For the possibilities that a young person has, the future which is in store for him?
No, thank you,' he will think. 'Instead of possibilities, I have realities in my past, not only the reality of work done and of love loved, but of sufferings bravely suffered. These sufferings are even the things of which I am most proud, although these are things which cannot inspire envy.' "
From "Logotherapy in a Nutshell", an essay"— Viktor E. Frankl, Man's Search for Meaning

2166.   "Stand firm in the Lord. Stand firm and let Him fight your battle. Do not try to fight alone."— Francine Rivers, A Voice in the Wind

2167.   "Start writing, no matter what. The water does not flow until the faucet is turned on."— Louis L'Amour

2168.   "Even if it's a dumb story, telling it changes people just the slightest little bit, just as living the story changes me. An infinitesimal change. And that infinitesimal change ripples outward —ever smaller but everlasting. I will get forgotten, but the stories will last. And so we all matter —maybe less than a lot, but always more than none."— John Green, An Abundance of Katherines

2169.   "In your own life it's important to know how spectacular you are."— Steve Maraboli, Unapologetically You: Reflections on Life and the Human Experience

2170.   "Pressure makes diamonds"— George S. Patton Jr.

2171.   "The best of a book is not the thought which it contains, but the thought which it suggests; just as the charm of music dwells not in the tones but in the echoes of our hearts."— Oliver Wendell Holmes Sr.

2172.   "No one lights a lamp in order to hide it behind the door: the purpose of light is to create more light, to open people's eyes, to reveal the marvels around."— Paulo Coelho

2173.   "The difference between me and other people is that they all walk around with onion skins wrapped around them. Pre-meditations, pretentions, the faces that they present to the world, the faces that they present to themselves.. onion skins that come in layer after layer. They're on the inside of all that. And I... I am the inside of the onion skin walking around. I am only me."— C. JoyBell C.

2174.　　　　"I feel very adventurous. There are so many doors to be opened, and I'm not afraid to look behind them."— Elizabeth Taylor

2175.　　　　"Life is sweet when you pay attention. When it doesn't seem sweet, put a sticker on your nose and do a funky dance."— Whitney Scott

2176.　　　　"Happiness has to do with your mindset, not with outside circumstance."— Steve Maraboli, Life, the Truth, and Being Free

2177.　　　　"You learn to write by writing, and by reading and thinking about how writers have created their characters and invented their stories. If you are not a reader, don't even think about being a writer."— Jean M. Auel

2178.　　　　"To know you are ignorant is the beginning of wisdom."— Marion Zimmer Bradley

2179.　　　　"It seems that a profound, impartial, and absolutely just opinion of our fellow-creatures is utterly unknown. Either we are men, or we are women. Either we are cold, or we are sentimental. Either we are young, or growing old. In any case life is but a procession of shadows, and God knows why it is that we embrace them so eagerly, and see them depart with such anguish, being shadows. And why, if this -- and much more than this is true -- why are we yet surprised in the window corner by a sudden vision that the young man in the chair is of all things in the world the most real, the most solid, the best known to us--why indeed? For the moment after we know nothing about him.Such is the manner of our seeing. Such the conditions of our love."— Virginia Woolf, Jacob's Room

2180.　　　　"There is no greater force for change than people inspired to live a better life."— Steve Maraboli, Life, the Truth, and Being Free

2181.　　　　"Today, many will choose to live free of conditions and rules governing their own happiness. Why not you? Do not let another day go by where your dedication to other people's opinions is greater than your dedication to your own emotions! Today's a new day!"— Steve Maraboli, Life, the Truth, and Being Free

2182.　　　　"Often, moreover, it is...that aspect of our being that society finds eccentric, ridiculous, or disagreeable, that holds our sweet waters, our secret well of happiness, the key to our equanimity in malevolent climes."— Tom Robbins, Still Life With Woodpecker

2183.　　　　"In the deepest hour of the night, confess to yourself that you would die if you were forbidden to write. And look deep into your heart where it spreads its roots, the answer, and ask yourself, must I write?"— Rainer Maria Rilke, Letters to a Young Poet

2184.   "The business of being happy requires making a conscious choice. People think being happy will just happen to them someday, if only they do this or that right. But it doesn't - you have to choose it. You choose happiness; you don't wait for it to choose you."— Bethenny Frankel, A Place of Yes: 10 Rules for Getting Everything You Want Out of Life

2185.   "A person is never as quiet or unrestrained as they seem, or as bad or good, as vulnerable or as strong, as sweet or as feisty; we are thickly layered, page lying upon page, behind simple covers. And love - it is not the book itself, but the binding. It can rip us apart or hold us together...Layers, by their nature, are fragile things."— Deb Caletti, Honey, Baby, Sweetheart

2186.   "Find a purpose to serve, not a lifestyle to live."— Criss Jami, Venus in Arms

2187.   "Success is something you experience when you act accordingly. Success is not something you have, it's something you do."— Steve Maraboli, Life, the Truth, and Being Free

2188.   "When choosing the lesser of two evils, always remember, it is still an evil."— Max Lerner

2189.   "LAW 25 Re-Create Yourself
Do not accept the roles that society foists on you. Re-create yourself by forging a new identity, one that commands attention and never bores the audience. Be the master of your own image rather than letting others define if for you. Incorporate dramatic devices into your public gestures and actions – your power will be enhanced and your character will seem larger than life."— Robert Greene, The 48 Laws of Power

2190.   "Keeping baggage from the past will leave no room for happiness in the future."— Wayne L. Misner

2191.   "Restlessness and impatience change nothing except our peace and joy. Peace does not dwell in outward things, but in the heart prepared to wait trustfully and quietly on Him who has all things safely in His hands."— Elisabeth Elliot

2192.   "Nobody sees a flower - really - it is so small it takes time - we haven't time - and to see takes time, like to have a friend takes time."— Georgia O'Keeffe, Georgia O'Keeffe

2193.   "Day after day, day after day,
We stuck, nor breath nor motion;
As idle as a painted ship
Upon a painted ocean."— Samuel Taylor Coleridge, The Rime of the Ancient Mariner

2194.   "Freedom is...the right to write the wrong words."— Patti Smith

2195.   "What's terrible is to pretend that second-rate is first-rate. To pretend that you don't need love when you do; or you like your work when you know quite well you're capable of better."— Doris Lessing, The Golden Notebook

2196.   "Let us labor for an inward stillness--
An inward stillness and an inward healing.
That perfect silence where the lips and heart
Are still, and we no longer entertain
Our own imperfect thoughts and vain opinions,
But God alone speaks to us and we wait
In singleness of heart that we may know
His will, and in the silence of our spirits,
That we may do His will and do that only"— Henry Wadsworth Longfellow

2197.   "Good ideas stay with you until you eventually write the story."— Brian Keene

2198.   "If you're serious about sanctification, you can expect to experience heart-wrenching moments that try your faith, your endurance, and your patience."— Sheri L. Dew, If Life Were Easy, It Wouldn't Be Hard: And Other Reassuring Truths

2199.   "I like Texas and Texans. In Texas, everything is bigger. When Texans win, they win big. And when they lose, it's spectacular.
If you really want to learn the attitude of how to handle risk, losing and failure, go to San Antonio and visit the Alamo. The Alamo is a great story of brave people who chose to fight, knowing there was no hope of success against overwhelming odds. They chose to die instead of surrendering. It's an inspiring story worthy of study; nonetheless, it's still a tragic military defeat. They got their butts kicked. A failure if you will. They lost. So how do Texans handle failure? They still shout, "Remember the Alamo!"
That's why I like Texans so much. They took a great failure and turned it into a tourist destination that makes them millions.
Texans don't bury their failures. They get inspired by them. They take their failures and turn them into rallying cries. Failure inspires Texans to become winners. But that formula is not just the formula for Texans. It is formula for all winners."— Robert T. Kiyosaki, Rich Dad, Poor Dad: What the Rich Teach Their Children About Money That the Poor and Middle Class Don't

2200.   "Champions are made from something they have deep inside of them- a desire, a dream, a vison."— Mahatma Gandhi

2201.   "Heavenly Father, we come before you today to ask your forgiveness and to seek your direction and guidance. We know Your Word says, 'Woe to those who call evil good,' but that is exactly what we have done. We have lost our spiritual equilibrium and reversed our values. We have exploited the poor and called it the lottery. We have rewarded laziness and called it welfare. We have killed our unborn and called it choice. We have shot abortionists and called it justifiable. We have neglected to discipline our children and called it building self-esteem. We have abused power and called it politics. We have coveted our neighbor's possessions and called it ambition. We have polluted the air with profanity and pornography and called it freedom of expression. We have ridiculed the time-honored values of our forefathers and called it enlightenment. Search us, Oh God, and know our hearts today; cleanse us from every sin and set us free. Amen!"— Billy Graham

2202.   "If you would not be forgotten, as soon as you are dead and rotten, either write things worth reading, or do things worth the writing."— Benjamin Franklin

2203.   "In life, you need either inspiration or desperation."— Anthony Robbins

2204.   "Some of our struggles involve making decisions, while others are a result of the decisions we have made. Some of our struggles result from choices others make that affect our lives. We cannot always control everything that happens to us in this life, but we can control how we respond. Many struggles come as problems and pressures that sometimes cause pain. Others come as temptations, trials, and tribulations."— L. Lionel Kendrick

2205.   "If it wasn't hard, everyone would do it. It's the hard that makes it great."— Tom Hanks

2206.   "When one flower blooms spring awakens everywhere"— John O'Donohue

2207.   "One way to define wisdom is the ability to see, into the future, the consequences of your choices in the present. That ability can give you a completely different perspective on what the future might look like."— Andy Andrews, The Noticer: Sometimes, All a Person Needs Is a Little Perspective.

2208.   "My dad always says, some people will treat you badly and you can't help that. But how you handle it and how it makes you feel, that's up to you."— Elise Broach, Shakespeare's Secret

2209.   "All great deeds and all great thoughts have a ridiculous beginning. Great works are often born on a street corner or in a restaurant's revolving door."— Albert Camus

2210.   "You gotta find what you like and let it kill you."— Charles Bukowski

2211.   "God's extraordinary work is most often done by ordinary people in the seeming obscurity of a home and family."— Neal A. Maxwell

2212.   "Patience is the only way you can endure the gray periods."— Teri Hatcher, Burnt Toast: And Other Philosophies of Life

2213.   "Each of our acts makes a statement as to our purpose."— Leo Buscaglia

2214.   "Guilt starts as a feeling of failure."— Frank Herbert

2215.	"I felt as if I were walking with destiny, and that all my past life had been but a preparation for this hour and for this trial... I thought I knew a good deal about it all, I was sure I should not fail."— Winston Churchill, The Second World War

2216.	"If faith never encounters doubt, if truth never struggles with error, if good never battles evil, how can faith know its own power? In my own pilgrimage, if I had to choose between a faith that has stared doubt in the eye and made it blink, or a naive faith that has never known the firing line of doubt, I will choose the former every time."— Gary Parker

2217.	"If you do whatever it takes to accomplish your goals to live the life you desire, It will be worth it. I promise! But if you find some excuse to justify quitting your journey, you will regret it. This is also a promise!" -gbb"— Glenn Brandon Burke

2218.	"Let us stand a little taller, if you don't, you will never strengthen yourself"— Gordon B. Hinckley, Stand a Little Taller

2219.	"It's a lie to think you're not good enough. It's a lie to think you're not worth anything."— Nick Vujicic

2220.	"Beauty is about being comfortable in your own skin. It's about knowing and accepting who you are."— Ellen DeGeneres, Seriously...I'm Kidding
"People who have a religion should be glad, for not everyone has the gift of believing in heavenly things. You don't necessarily even have to be afraid of punishment after death; purgatory, hell, and heaven are things that a lot of people can't accept, but still a religion, it doesn't matter which, keeps a person on the right path. It isn't the fear of God but the upholding of one's own honor and conscience. How noble and good everyone could be if, every evening before falling asleep, they were to recall to their minds the events of the whole day and consider exactly what has been good and bad. Then, without realizing it you try to improve yourself at the start of each new day; of course, you achieve quite a lot in the course of time. Anyone can do this, it costs nothing and is certainly very helpful. Whoever doesn't know it must learn and find by experience that: "A quiet conscience makes one strong!"— Anne Frank, The Diary of a Young Girl

2221.	"Jesus Christ lived in the midst of his enemies. At the end all his disciples deserted him. On the Cross he was utterly alone, surrounded by evildoers and mockers. For this cause he had come, to bring peace to the enemies of God. So the Christian, too, belongs not in the seclusion of a cloistered life but in the thick of foes. There is his commission, his work. 'The kingdom is to be in the midst of your enemies. And he who will not suffer this does not want to be of the Kingdom of Christ; he wants to be among friends, to sit among roses and lilies, not with the bad people but the devout people. O you blasphemers and betrayers of Christ! If Christ had done what you are doing who would ever have been spared' (Luther)."— Dietrich Bonhoeffer, Life Together: The Classic Exploration of Faith in Community

2222.   "And the worst part is before it gets any better we're heading for a cliff. And in the free fall I will realize I'm better off when I hit the bottom"— Hayley Williams

2223.   "Give freely to the world these gifts of love and compassion. Do not concern yourself with how much you receive in return, just know in your heart it will be returned."— Steve Maraboli, Life, the Truth, and Being Free

2224.   "All I have is all I need and all I need is all I have in this moment."— Byron Katie

2225.   "The soul hardly ever realizes it, but whether he is a believer or not, his loneliness is really a homesickness for God."— Hubert Van Zeller

2226.   "the shell must break before the bird can fly."— Alfred Tennyson

2227.   "That's one small step for [a] man, one giant leap for mankind"— Neil Armstrong

2228.   "I don't believe in hate. To me it wastes too much time. People who hate waste so much of their life hating that they miss out on all the other stuff out here."— Jaycee Dugard, A Stolen Life

2229.   "A girl expecting rescue never learns to save herself"— Kate Morton, The Forgotten Garden

2230.   "If I work hard enough, there will be things I can do tomorrow that I can't do today."— Randy Pausch, The Last Lecture

2231.   "A grateful mindset can set you free from the prison of disempowerment and the shackles of misery."— Steve Maraboli, Unapologetically You: Reflections on Life and the Human Experience

2232.   "Never say 'I can't.' 'I can't' is a limit, and life is about breaking through limits. Say 'I will' instead."— Heather Vogel Frederick, Pies & Prejudice

2233.   "Some men have thousands of reasons why they cannot do what they want to, when all they need is one reason why they can"— Martha Graham

2234.   "God never gives us discernment in order that we may criticize, but that we may intercede."— Oswald Chambers

2235.   "Some of us go full circle. Some of us blindly go nowhere. The circle doesn't have to be very large to make a point, kick your ass and/or be entertaining. Remember that and stay light. Even the deaf know good music when they hear it."— Jason Mraz

2236.   "at your weakest, you end up showing more strength; at your lowest, you are suddenly lifted higher than you've ever been. They all border one another, these opposites and show how quickly we can be altered."— Cecelia Ahern, Thanks for the Memories

2237.   "Bunkum and tummyrot! You'll never get anywhere if you go about what-iffing like that. Would Columbus have discovered America if he'd said 'What if I sink on the way over? What if I meet pirates? What if I never come back?' He wouldn't even have started."— Roald Dahl

2238.   "This world demands the qualities of youth; not a time of life but a state of mind, a temper of the will, a quality of the imagination, a predominance of courage over timidity, of the appetite for adventure over the life of ease."— Robert F. Kennedy

2239.   "Of course, we all inevitably work too hard, then we get burned out and have to spend the whole weekend in our pajamas, eating cereal straight out of the box and staring at the TV in a mild coma (which is the opposite of working, yes, but not exactly the same thing as pleasure)."— Elizabeth Gilbert, Eat, Pray, Love

2240.   "Age is a very high price to pay for maturity."— Tom Stoppard

2241.   "There are so many moments to remember and sometimes I think that maybe we're not really people at all. Maybe moments are what we are.... Sometimes I just survive. But sometimes I stand on the rooftop of my existence, arms stretched out, begging for more."— Markus Zusak, Getting the Girl

2242.   "We're all water from different rivers,
That's why it's so easy to meet,
We're all water in this vast, vast ocean,
Someday we'll evaporate together."— Yoko Ono

2243.   "The tools are real. The viewer is real, you, the artist, is real and a part of everything you paint. You connect yourself to the viewer by sharing something that is inside of you that connects with something inside of him. All you have as your guide is that you know what moves you. All you have to do it with is a brush, some chemical and canvas, and technique."— Steven Brust

2244.   "It is necessary to hope... for hope itself is happiness."— Samuel Johnson

2245.   "Here's the life lesson I've learned, Fifi: Some people are born to play the hero, and some are born to play the bad guy. Fighting your destiny only makes life harder than it needs to be. Besides, people remember the villain long after they've forgotten the hero."— Susan Elizabeth Phillips

2246.   "There are only two possibilities in life:1. Things don't always go the way you want, and you don't understand why you're having trouble; yet there is a hand of providence behind everything and a purpose for all that happens.2. Things don't always go the way you want, and you don't understand why you're having trouble; but there is no hand of providence behind everything and no purpose for all that happens. The first possibility gives hope in the midst of trials, the second produces only despair."— Fred Klett

2247.   "Nella vita: chi non risica, non rosica," he said finally, his voice quiet. "In life: nothing ventured, nothing gained. My mom used to tell us that. It's been a long time, but I can still hear her saying it."— J.M. Darhower, Sempre

2248.   "There, peeping among the cloud-wrack above a dark tower high up in the mountains, Sam saw a white star twinkle for a while. The beauty of it smote his heart, as he looked up out of the forsaken land, and hope returned to him. For like a shaft, clear and cold, the thought pierced him that in the end the Shadow was only a small and passing thing: there was light and high beauty forever beyond its reach."— J.R.R. Tolkien, The Return of the King

2249.   "We're on the same boat but in different cabin"— Hlovate, Rooftop Rant

2250.   "The treacherous are ever distrustful."— J.R.R. Tolkien, The Two Towers

2251.   "By declaring that man is responsible and must actualize the potential meaning of his life, I wish to stress that the true meaning of life is to be discovered in the world rather than within man or his own psyche, as though it were a closed system. I have termed this constitutive characteristic "the self-transcendence of human existence." It denotes the fact that being human always points, and is directed, to something or someone, other than oneself--be it a meaning to fulfill or another human being to encounter. The more one forgets himself--by giving himself to a cause to serve or another person to love--the more human he is and the more he actualizes himself. What is called self-actualization is not an attainable aim at all, for the simple reason that the more one would strive for it, the more he would miss it. In other words, self-actualization is possible only as a side-effect of self-transcendence."— Viktor E. Frankl, Man's Search for Meaning

2252.   "Mother is a verb. It's something you do. Not just who you are."— Cheryl Lacey Donovan, The Ministry of Motherhood

2253.   "Never give up on what you really want to do. The person with big dreams is more powerful than one with all the facts."— H. Jackson Brown Jr., Life's Little Instruction Book: 511 Suggestions, Observations, and Reminders on How to Live a Happy and Rewarding Life

2254.   "True beauty lies in purity of the heart."— Mahatma Gandhi

2255.   "Loyalty and obedience to wisdom and justice are fine; but it is still finer to defy arbitrary power, unjustly and cruelly used--not on behalf of ourselves, but on behalf of others more helpless."— Elizabeth Gaskell, North and South

2256.   "Service is the rent we pay for being. It is the very purpose of life, and not something you do in your spare time."— Marian Wright Edelman

2257.   "This is not the end, this is not even the beginning of the end, this is just perhaps the end of the beginning."— Winston Churchill

2258.   "The paths to liberation are numerous, but the bank along the way is always the same, the Bank of Karma, where the liberation account of each of us is credited or debited depending on our actions."— Yann Martel, Life of Pi

2259.   "Making others happy, through kindness of speech and sincerity of right advice, is a sign of true greatness. To hurt another soul by sarcastic words, looks, or suggestions, is despicable."— Paramahansa Yogananda, Where There is Light: Insight and Inspiration for Meeting Life's Challenges

2260.   "I'm not going to die, I'm going home like a shooting star."— Sojourner Truth

2261.   "I hated the mountains and the hills, the rivers and the rain. I hated the sunsets of whatever color, I hated its beauty and its magic and the secret I would never know. I hated its indifference and the cruelty which was part of its loveliness. Above all I hated her. For she belonged to the magic and the loveliness. She had left me thirsty and all my life would be thirst and longing for what I had lost before I found it."— Jean Rhys, Wide Sargasso Sea

2262.   "Life is largely a matter of expectation."— Homer

2263.   "I will cling to the rope God has thrown me in Jesus Christ, even when my numb hands can no longer feel it."— Sophie Scholl

2264.   "And what, incidentally, do you think integrity is? The ability not to pick a watch out of your neighbor's pocket? No, it's not as easy as that. If that were all, I'd say ninety-five percent of humanity were honest, upright men. Only, as you can see, they aren't. Integrity is the ability to stand by an idea."— Ayn Rand, The Fountainhead

2265.   "Faith is accepting what makes no sense, what we cannot prove, but know down deep in our souls is real."— Megan McCafferty, Bumped

2266.   "How is love between two people a sin? Love isn't about gender; it's about two souls uniting."— Alex Sanchez, The God Box

2267.   "CLAUDIA: I love you as high as the sky and as deep as the sea. MICHAEL: Multiply my love by infinity and take it to the depths of forever, and you still have only a glimpse of how much I feel for you. I love you more."— Mary Ting, Crossroads

2268.   "The world is your exercise book, the pages on which you do your sums. It is not reality, though you may express reality there if you wish. You are also free to write lies, or nonsense, or to tear the pages."— Richard Bach, Illusions: The Adventures of a Reluctant Messiah

2269.   "This pool is a triumph of imagination. That's how you win at life, Gin. You have to imagine your way through. Never say something can't be done. There's always a solution, even if it's weird."— Maureen Johnson, The Last Little Blue Envelope

2270.   "It seemed to travel with her, to sweep her aloft in the power of song, so that she was moving in glory among the stars, and for a moment she, too, felt that the words Darkness and Light had no meaning, and only this melody was real."— Madeleine L'Engle, A Wrinkle in Time

2271.   "And exactly how does a miserable face help the war effort?" he asked sharply, his mood beginning to change. "Will a frown bring back the dead or fortify a town? If I allow myself to laugh in the face of misery, I rest my mind from the stress of it all, and then it'll work the better for you and your war. And if I'm really to be one of your advisers, Your Majesty, accept this piece of advice: Take happiness where and when you find it, because there is going to be precious little of it in the next few months!"— Stuart Hill, The Cry of the Icemark

2272.   "So long as governments set the example of killing their enemies, private individuals will occasionally kill theirs."— Elbert Hubbard, Elbert Hubbard's Scrap Book

2273.   "Before I die, I want to fight for life."— Paulo Coelho

2274.   "The American story has never been about things coming easy. It has been about rising to the moment when the moment is hard. About rejecting panicked division for purposeful unity. About seeing a mountaintop from the deepest valley. That is why we remember that some of the most famous words ever spoken by an American came from a president who took office in a time of turmoil: "The only thing we have to fear is fear itself."— Barack Obama

2275.   "The size of your body is just right. The only question is whether you're big enough inside."— Patrick Carman, The Dark Hills Divide

2276.   "Love the trees until their leaves fall off, then encourage them to try again next year."— Chad Sugg

2277.   "It's very dramatic when two people come together to work something out. It's easy to take a gun and annihilate your opposition, but what is really exciting to me is to see people with differing views come together and finally respect each other."— Fred Rogers, The World According to Mister Rogers: Important Things To Remember

2278.   "close some doors today. not because of pride, incapacity or arrogance, but simply because they lead you nowhere"— Paulo Coelho

2279.   "Do not wait: the time will never be 'just right'. Start where you stand, and work whatever tools you may have at your command and better tools will be found as you go along."— Napoleon Hill

2280.   "I don't regret the painful times; I bare my scars as if they were medals."— Paulo Coelho

2281.   "Dance for yourself. If someone understands, good. If not, no matter. Go right on doing what interests you, and do it until it stops interesting you."— Louis Horst

2282.   "I suffer because my interactions with others do not meet the expectations I did not know I had."— Jim McDonald

2283.   "Though we tremble before uncertain futures may we meet illness, death and adversity with strength may we dance in the face of our fears. "— Gloria E. Anzaldúa

2284.   "Keep good company, read good books, love good things and cultivate soul and body as faithfully as you can"— Louisa May Alcott, Rose in Bloom

2285.   "In the final analysis it is between you and God, it was never between you and them anyway."— Mother Teresa

2286.   "You've got to think about big things while you're doing small things, so that all the small things go in the right direction."— Alvin Toffler

2287.   "A dream you dream alone is only a dream. A dream you dream together is reality."— Yoko Ono, Grapefruit: A Book of Instructions and Drawings

2288.   "A boy said, "Everybody is my friend. "Beloved said, "No, not everybody can be your friend." Boy said, "Each one of them is gifted to teach me something new in my life." Beloved said, "I still don't agree." Boy again smilingly said, "Don't divide human ...divide your soul, you will have everybody as friend. In short, Friends are your own soul divided from you, who will guide you when you will move away from your path."— Santosh Kalwar, Quote Me Everyday

2289.   "At the heart of the matter is a battle between wish and fear. Fear generally proves stronger than a wish, but it leaves a taste of disappointment on the tongue."— George Packer

2290.   "When we lose one we love, our bitterest tears are called forth by the memory of hours when we loved not enough."— Maurice Maeterlinck

2291.   "Every single being, even those who are hostile to us, is just as afraid of suffering as we are, and seeks happiness in the same way we do. Every person has the same right as we do to be happy and not to suffer. So let's take care of others wholeheartedly, of both our friends and our enemies. This is the basis for true compassion."— Dalai Lama XIV

2292.   "Perhaps life is just that... a dream and a fear"— Joseph Conrad

2293.   "God is a slick god. Temple Knows. She knows because of all the crackerjack miracles still to be seen on this ruined globe."— Alden Bell, The Reapers Are the Angels

2294.   "If you write it down, you can make it happen."— Staness Jonekos

2295.   "I dreamt a limitless book, A book unbound, Its leaves scattered in fantastic abundance On every line there was a new horizon drawn, New heavens supposed; New states, new souls."— Clive Barker

2296.   "The old woman I shall become will be quite different from the woman I am now. Another I is beginning."— George Sand

2297.   "Seek always to do some good, somewhere... Even if it's a little thing, so something for those that need help, something for which you get no pay but the privilege of doing it."— Albert Schweitzer

2298.   "Let nothing disturb you. Let nothing frighten you. Everything passes away except God."— Teresa of Ávila

2299.   "While it is true that most people never see or understand the difference they make, or sometimes only imagine their actions having a tiny effect, every single action a person takes has far-reaching consequences."— Andy Andrews, The Noticer: Sometimes, All a Person Needs Is a Little Perspective.

2300.   "Who are they to give stars or dots? They're Wemmicks just like you." Eli to Punchinello (p. 25)"— Max Lucado, You Are Special

2301.   "Life is a bitter sweet journey my friend, a bitter sweet journey."— Luellen Hoffman

2302.   "Work It Harder Make It Better
Do It Faster, Makes Us stronger
More Than Ever Hour After
Our Work Is Never Over
-Harder, Better, Faster, Stronger, lyrics and music by Daft Punk"— Daft Punk

2303.   "Life without risk is life wasted."— Santosh Kalwar

2304.   "Isn't it the unexpected that teaches us the most?"— Marwa Ayad

2305.   "Love, I thought to myself abstractedly. Not 'This is love' or 'Is this love?' Not a sentence, not a certainty, not a thought with moving parts or direction. Just love, all of it, as it is. Whether it's enough or not. Whether it's real or we're making it up. However shoddy it gets, or bent out of shape. It's still extraordinary. However foolish, however vain. However badly it ends. Love."— Julian Gough, Juno & Juliet

2306.   "I promise you nothing is as chaotic as it seems. Nothing is worth your health. Nothing is worth poisoning yourself into stress, anxiety, and fear."— Steve Maraboli, Unapologetically You: Reflections on Life and the Human Experience

2307.   "Love doesn't have to be on Valentine's Day. It doesn't have to be by the time you turn eighteen or thirty-three or fifty-nine. It doesn't have to conform to whatever is usual. It doesn't have to be kismet at once or rhapsody by the third day. It just has to be. In time. In place. In spirit. It just has to be."— David Levithan, How They Met, and Other Stories

2308.   "The sea's only gifts are harsh blows, and occasionally the chance to feel strong. Now I don't know much about the sea, but I do know that that's the way it is here. And I also know how important it is in life not necessarily to be strong but to feel strong. To measure yourself at least once. To find yourself at least once in the most ancient of human conditions. Facing the blind death stone alone, with nothing to help you but your hands and your own head."— Jon Krakauer, Into the Wild

2309.   "A concept is a brick. It can be used to build a courthouse of reason. Or it can be thrown through the window."— Gilles Deleuze, Thousand Plateaus: Capitalism and Schizophrenia

2310.   "Indeed, the more we find to love, the more we add to the measure of our hearts."— Lloyd Alexander, The Black Cauldron

2311.   "Go and get your things,' he said. 'Dreams mean work."— Paulo Coelho, By the River Piedra I Sat Down and Wept

2312.   "We're on this planet for too short a time. And at the end of the day, what's more important? Knowing that a few meaningless figures balanced—or knowing that you were the person you wanted to be?"— Sophie Kinsella

2313.   "Failing sucks. But it's better than the alternative."
"Which is?"
"Not even trying." Now he did look at me, straight on. "Life's short, you know?"— Sarah Dessen, Along for the Ride

2314.   "The consequences of every act are included in the act itself."— George Orwell, 1984

2315.   "I'd rather welcome change than cling to the past."— Robert T. Kiyosaki, Rich Dad, Poor Dad

2316.   "… Without a sense of identity, there can be no real struggle…"— Paulo Freire, Pedagogy of the Oppressed

2317.   "Life never end when you are in it."— Lemony Snicket, The Beatrice Letters

2318.   "You know what? I was wrong. You are an idiot. My life happens to, on occasion, suck beyond the telling of it. Sometimes more than I can handle. And it's not just mine. Every single person down there is ignoring your pain because they're too busy with their own. The beautiful ones. The popular ones. The guys that pick on you. Everyone. If you could hear what they were feeling. The loneliness. The confusion. It looks quiet down there. It's not. It's deafening… You know, I could've taken that by now. "Edit"— Joss Whedon

2319.   "Do your work, then step back. The only path to serenity."— Lao Tzu

2320.   "I know quite certainly that I myself have no special talent; curiosity, obsession and dogged endurance, combined with self-criticism, have brought me to my ideas."— Albert Einstein

2321.   "When was the last time you woke up and realized that today could be the best day of your life?"— Steve Maraboli, Unapologetically You: Reflections on Life and the Human Experience

2322.   "Most of us lead far more meaningful lives than we know. Often finding meaning is not about doing things differently; it is about seeing familiar things in new ways. "— Rachel Naomi Remen, My Grandfather's Blessings : Stories of Strength, Refuge, and Belonging

2323.   "Love, he realized, was like the daggers he made in his forge: When you first got one it was shiny and new and the blade glinted bright in the light. Holding it against your palm, you were full of optimism for what it would be like in the field, and you couldn't wait to try it out. Except those first couple of nights out were usually awkward as you got used to it and it got used to you. Over time, the steel lost its brand-new gleam, and the hilt became stained, and maybe you nicked the shit out of the thing a couple of times. What you got in return, however, saved your life: Once the pair of you were well acquainted, it became such a part of you that it was an extension of your own arm. It protected you and gave you a means to protect your brothers; it provided you with the confidence and the power to face whatever came out of the night; and wherever you went, it stayed with you, right over your heart, always there when you needed it.
You had to keep the blade up, however. And rewrap the hilt from time to time. And double-check the weight.
Funny...all of that was well, duh when it came to weapons. Why hadn't it dawned on him that mattings were the same?
(From the thoughts of Vishous)"— J.R. Ward, Lover Unleashed

2324.   "I love finding gems. However I'm not talking about ludicrously expensive diamonds, or priceless sapphires. I mean the impetuous, primitive rushes of passion and love we experience so rarely that they become impossible to ignore. That overwhelming sense of selflessness and beauty. Hope and desire. Happiness and strength. These are the moments that define us as people. As individuals. Should it be falling in love, playing a guitar for the first time, donating to charity, meeting new people, staying up till three in the morning listening to old Bob Marley Vinyls or beating the elite 4 on Pokemon. Whatever it is, it's moments like these that are worth more than any gem or diamond. Treasure or material goods."— George MacDonald (The Runaway State)

2325.   "There's always a choice,' said Torak, and walked backward off the cliff."— Michelle Paver

2326.   "Trying is always enough."— Patricia Briggs, Dragon Bones

2327.   "Without the gods, how would I sing?' I asked. With your own voice,' he said."— Erica Jong, Sappho's Leap

2328.	"There are always possibilities."— Jack B. Sowards, Star Trek II: The Wrath Of Khan: Photostory

2329.	"With stillness comes the benediction of Peace."— Eckhart Tolle, A New Earth: Awakening to Your Life's Purpose

2330.	"So I started out for God knows where. I guess I'll know when I get there."— Tom Petty

2331.	"...one had to expect very little—almost nothing—from life, Aaron knew, one had to be grateful, not always trying to seize the days like some maniac of living, but to give oneself up, be seized by the days, the months and years, be taken up in the froth of sun and moon, some pale and smoothie-ed river-cloud of life, a long, drawn-out, gray sort of enlightenment, so that when it was time to die, one did not scream swear words and knock things down, did not make a scene, but went easily with understanding and tact, and quietly, in a lightly pummeled way, having been consoled–having allowed to be consoled–by the soft, generous, worthlessness of it all, having allowed to be massaged by the daily beating of life, instead of just beaten."— Tao Lin, Bed: Stories

2332.	"Work will win when wishy washy wishing won't."— Thomas S. Monson

2333.	"See what I mean? You gotta be crazy. Ain't no time to be sane."— Robin P. Williams

2334.	"No one is ever satisfied where he is."— Antoine de Saint-Exupéry, The Little Prince

2335.	"Vote for the man who promises least; he'll be the least disappointing."— Bernard M. Baruch

2336.	"Three passions, simple but overwhelmingly strong, have governed my life: the longing for love, the search for knowledge, and unbearable pity for the suffering of mankind. These passions, like great winds, have blown me hither and thither, in a wayward course, over a great ocean of anguish, reaching to the very verge of despair.
I have sought love, first, because it brings ecstasy - ecstasy so great that I would often have sacrificed all the rest of life for a few hours of this joy. I have sought it, next, because it relieves loneliness--that terrible loneliness in which one shivering consciousness looks over the rim of the world into the cold unfathomable lifeless abyss. I have sought it finally, because in the union of love I have seen, in a mystic miniature, the prefiguring vision of the heaven that saints and poets have imagined. This is what I sought, and though it might seem too good for human life, this is what--at last--I have found.
With equal passion I have sought knowledge. I have wished to understand the hearts of men. I have wished to know why the stars shine. And I have tried to apprehend the Pythagorean power by which number holds sway above the flux. A little of this, but not much, I have achieved.
Love and knowledge, so far as they were possible, led upward toward the heavens. But always pity brought me back to earth. Echoes of cries of pain reverberate in my heart. Children in famine, victims tortured by oppressors,

helpless old people a burden to their sons, and the whole world of loneliness, poverty, and pain make a mockery of what human life should be. I long to alleviate this evil, but I cannot, and I too suffer.
This has been my life. I have found it worth living, and would gladly live it again if the chance were offered me."— Bertrand Russell

2337.   "Forgive me for being so ordinary while claiming to know so extraordinary a God."— Jim Elliot

2338.   "Only he who attempts the absurd is capable of achieving the impossible."— Miguel de Unamuno

2339.   "Total paranoia is just total awareness."— Charles Manson

2340.   "Don't get set into one form, adapt it and build your own, and let it grow, be like water."— Bruce Lee

2341.   "Fear not the path of Truth for the lack of People walking on it."— Robert F. Kennedy

2342.   "When you have a great and difficult task, something perhaps almost impossible, if you only work a little at a time, every day a little, suddenly the work will finish itself."— Isak Dinesen

2343.   "He who robs us of our dreams robs us of our life."— Virginia Woolf, Orlando

2344.   "There is no wealth like knowledge, no poverty like ignorance"— Ali Bin Abi Thalib

2345.   "Exuberance is beauty."— William Blake

2346.   "Literature is my Utopia. Here I am not disenfranchised. No barrier of the senses shuts me out from the sweet, gracious discourses of my book friends. They talk to me without embarrassment or awkwardness. "— Helen Keller

2347.   "If you're really listening, if you're awake to the poignant beauty of the world, your heart breaks regularly. In fact, your heart is made to break; its purpose is to burst open again and again so that it can hold evermore wonders."— Andrew Harvey

2348.   "Open up and wake up with blazing beauty just remember no one is perfect and you are the most beautiful creature on this planet."— Santosh Kalwar

2349.   "At any given moment the choice to be happy is present- we just have to choose to be happy."— Steve Maraboli, Life, the Truth, and Being Free

2350.   "To forgive is not to forget. The merit lies in loving in spite of the vivid knowledge that one that must be loved is not a friend. There is not merit in loving an enemy when you forget him for a friend. "— Mahatma Gandhi

2351.   "and the world we live in will be either better or worse, depending on whether we become better or worse. And that's where the power of love comes in. Because when we love, we always strive to become better than we are."— Paulo Coelho, The Alchemist

2352.   "what other people think of me is not my business."— Michael J. Fox

2353.   "People either have comedy or they don't. You can't teach it to them."— Lucille Ball

2354.   "She was never going to seek gainful employment again, that was for certain. She'd remain outside the public sector. She'd be an anarchist, she'd travel with jaguars. She was going to train herself to be totally irrational. She'd fall in love with a totally inappropriate person. She'd really work on it, but abandon would be involved as well. She'd have different names, a.k.a. Snake, a.k.a. Snow - no that was juvenile. She wanted to be extraordinary, to possess a savage glitter."— Joy Williams

2355.   "Change is in the air. This change reminds us that we are made and beautifully sculpted by the same power that orchestrates the change of season. Let this be the season you embrace and align yourself with this change."— Steve Maraboli, Life, the Truth, and Being Free

2356.   "I am really very grateful for this Award. It is one of the first given to a woman, and to two women at that. When I first started getting work published, I used to have wistful thoughts at the way all important awards were given to men. Women, I used to think, could be as innovative, imaginative and productive as possible - and women were the ones mostly at work in the field of fantasy for children and young adults - but only let a man enter the field, and people instantly regarded what he had to say and what he did as more Important. He got respectful reviews as well as awards, even if what he was doing - which it often was - was imitating the women. But you have changed all that.Thank you for being so enlightened.

2357.   Women, large-minded, formidable women, have played an almost exclusive part in helping my career. I have hardly ever dealt with a man - at least, when it came to publishing: "— Diana Wynne Jones

2358.   "The value of a moment is immeasurable. The power of just ONE moment can propel you to success and happiness or chain you to failure and misery."— Steve Maraboli, Life, the Truth, and Being Free

2359.   "I had the feeling she was going to say something big. One of us had to say it. What happened to us? Where are we going? It was like this silence between us was frozen and we were both feeling our way around it. How is it that two people can need each other so absolutely and then, in moments, not even know how to be next to each other and just be quiet?"— Heather Duffy Stone, This Is What I Want to Tell You

2360.   "Here's to opening and upward...and to yourself and up with you and up with and up with laughing."— E.E. Cummings

2361.   "How life teaches us, breaks us, rewards us, and tears us apart... how it lifts us up and brings us down... the wonder of life."— Marwa Ayad

2362.   "Participate in your own dreams, don't just say what you want or complain about what you don't have."— Steve Maraboli, Life, the Truth, and Being Free

2363.   "Maybe it's not about having a plan, or even a plan B. Maybe it's about seeing where life takes you and learning to enjoy the ride."— Jenny O'Connell

2364.   "Leap and the net will appear"— John Burroughs

2365.   "We are all equal in the fact that we are all different. We are all the same in the fact that we will never be the same. We are united by the reality that all colors and all cultures are distinct & individual. We are harmonious in the reality that we are all held to this earth by the same gravity. We don't share blood, but we share the air that keeps us alive. I will not blind myself and say that my black brother is not different from me. I will not blind myself and say that my brown sister is not different from me. But my black brother is he as much as I am me. But my brown sister is she as much as I am me."— C. JoyBell C.

2366.   "Am I weird?"
"Yeah. But so what? Everybody's weird."— Stephen King, Different Seasons

2367.   "Love is like a good cake; you never know when it's coming, but you'd better eat it when it does!"— C. JoyBell C.

2368.   "A winner is a dreamer who never gives up"— Nelson Mandela

2369.   "In order to write the book you want to write, in the end you have to become the person you need to become to write that book."— Junot Díaz

2370.   "It is worse to stay where one does not belong at all than to wander about lost for a while and looking for the psychic and soulful kinship one requires"— Clarissa Pinkola Estés, Women Who Run With the Wolves: Myths and Stories of the Wild Woman Archetype

2371.   "This first glance of a soul which does not yet know itself is like dawn in the heavens; it is the awakening of something radiant and unknown."— Victor Hugo, Les Misérables

2372.   "A scar is a sign of strength . . . the sign of a survivor."— Laurie Halse Anderson, Chains

2373.   "Humans have come into being for the sake of each other, so either teach them, or learn to bear them."— Marcus Aurelius, Meditations

2374.   "Though fairy tales end after ten pages, our lives do not. We are multi-volume sets. In our lives, even though one episode amounts to a crash and burn, there is always another episode awaiting us and then another. There are always more opportunities to get it right, to fashion our lives in the ways we deserve to have them. Don't waste your time hating a failure. Failure is a greater teacher than success."— Clarissa Pinkola Estés, Women Who Run With the Wolves: Myths and Stories of the Wild Woman Archetype

2375.   "I tell people not to be afraid of their fears; because their fears are not there to scare them, they're there to let them know that something is worth it. Yet I am often afraid. I guess that means in my life, lots of things have been worth it!"— C. JoyBell C.

2376.   "By reading the scriptures I am so renewed that all nature seems renewed around me and with me. The sky seems to be a pure, a cooler blue, the trees a deeper green. The whole world is charged with the glory of God and I feel fire and music under my feet. "— Thomas Merton

2377.   "You will always define events in a manner which will validate your agreement with reality."— Steve Maraboli, Life, the Truth, and Being Free

2378.   "The universe is so well balanced that the mere fact that you have a problem also serves as a sign that there is a solution."— Steve Maraboli, Life, the Truth, and Being Free

2379.   "Your best days are still out in front of you"— Joel Osteen

2380.   "So you think that money is the root of all evil? [...] Have you ever asked what is the root of money? Money is a tool of exchange, which can't exist unless there are goods produced and men able to produce them. Money is the material shape of the principle that men who wish to deal with one another must deal by trade and give value for value. Money is not the tool of the moochers, who claim your product by tears, or of the looters, who take it from you by force. Money is made possible only by the men who produce. Is this what you consider evil?"— Ayn Rand, Atlas Shrugged

2381.   "There are few sources of energy so powerful as a procrastinating college student."— Paul Graham, Hackers & Painters: Big Ideas from the Computer Age

2382.   "I have a self-made quote: Celebrate diversity, practice acceptance and may we all choose peaceful options to conflict."— Donzella Michele Malone

2383.   "Just because I've walked into this crazy fantasy doesn't mean I can just abandon my other plans, much as I might want to."— Alexandra Adornetto, Halo

2384.   "The most important thing in life is to learn how to give out love, and to let it come in.
2. Forgive yourself before you die. Then forgive others.
3. Death ends a life, not a relationship.
4. Once you learn how to die, you learn how to live.
5. Sometimes you cannot believe what you see, you have to believe what you feel. And if you are ever going to have other people trust you, you must feel that you can trust them too-even when you are in the dark. Even when you're falling.

6. As you grow old, you learn more. If you stayed at twenty-two, you'd always be as ignorant as you were at twenty-two. Aging is not just decay, you know. It's growth. It's more than the negative that you're going to die, it's also the positive that you understand you're going to die, and that you live a better life because of it."— Morrie Schwartz

2385.   "God picks up the reed-flute world and blows.
Each note is a need coming through one of us,a passion, a longing pain.
Remember the lips where the wind-breath originated,and let your note be clear.
Don't try to end it.
Be your note."— Rumi

2386.   "A miracle, my friend, is an event which creates faith."— George Bernard Shaw

2387.   "Don't let your character change color with your environment. Find out who you are and let it stay its true color."— Rachel Scott

2388.   "Let the revolution begin."— Ron Paul, The Revolution: A Manifesto

2389.   "Every creator painfully experiences the chasm between his inner vision and its ultimate expression. The chasm is never completely bridged. We all have the conviction, perhaps illusory, that we have much more to say than appears on the paper."— Isaac Bashevis Singer

2390.   "War is not the answer, for only love can conquer hate"— Marvin Gaye

2391.   "Language is the armory of the human mind, and at once contains the trophies of its past and the weapons of its future conquests."— Samuel Taylor Coleridge

2392.   "To travel a circle is to journey over the same ground time and time again. To travel a circle wisely is to journey over the same ground for the first time. In this way, the ordinary becomes extraordinary, and the circle, a path to where you wish to be. And when you notice at last that the path has circled back into itself, you realize that where you wish to be is where you have already been ... and always were."— Neale Donald Walsch

2393.   "The reasoning man who scorns the prejudices of simpletons necessarily becomes the enemy of simpletons; he must expect as much, and laugh at the inevitable."— Marquis de Sade

2394.   "I learned to love the fool in me. The one who feels too much, talks too much, takes too many chances, wins sometimes & loses often, lacks self-control, loves & hates, hurts & gets hurt, promises & breaks promises, laughs & cries."— Theodore Isaac Rubin

2395.   "I was giving up. I would have given up - if a voice hadn't made itself heard in my heart. The voice said "I will not die. I refuse it. I will make it through this nightmare. I will beat the odds, as great as they are. I have survived so far, miraculously. Now I will turn miracle into routine. The amazing will be seen every day. I will put in all the hard work necessary. Yes, so long as God is with me, I will not die. Amen."— Yann Martel, Life of Pi

2396.   "If you're the kind of person who has no guts, you just give up every time life pushes you. If you're that kind of person, you'll live all your life playing it safe, doing the right things, saving yourself for something that never happens. Then, you die a boring old man."— Robert T. Kiyosaki, Rich Dad, Poor Dad

2397.   "The most difficult thing is the decision to act, the rest is merely tenacity. The fears are paper tigers. You can do anything you decide to do. You can act to change and control your life; and the procedure, the process is its own reward."— Amelia Earhart

2398.   "The future doesn't belong to the light-hearted. It belongs to the brave."— Ronald Reagan

2399.   "Spirituality is not to be learned by flight from the world, or by running away from things, or by turning solitary and going apart from the world. Rather, we must learn an inner solitude wherever or with whomsoever we may be. We must learn to penetrate things and find God there."— Meister Eckhart

2400.   "Intense, unexpected suffering passes more quickly than suffering that is apparently bearable; the latter goes on for years and, without our noticing, eats away at our souls, until, one day, we are no longer able to free ourselves from the bitterness and it stays with us for the rest of our lives."— Paulo Coelho, The Alchemist

2401.   "Philosophy of science is about as useful to scientists as ornithology is to birds."— Richard P. Feynman

2402.   "It is better to live one day as a lion than 100 years as a sheep."— Benito Mussolini

2403.   "How strange that we should ordinarily feel compelled to hide our wounds when we are all wounded! Community requires the ability to expose our wounds and weaknesses to our fellow creatures. It also requires the ability to be affected by the wounds of others... But even more important is the love that arises among us when we share, both ways, our woundedness."— M. Scott Peck

2404.   "How many people you bless is how you measure success"— Rick Ross

2405.   "Behind your image, below your words, above your thoughts, the silence of another world waits."— John O'Donohue, Anam Cara: A Book of Celtic Wisdom

2406.   "Perhaps this is what it was all about. Leaning on God when life made no sense, as well as when the answers seem clear."— Tracie Peterson, A Lady of Secret Devotion

2407.   "If you need a miracle, be a miracle."— Phillip C. McGraw

2408.   "There is a terrible hunger for love. We all experience that in our lives - the pain, the loneliness. We must have the courage to recognize it. The poor you may have right in your own family. Find them. Love them."— Mother Teresa

2409.   "And to all this she must yet add something more substantial, in the improvement of her mind by extensive reading."— Jane Austen, Pride and Prejudice

2410.   "Nothing is impossible. With so many people saying it couldn't be done, all it takes is an imagination."— Michael Phelps

2411.   "I don't need any plastic in my body to validate me as a woman."— Courtney Love

2412.   "Like a good chess player, Satan is always trying to maneuver you into a position where you can save your castle only by losing your bishop."— C.S. Lewis

2413.   "There were eleven of us. Each more different than the next. All with the same mindset. Things weren't the way they were meant to be. It was our job to make things right. We were the soldiers of Halla.It was time for us to take it back."— D.J. MacHale

2414.   "That knowledge humbles me, melts my bones, closes my ears, and makes my teeth rock loosely in their gums. And it also liberates me. I am a big bird winging over high mountains, down into serene valleys. I am ripples of waves on silver seas. I'm a spring leaf trembling in anticipation."— Maya Angelou, Wouldn't Take Nothing for My Journey Now

2415.   "See, the 'small stuff' is what makes up the larger picture of our lives. Many people are like you, young man. But their perspective is distorted. They ignore 'small stuff,' claiming to have an eye on the bigger picture, never understanding that the bigger picture is composed of nothing more than-are you ready? - 'small stuff'."— Andy Andrews, The Noticer: Sometimes, All a Person Needs Is a Little Perspective.

2416.   "Pray that God is the most important thing in your life, so much so that hurting him would hurt you. When that happens, and your choices line up with his, it produces an amazing ripple effect of blessings--in your life, that of your family, and for the man you eventually marry."— Julie Lessman, A Passion Denied

2417.   "I'm not really silly enough to think that chocolate solves anything. But it calms me. It's a soothing assurance, that this hectic life I have worked myself into is also full of wonderful surprises and unexpected sweetness. It reminds me that a hefty percentage of my "problems" don't really need to be solved at all, just outlasted."— Emily Watts, Take Two Chocolates and Call Me in the Morning: 12 Semi-Practical Solutions for the Really Busy Woman

2418.   "Writing a long and substantial book is like having a friend and companion at your side, to whom you can always turn for comfort and amusement, and whose society becomes more attractive as a new and widening field of interest is lighted in the mind."— Winston Churchill

2419.	"Work without vision is drudgery. Vision without work is dreaming. Work plus vision-this is destiny."— Gordon B. Hinckley

2420.	"Love is photogenic, it develops in the dark."— Lorraine Gokul

2421.	"Mercy Falls was all about rumors, and the rumor on Jack was that he got his short fuse from his dad. I didn't know about that. It seemed like you ought to pick the sort of person you would be, no matter what your parents were like."— Maggie Stiefvater, Shiver

2422.	"If they give you ruled paper, write the other way."— Juan Ramon Jimenez

2423.	"...you have to have faith that you are doing God's will. Sometimes you will not understand. Sometimes you will doubt. But if you are doing God's will, you can't be wrong, you can't go wrong."— Philippa Gregory, The Constant Princess

2424.	"It takes a huge effort to free yourself from memory"— Paulo Coelho, Aleph

2425.	"It's not very easy to grow up into a woman. We are always taught, almost bombarded, with ideals of what we should be at every age in our lives: "This is what you should wear at age twenty", "That is what you must act like at age twenty-five", "This is what you should be doing when you are seventeen." But amidst all the many voices that bark all these orders and set all of these ideals for girls today, there lacks the voice of assurance. There is no comfort and assurance. I want to be able to say, that there are four things admirable for a woman to be, at any age! Whether you are four or forty-four or nineteen! It's always wonderful to be elegant, it's always fashionable to have grace, it's always glamorous to be brave, and it's always important to own a delectable perfume! Yes, wearing a beautiful fragrance is in style at any age!"— C. JoyBell C.

2426.	"Maybe we shouldn't be looking for love. Maybe we should be looking for a person. Because maybe you can find love in a person, but not have that person. So if you look for love, what you will find is love. But if you want to belong to someone, and you want someone to belong to you, you should look for a person."— C. JoyBell C.

2427.	"... if you don't have peace, it isn't because someone took it from you; you gave it away. You cannot always control what happens to you, but you can control what happens in you."— John C. Maxwell, Be a People Person

2428.	"If you fuel your journey on the opinions of others, you are going to run out of gas."— Steve Maraboli, Unapologetically You: Reflections on Life and the Human Experience

2429.   "don't trouble the trouble if you don't want the trouble to trouble you."—
Hlovate

2430.   "I don't have a diary, I don't write things into a diary. I imprint myself
into the sky and when the sunlight shines brightly, I can stand under the sun's
rays and everything I have imprinted of myself into the sky, I will begin to see
again, feel again, remember. And when the wind begins to blow, it blows the
details over my face, and I remember everything I left in the sky and see new
things being born. I am unwritten."— C. JoyBell C.

2431.   "Books didn't make me wallow in darkness, darkness made me wallow
in books."— Jackson Pearce

2432.   "Happiness is pretty simple: someone to love, something to do,
something to look forward to."— Rita Mae Brown, Hiss of Death

2433.   "A clown on a throne is still a clown. A king in rags is still a king."— C.
JoyBell C., The Sun Is Snowing: Poetry & Prose by C. Joybell C

2434.   "The words get easier the moment you stop fearing them."— Tahereh
Mafi

2435.   "Adversity introduces a man to himself."— Albert Einstein

2436.   "Everything changes, but beauty remains."— Kelly Clarkson

2437.   "Do you know what my father used to say?" I ask her. "He used to say
that songs had a heart. A crescendo that can make all your blood rush from your
head to your toes."— Lauren DeStefano, Fever

2438.   "Writing means not just staring ugliness in the face, but finding a way
to embrace it."— Veronica Roth

2439.   "Why should a man be scorned, if, finding himself in prison, he tries to
get out and go home? Or if, when he cannot do so, he thinks and talks about
other topics than jailers and prison-walls? The world outside has not become less
real because the prisoner cannot see it. In using Escape in this way the critics
have chosen the wrong word, and, what is more, they are confusing, not always
by sincere error, the Escape of the Prisoner with the Flight of the Deserter. Just
so a Party-spokesman might have labeled departure from the misery of the
Fuhrer's or any other Reich and even criticism of it as treachery.... Not only do
they confound the escape of the prisoner with the flight of the deserter; but they
would seem to prefer the acquiescence of the "quisling" to the resistance of the
patriot."— J.R.R. Tolkien, On Fairy-Stories

2440.   "If at first you don't succeed, failure may be your style."— Quentin
Crisp, The Naked Civil Servant; How To Become A Virgin; Resident Alien

2441.   "We Greeks believe that a man who takes no part in public affairs is
not merely lazy, but good for nothing"— Thucydides

2442.   "Because the hardest boss a man can ever have is himself."—
Stephen King, Duma Key

2443.   "For a hundred years or more the world, our world, has been dying.
And not one man, in these last hundred years or so, has been crazy enough to
put a bomb up the asshole of creation and set it off. The world is rotting away,
dying piecemeal. But it needs the coup de grace, it needs to be blown to
smithereens. Not one of us is intact, and yet we have in us all the continents and
the seas between the continents and the birds of the air. We are going to put it
down — the evolution of this world which has died but which has not been
buried."— Henry Miller, Tropic of Cancer

2444.   "But she loves me. Me. Just the way I am."— P.C. Cast, Destined

2445.   "I sometimes think my head is so large because it is so full of
dreams."— Joseph Merrick, How To Write Mysteries: A Writer's Notebook

2446.   "Constant kindness can accomplish much. As the sun makes ice melt,
kindness causes misunderstanding, mistrust, and hostility to evaporate. "—
Albert Schweitzer

2447.   "A person doesn't have to change who he is to become better."—
Sidney Poitier, The Measure of a Man: A Spiritual Autobiography

2448.   "When we sin and mess up our lives, we find that God doesn't go off
and leave us- he enters into our trouble and saves us."— Eugene H. Peterson

2449.   "Scientists have discovered that the small brave act of cooperating with
another person, of choosing trust over cynicism, generosity over selfishness,
makes the brain light up with quiet joy."— Natalie Angier

2450.   "I believe that love is better than hate. And that there is more nobility in
building a chicken coop than in destroying a cathedral."— Betty Greene

2451.   "The issue is truth, my dear brothers and sisters, and the only way to
find truth is through uncompromising self-education toward self-honesty to see
the original "real me," the child of God, in its innocence and potential in contrast
to the influence from the other part of me, "the flesh," with its selfish desires and
foolishness. Only in that state of pure honesty are we able to see truth in its
complete dimension. Honesty may not be everything, but everything is nothing
without honesty. In its final state, honesty is a gift of the Spirit through which the
true disciples of Christ"— Elder F. Enzio Busche

2452.   "This day I call heaven and earth as witnesses against you that I have
set before your life and death, blessings and curses. Now choose life, so that you
and your children may live 20 and that you may love the LORD your God, listen
to his voice, and hold fast to him. For the LORD is your life, and he will give you
many years in the land he swore to give to your fathers, Abraham, Isaac and
Jacob. Deuteronomy 30:19-20 (NIV)"— Anonymous, Holy Bible: The New King
James Version

2453.   "Death is a butterfly in its cocoon waiting to fly . . ."— Maria Housden, Hannah's Gift: Lessons from a Life Fully Lived

2454.   "So many people live within unhappy circumstances and yet will not take the initiative to change their situation because they are conditioned to a life of security, conformity, and conservatism, all of which may appear to give one peace of mind, but in reality nothing is more damaging to the adventurous spirit within a man than a secure future. The very basic core of a man's living spirit is his passion for adventure. The joy of life comes from our encounters with new experiences and hence there is no greater joy than to have an endlessly changing horizon, for each day to have a new and different sun."— Christopher McCandless

2455.   "Lord, grant me the strength to accept the things I cannot change, he courage to change the things I can, and the wisdom to know the difference."— St. Francis of Assisi

2456.   "If we recognize our talents and use them appropriately, and choose a field that uses those talents, we will rise to the top of our field."— Ben Carson

2457.   "Life's managed, not cured."— Phillip C. McGraw

2458.   "A monkey glances up and sees a banana, and that's as far as he looks. A visionary looks up and sees the moon."— Eoin Colfer, Airman

2459.   "If your life is worth thinking about, it is worth writing about."— Robin S. Sharma

2460.   "To do something that you feel in your heart that's great, you need to make a lot of mistakes. Anything that's successful is a series of mistakes."— Billie Joe Armstrong

2461.   "The day you become old is the day you're not looking for new experiences anymore."— Billie Joe Armstrong

2462.   "There are two things that men should never weary of, goodness and humility; we get none too much of them in this rough world among cold, proud people."— Robert Louis Stevenson, Kidnapped

2463.   "And like a colorful bloom of temporary lights in the sky, you will shine."— Chad Sugg

2464.   "O love, O fire! Once he drew
With one long kiss my whole soul through
My lips, as sunlight drinketh dew."— Alfred Tennyson

2465.   "You can't do anything about the length of your life, but you can do something about its width and depth."— H.L. Mencken

2466.   "The most beautiful people we have known are those who have known defeat, known suffering, known struggle, known loss, and have found their way out of the depths. These persons have an appreciation, sensitivity, and an understanding of life that fills them with compassion, gentleness, and a deep loving concern. Beautiful people do not just happen."— Elizabeth Kubler-Ross

2467.   "If we hold tightly to anything given to us unwilling to allow it to be used as the Giver means it to be used we stunt the growth of the soul. What God gives us is not necessarily "ours" but only ours to offer back to him, ours to relinquish, ours to lose, ours to let go of, if we want to be our true selves. Many deaths must go into reaching our maturity in Christ, many letting goes."— Elisabeth Elliot, Passion and Purity: Learning to Bring Your Love Life Under Christ's Control

2468.   "The most wonderful and the strongest things in the world, you know, are just the things which no one can see."— Charles Kingsley, The Water-Babies

2469.   "Ritsu: "I'm a complete failure. At everything I do, I'm absolutely worthless. I know this, and yet I continue to burden the human race with my presence. Every day I rob the world of valuable air by breathing. I'm a thief, and I hate myself for it. I don't deserve to exist. But even though I know it's the right thing to do, I'm such a useless coward. I don't even have the courage to jump!" Tohru: "No, don't! Don't jump! It's okay that you don't have that kind of courage. The important thing is you're alive. And life hurts sometimes and sometimes it can be hard, but it won't always be that way. There's gotta be a reason for you to live."— Natsuki Takaya

2470.   "It is often advantageous to forget. Forget your wincing humiliations, forget life's blows, and get on. For blocks in every direction, down every street in the city, people not yet old enough to have lines on their foreheads were laughing away memory, warmly ensconced in shrines of forgetfulness. Those who followed the word of God and those who preferred what the priests called "hoodoo" alike. People everywhere forgetting with drink or forgetting with religion or forgetting with the numbing quality of their many heaps of things. They looked forward and imagined rosy tomorrows, and gave up whatever horrors heckled their dreams, and listened to the pretty stories of whoever ruled their pulpit."— Anna Godbersen, Bright Young Things

2471.   "Be content with who you are and where you are, and do whatever you can do to bring to others such contentment, and joy, and understanding that you have managed to find yourself."— Alexander McCall Smith, The Double Comfort Safari Club

2472.   "Where you are right now doesn't have to determine where you'll end up"— Barack Obama

2473.   "Our deepest calling is to grow into our own authentic self-hood, whether or not it conforms to some image of who we ought to be. As we do so, we will not only find the joy that every human being seeks--we will also find our path of authentic service in the world."— Parker J. Palmer

2474.   "Make the choice to embrace this day. Do not let your TODAY be stolen by the ghost of yesterday or the "To-Do" list of tomorrow! It's inspiring to see all the wonderfully amazing things that can happen in a day in which you participate."— Steve Maraboli, Life, the Truth, and Being Free

2475.   "The things we truly love stay with us always, locked in our hearts as long as life remains."— Josephine Baker

2476.   "Man can live about forty days without food, about three days without water, about eight minutes without air...but only for one second without hope."— Hal Lindsey

2477.   "Let me tell you something you haven't learnt yet, something you learn only by living awhile. As you get older, you find that life begins to wear you down. Doesn't matter who you are or what you do, it happens. Experience, time, events - they all conspire against you to steal away your energy, to erode your confidence, to make you question things you wouldn't have given a second thought to when you were young. It happens gradually, a chipping away that you don't even notice at first, and then one day it's there. You wake up and you just don't have the fire anymore...Then you have a choice. You can either give in to what you're feeling, just say "okay, enough is enough" and be done with it, or you can fight it. You can accept that every day you're alive you're going to have to face it down, that you're going to have to say to yourself that you don't care what you feel, that it doesn't matter what happens anyway, that you're going to do what you have to because otherwise you're defeated and life doesn't have any real purpose left. When you can do that, little Wren, when you can accept the wearing down and the eroding, then you can do anything. How did I manage to keep going out nights? I just told myself I didn't matter all that much - that those in here mattered more. You know something? It's not so hard really. You just have to get past the fear."— Terry Brooks

2478.   "...because where we are is always the most important place."— Philip Pullman, The Amber Spyglass

2479.   "A man's ego is the fountainhead of human progress."— Ayn Rand

2480.   "Search for contentment in each person you meet."— Steve Maraboli, Life, the Truth, and Being Free

2481.   "The key to your happiness is to...own who you are, own how you look, own your family, own the talents you have, and own the ones you don't. [Otherwise] you'll die searching, you'll die bitter, always feeling you were promised more. Not only our actions, but also our omissions, become our destiny."— Abraham Verghese

2482.   "my child, if you want to have a beautiful and happy life... 2 things you need... learn the art of love and practice it with your beloved one."— Carlos Barrios

2483.   "There is in God, some say, a deep but dazzling darkness."— Madeleine L'Engle, A Ring of Endless Light

2484.   "Maybe this is why we read, and why in moments of darkness we return to books: to find words for what we already know."— Alberto Manguel, A Reading Diary: A Passionate Reader's Reflections on a Year of Books

2485.   "It's total bullshit," he said. "The whole thing. Eighty percent survival rate and he's in the twenty percent? Bullshit. He was such a bright kid. It's bullshit. I hate it. But it was sure a privilege to love him, huh?"— John Green, The Fault in Our Stars

2486.   "How should we be able to forget those ancient myths that are at the beginning of all peoples, the myths about dragons that at the last moment turn into princesses; perhaps all the dragons of our lives are princesses who are only waiting to see us once beautiful and brave. Perhaps everything terrible is in its deepest being something helpless that wants help from us. So you must not be frightened if sadness rises up before you larger than any you have ever seen; if a restiveness, like light and cloud shadows, passes over your hands and over all you do. You must think that something is happening with you, that life has not forgotten you, that it holds you in its hand; it will not let you fall. Why do you want to shut out of your life any uneasiness, any miseries, or any depressions? For after all, you do not know what work these conditions are doing inside you."— Rainer Maria Rilke, Letters to a Young Poet

2487.   "I believe the simplest explanation is, there is no God. No one created the universe and no one directs our fate. This leads me to a profound realization that there probably is no heaven and no afterlife either. We have this one life to appreciate the grand design of the universe and for that, I am extremely grateful."— Stephen Hawking

2488.   "Don't ever give up. Don't ever give in. Don't ever stop trying. Don't ever sell out. And if you find yourself succumbing to one of the above for a brief moment, pick yourself up, brush yourself off, whisper a prayer, and start where you left off.
But never, ever, ever give up."— Richelle E. Goodrich, Eena: The Tempter's Snare

2489.   "Libraries store the energy that fuels the imagination. They open up windows to the world and inspire us to explore and achieve, and contribute to improving our quality of life. Libraries change lives for the better."— Sidney Sheldon

2490.   "It is not uncommon for people to spend their whole life waiting to start living."— Eckhart Tolle, The Power of Now: A Guide to Spiritual Enlightenment

2491.   "If you truly expect to realize your dreams, abandon the need for blanket approval. If conforming to everyone's expectations is the number one goal, you have sacrificed your uniqueness, and therefore your excellence."— Hope Solo

2492.   "Me, I want to bloody kick this moronic bloody world in the bloody teethover and over till it bloody understands that not hurting people is ten bloody thousand times more bloody important than being right."— David Mitchell, Black Swan Green

2493.   "God is God. He knows what he is doing. When you can't trace his hand, trust his heart."— Max Lucado

2494.   "As long as I am breathing, in my eyes, I am just beginning."— Criss Jami

2495.   "Better to illuminate than merely to shine to deliver to others contemplated truths than merely to contemplate."— St. Thomas Aquinas

2496.   ""You shouldn't feel so bad about being afraid of so many things." "Why not?" "Because if you weren't afraid never ever, then you couldn't be brave never ever."— C. JoyBell C.

2497.   "And a beautiful world we live in, when it is possible, and when many other such things are possible, and not only possible, but done-- done, see you! -- under that sky there, every day."— Charles Dickens, A Tale of Two Cities

2498.   "I believe that life is a prize, but to live doesn't mean you're alive."— Nicki Minaj

2499.   "Hurl yourself at goals above your head and bear the lacerations that come when you slip and make a fool of yourself. Try always, as long as you have breath in your body, to take the hard way—and work, work, work to build yourself into a rich, continually evolving entity."— Sylvia Plath

2500.   "The only difference between a wish and a prayer is that you're at the mercy of the universe for the first, and you've got some help with the second."— Jodi Picoult, Sing You Home

2501.   "If you're walking the path of the dreamer... everything is possible."— Jared Leto

2502.   "The Highest Thought is always that thought which contains joy. The Clearest Words are those words which contain truth. The Grandest Feeling is that feeling which you call love."— Neale Donald Walsch

2503.   "If you are a writer you locate yourself behind a wall of silence and no matter what you are doing, driving a car or walking or doing housework you can still be writing, because you have that space."— Joyce Carol Oates

2504.   "Change is the parent of progress."— Steve Maraboli, Life, the Truth, and Being Free

2505.   "Success always leaves footprints."— Booker T. Washington

2506.   "There are few things in life that bring as much joy as the joy that comes from assisting another improves his or her life."— Richard G. Scott

2507.   "Every man builds his world in his own image; he has the power to choose, but no power to escape the necessity of choice. If he abdicates his power, he abdicates the status of man, and the grinding chaos of the irrational is what he achieves as his sphere of existence—by his own choice."— Ayn Rand

2508.   "Independent will is our capacity to act. It gives us the power to transcend our paradigms, to swim upstream, to rewrite our scripts, to act based on principle rather than reacting based on emotion or circumstance."— Stephen R. Covey

2509.   "Even a moment's reflection will help you see that the problem of using your time well is not a problem of the mind but of the heart. It will only yield to a change in the very way we feel about time. The value of time must change for us. And then the way we think about it will change, naturally and wisely. That change in feeling and in thinking is combined in the words of a prophet of God in this dispensation. It was Brigham Young, and the year was 1877, and he was speaking at April general conference. He wasn't talking about time or schedules or frustrations with too many demands upon us. Rather, he was trying to teach the members of the Church how to unite themselves in what was called the united order. The Saints were grappling with the question of how property should be distributed if they were to live the celestial law. In his usual direct style, he taught the people that they were having trouble finding solutions because they misunderstood the problem. Particularly, he told them they didn't understand either property or the distribution of wealth. Here is what he said: With regard to our property, as I have told you many times, the property which we inherit from our Heavenly Father is our time, and the power to choose in the disposition of the same. This is the real capital that is bequeathed unto us by our Heavenly Father; all the rest is what he may be pleased to add unto us. To direct, to counsel and to advise in the disposition of our time pertains to our calling as God's servants, according to the wisdom which he has given and will continue to give unto us as we seek it. [JD 18:354]Time is the property we inherit from God, along with the power to choose what we will do with it. President Young calls the gift of life, which is time and the power to dispose of it, so great an inheritance that we should feel it is our capital. The early Yankee families in America taught their children and grandchildren some rules about an inheritance. They were always to invest the capital they inherited and live only on part of the earnings. One rule was "Never spend your capital." And those families had confidence the rule would be followed because of an attitude of responsibility toward those who would follow in later generations. It didn't always work, but the hope was that inherited wealth would be felt a trust so important that no descendent would put pleasure ahead of obligation to those who would follow. Now, I can see and hear Brigham Young, who was as flinty a New Englander as the Adams or the Cabots ever hoped to be, as if he were leaning over this pulpit tonight. He would say something like this, with a directness and power I wish I could approach: "Your inheritance is time. It is capital far more precious than any lands or stocks or houses you will ever get. Spend it foolishly, and you will bankrupt yourself and cheapen the inheritance of those that follow you. Invest it wisely, and you will bless generations to come. "A Child of Promise", BYU Speeches, 4 May 1986"— Henry B. Eyring

2510.   "There is no refuge from confession but suicide; and suicide is confession"— Daniel Webster

2511.   "So when you feel like hope is gone, look inside you and be strong, and you'll finally see the truth -that a hero lies in you."— Mariah Carey

2512.   "Beyond work and love, I would add two other ingredients that give meaning to life. First, to fulfill whatever talents we are born with. However blessed we are by fate with different abilities and strengths; we should try to develop them to the fullest, rather than allow them to atrophy and decay. We all know individuals who did not fulfill the promise they showed in childhood. Many of them became haunted by the image of what they might have become. Instead of blaming fate, I think we should accept ourselves as we are and try to fulfill whatever dreams are within our capability. Second, we should try to leave the world a better place than when we entered it. As individuals, we can make a difference, whether it is to probe the secrets of Nature, to clean up the environment and work for peace and social justice, or to nurture the inquisitive, vibrant spirit of the young by being a mentor and a guide."— Michio Kaku

2513.   "Leaders must be close enough to relate to others, but far enough ahead to motivate them."— John C. Maxwell

2514.   "In the external scheme of things, shining moments are as brief as the twinkling of an eye, yet such twinklings are what eternity is made of -- moments when we human beings can say "I love you," "I'm proud of you," "I forgive you," "I'm grateful for you." That's what eternity is made of: invisible imperishable good stuff."— Fred Rogers, The World According to Mister Rogers: Important Things To Remember

2515.   "Life doesn't just happen to you; you receive everything in your life based on what you've given."— Rhonda Byrne

2516.   "Then let us all do what is right, strive with all our might toward the unattainable, develop as fully as we can the gifts God has given us, and never stop learning"— Ludwig van Beethoven

2517.   "Until you have suffered much in your heart, you cannot learn humility."— Elder Thaddeus of Vitovnica, Our Thoughts Determine Our Lives: The Life and Teachings of Elder Thaddeus of Vitovnica

2518.   "If freedom is short of weapons, we must compensate with willpower."— Adolf Hitler

2519.   "Voyager, there are no bridges, one builds them as one walks."— Gloria E. Anzaldúa

2520.   "Grace isn't a little prayer you chant before receiving a meal. It's a way to live."— Jacqueline Winspear

2521.   "Are You Living or Just Existing?"-Tyler Perry The Family That Preys"— Tyler Perry

2522.	"Better to shun the bait than struggle in the snare."— William Blake

2523.	"Get this in mind early: We never grow up."— Richard Bach

2524.	"So long as you do no harm to another, change your opinion once in a while. Contradict yourself without being embarrassed. This is your right. It doesn't matter what others think -because that's what they will think, in any case."— Paulo Coelho, Maktub

2525.	"While intent is the seed of manifestation, action is the water that nourishes the seed. Your actions must reflect your goals in order to achieve true success."— Steve Maraboli, Life, the Truth, and Being Free

2526.	"What's the point of playing if winning isn't the goal?"— J.D. Robb, Fantasy in Death

2527.	"Because I am a woman, I must make unusual efforts to succeed. If I fail, no one will say, 'She doesn't have what it takes.'' ~ ' They will say, 'Women don't have what it takes.'' -"— Clare Boothe Luce

2528.	"Some people will dream big dreams while others will wake up and do them."— John Bytheway

2529.	"This is a photograph of me as I wish I looked all the time. Then I might have a chance of getting in Hollywood."— Anne Frank, The Diary of a Young Girl

2530.	"Not knowing a thing is not ignorance. Feigning knowledge you don't have can be--Sholto"— Laurell K. Hamilton, A Kiss of Shadows

2531.	"Free yourself from the complexities of your life! A life of simplicity and happiness awaits you."— Steve Maraboli, Life, the Truth, and Being Free

2532.	"Just because you're in a situation, doesn't mean you have to be that situation. You're not the situation you're in!"— K.M. Johnson, Knowing the Struggle Is Over!

2533.	"People who you are close with don't understand you. The people you usually lean on have changed. You rely on your other friends that you usually wouldn't tell your secretes, but still, they are there. You move away from the people you trust toward your new found trustees, and the people you called close are mad you because YOU'VE changed. So now you're confused, and now you think you've changed. Tell whoever told you that to kiss you on the cheek, and wave good-bye for good."— Megan Johnson

2534.	"We're all confused, Samantha. We all need more time to think. That's life. Get over it. "— Sophie Kinsella, The Undomestic Goddess

2535.	"The act of laughing releases some nice chemical into your brain, you feel good and it's free."— James Patterson, Sam's Letters to Jennifer

2536.	"I think now that fate is half shaped by expectation, half by inattention. But somehow, when you lose something you love, faith takes over. You have to pay attention to what you lost. You have to undo the expectation."— Amy Tan, The Joy Luck Club

2537.	"All this will not be finished in the first one hundred days. Nor will it be finished in the first one thousand days . . . nor even perhaps in our lifetime on this planet. But let us begin."— John F. Kennedy

2538.	"He gave her his phone number, in a peculiar reversal of dating procedure. She might have considered kissing him, even after the horrible first date, but he just didn't seem to know what to do. However, Jeremy does have one outstanding quality. He likes her. And this quality in a person makes them infinitely interesting to the person who is being liked."— Steve Martin, Shopgirl

2539.	"Today stretches ahead of you waiting to be shaped. You are the sculptor who gets to do the shaping. What today will be like is up to you."— Steve Maraboli, Life, the Truth, and Being Free

2540.	"Life is like a recycling center, where all the concerns and dramas of humankind get recycled back and forth across the universe. But what you have to offer is your own sensibility, maybe your own sense of humor or insider pathos or meaning. All of us can sing the same song, and there will still be four billion different renditions."— Anne Lamott

2541.	"Stand tall and be strong in defense of those great virtues which have been the backbone of our social progress. When you are united, your power is limitless. You can accomplish anything you wish to accomplish. -President Gordon B. Hinckley, Church of Jesus Christ of Latter Day Saints"— Gordon B. Hinckley

2542.	"Get comfortable with being uncomfortable!"— Jillian Michaels

2543.	"Friends can make you feel that the world is smaller and less sneaky than it really is, because you know people who have similar experiences."— Lemony Snicket, The Austere Academy

2544.	"The primary thing when you take a sword in your hands is your intention to cut the enemy, whatever the means. Whenever you parry, hit, spring, strike or touch the enemy's cutting sword, you must cut the enemy in the same movement. It is essential to attain this. If you think only of hitting, springing, striking or touching the enemy, you will not be able actually to cut him."— Miyamoto Musashi, The Book of Five Rings

2545.	"It's a sad day when you find out that it's not accident or time or fortune, but just yourself that kept things from you."— Lillian Hellman

2546.	"If you change the way you look at things, the things you look at will change."— Wayne W. Dyer

2547.   "When people see some things as beautiful, other things become ugly. When people see some things as good, other things become bad."— Lao Tzu, Tao Te Ching

2548.   "Nobody ever lives their life all the way up except bullfighters."— Ernest Hemingway, The Sun Also Rises

2549.   "Genius is eternal patience."— Michelangelo Buonarroti

2550.   "It is wisdom to recognize necessity when all other courses have been weighed, though as folly it may appear to those who cling to false hope."— J.R.R. Tolkien, The Fellowship of the Ring

2551.   "Live as if you'd drop dead in ten seconds."— Ray Bradbury, Fahrenheit 451

2552.   "It is not every day that the world arranges itself into a poem."— Wallace Stevens

2553.   "There is no instinct like that of the heart."— George Gordon Byron

2554.   "When given an opportunity, deliver excellence and never quit."— Robert Rodriguez, Rebel Without a Crew, or How a 23-Year-Old Filmmaker With $7,000 Became a Hollywood Player

2555.   "To oppose something is to maintain it... You must go somewhere else; you must have another goal; then you walk a different road."— Ursula K. Le Guin

2556.   "I prepare for the worst, but hope for the best."— Jackie Chan

2557.   "Remember that the most beautiful things in the world are the most useless."— John Ruskin

2558.   "Each of us is an innkeeper who decides if there is room for Jesus!"— Neal A. Maxwell

2559.   "A man, whilst he is dreaming, believes in his dream; he is undeceived only when he is awakened from his slumber."— Mahatma Gandhi, Hind Swaraj or Indian Home Rule

2560.   "None of us come to this earth to gain our worth; we brought it with us."— Sheri L. Dew

2561.   "In the things that really matter--our covenants, the commandments, and following the prophet--we need to be completely united. In the non-essentials, we have our agency to handle things as we see fit. But, in all things, regardless of whether we make the same choices or not, we are to treat each other with dignity and respect, both of which are evidences of charity in our hearts and lives."— Sheri L. Dew, If Life Were Easy, It Wouldn't Be Hard: And Other Reassuring Truths

2562.   "The goodbyes we speak and the goodbyes we hear are the good byes that tell us we're still alive."— Steven King

2563.   "Are you born again?" he asked, as we taxied down the runway. He was rather prim and tense, maybe a little like David Eisenhower with a spastic colon. I did not know how to answer for a moment.
"Yes," I said. "I am."
My friends like to tell each other that I am not really a born-again Christian. They think of me more along the lines of that old Jonathan Miller routine, where he said, "I'm not really a Jew -- I'm Jew-ish." They think I am Christian-ish. But I'm not. I'm just a bad Christian. A bad born-again Christian. And certainly, like the apostle Peter, I am capable of denying it, of presenting myself as a sort of leftist liberation-theology enthusiast and maybe sort of a vaguely Jesusy bon vivant. But it's not true. And I believe that when you get on a plane, if you start lying you are totally doomed.
So I told the truth; that I am a believer, a convert. I'm probably about three months away from slapping an aluminum Jesus-fish on the back of my car, although I first want to see if the application or stickum in any way interferes with my lease agreement. And believe me, all this boggles even *my* mind. But it's true. I could go to a gathering of foot-wash Baptists and, except for my dreadlocks, fit right in. I would wash their feet; I would let them wash mine."— Anne Lamott

2564.   "Lord, to the degree I don't want to do this, bless me."— Luci Swindoll

2565.   "When power leads man toward arrogance, poetry reminds him of his limitations. When power narrows the area of man's concern, poetry reminds him of the richness and diversity of existence. When power corrupts, poetry cleanses."— John F. Kennedy

2566.   "Am I the woman I think I am, the woman I want to be? More importantly, am I the woman the Savior needs me to be?"— Sheri L. Dew

2567.   "He is a great enough magician to tap our most common nightmares, daydreams and twilight fancies, but he never invented them either: he found them a place to live, a green alternative to each day's madness here in a poisoned world. We are raised to honor all the wrong explorers and discoverers - thieves planting flags, murderers carrying crosses. Let us at last praise the colonizers of dreams."— Peter S. Beagle, The Tolkien Reader

2568.   "... perhaps the clock hands had become so tired of going in the same direction year after year that they had suddenly begun to go the opposite way instead..."— Jostein Gaarder, The Christmas Mystery

2569.   "Have you ever loved someone so much that when you drew a breath you knew it was his?"— Barbara Boyer, Courage of Fear

2570.   "Your life is always under construction. It is your job to learn how to untangle the threads and weave a tapestry that matches your desires."— Dannye Williamsen

2571.   "You are the guiding star of someone's existence"— Carroll Bryant

2572.   "The starting point of all achievement is DESIRE. Keep this constantly in mind. Weak desire brings weak results, just as a small fire makes a small amount of heat."— Napoleon Hill, Think and Grow Rich

2573.   "No man ever threw away life while it was worth keeping."— David Hume, Essays On Suicide And The Immortality Of The Soul

2574.   "Grace is what picks me up and lifts my wings high above and I fly! Grace always conquers! Be graceful in everything; in anger, in sadness, in joy, in kindness, in unkindness, retain grace with you!"— C. JoyBell C.

2575.   "We all want progress. But progress means getting nearer to the place where you want to be. And if you have taken a wrong turning, then to go forward does not get you any nearer. If you are on the wrong road, progress means doing an about-turn and walking back to the right road; and in that case the man who turns back soonest is the most progressive man."— C.S. Lewis, Mere Christianity

2576.   "A man with charm is an entertaining thing, and a man with looks is, of course, a sight to behold, but a man with honor - ah, he is the one, dear reader, to which young ladies should flock."— Julia Quinn, The Viscount Who Loved Me

2577.   "Sometimes the little things in life mean the most."— Ellen Hopkins, Glass

2578.   "No matter how many people believe or don't believe in you, you must be the ultimate believer in yourself!"— Pablo

2579.   "A man does not have to be an angel to be a saint."— Albert Schweitzer

2580.   "Imagination is what you do with your inspiration."— Violet Haberdasher

2581.   "It is beautiful to discover our wings and learn how to fly; flight is a beautiful process. But then to rest on the wings of God as He flies: this is divine."— C. JoyBell C.

2582.   "Each new day greets us with no rules except for the rules we place on it. Greet this new day with open arms and endless possibility."— Steve Maraboli, Life, the Truth, and Being Free

2583.   "Inner peace is impossible without patience. Wisdom requires patience. Spiritual growth implies the mastery of patience. Patience allows the unfolding of destiny to proceed at its own unhurried pace."— Brian L. Weiss, Muchas Vidas, Muchos Maestros

2584.   "And yet their wills did not yield, and they struggled on."— J.R.R. Tolkien, The Return of the King

2585.   "I adore Life. What do all the fools matter and all the stupidity. They do matter but somehow for me they cannot touch the body of Life. Life is marvelous. I want to be deeply rooted in it - to live - to expand - to breathe in it - to rejoice - to share it. To give and to be asked for Love."— Katherine Mansfield

2586.   "We can't look to the world to restore our worth; we're here to restore our worth to the world. The world outside us can reflect our glory, but it cannot create it. It cannot crown us. Only God can crown us, and he already has."— Marianne Williamson

2587.   "You should be concerned about the state of your soul, not the state of your bank account."— Jennifer Weiner, Little Earthquakes

2588.   "Today is yours to shape. Create a masterpiece!"— Steve Maraboli, Life, the Truth, and Being Free

2589.   "You are beautiful. Your beauty, just like your capacity for life, happiness, and success, is immeasurable."— Steve Maraboli, Life, the Truth, and Being Free

2590.   "Seek out the company of those who will never ask you to jump," the earth advised.
Bertie remembered the rush of feathers as she soared above the audience. "I can catch myself."
"Of those whose love will never fill your lungs with water-" the earth argued.
"But it did not kill me."
"there should be more to love," said the earth, "than 'it did not kill me.' More than 'I survived it."— Lisa Mantchev, Perchance to Dream

2591.   "God is Good...Jesus is Lord
Be Good to Yourself and each Other
J-Jesus...O-Others...Y-Yourself"— Joyce Meyer, Starting Your Day Right: Devotions for Each Morning of the Year

2592.   "We have messed-up lives, but we're good people and we have grace. And even though we don't have to do good for God to love us, I want to do good for Him."— Lacey Mosley

2593.   "A life of happiness, peace, and love is all within our grasp."— Steve Maraboli, Life, the Truth, and Being Free

2594.   "A woman can run, hide, play and have fun but she will shine far better when she just smiles without any."— Santosh Kalwar, Quote Me Everyday

2595.   "one word could change the whole world"— Sarah Dessen

2596.   "Funny, how one good cookie could calm the mind and even elevate a troubled soul."— Dean Koontz, False Memory

2597.   "Sit down every day and DO IT. Writing is a self-taught craft; the more you work at it, the more skilled you become. And when you're not writing, READ."— Lois Duncan

2598.   "Live the life you wish to, date the man you wish to date, and stop looking to your family for affirmation for the choices that you make. Life is full of risks. You can't live your life in fear of how people will judge you for following your dreams."— David Sullivan, The Sound of Your Voice

2599.   "All we can do is make the best decisions we can with the best information we have at that time and place. And learn how to rebound, reinvent, and regroup. Remember—people who seem to move through life with confidence aren't confident about the outcome of a decision; they're confident that they can deal with the outcome, good or bad."— Stephanie Bond

2600.   "When life gives you lemons, you make lemonade. Then find someone whose life is givin' them vodka and have a party!"— Ron White, I Had the Right to Remain Silent...But I Didn't Have the Ability

2601.   "Maybe we ought to look at a guy's response to our microwave from now on." Aunt Annie said. Really." Mom said. "The narcissist looks at his reflection in it. The OCD guy thinks you don't keep it clean enough. The antisocial--"Puts his fist through it because it reminds him of his father." Annie said. She'd read all of mom's books, too.
And the paranoid one would be jealous of the amount of time you spend cooking." Mom said
Were you using that microwave again? Is something going on between the two of you? I caught you looking right at its clock." Annie said."— Deb Caletti, The Secret Life of Prince Charming

2602.   "Some people insist that 'mediocre' is better than 'best.' They delight in clipping wings because they themselves can't fly. They despise brains because they have none."— Robert A. Heinlein, Have Space Suit—Will Travel

2603.   "Miracles are what happen when you get out of the way of yourself."— Brad Szollose

2604.   "If you hear the dogs, keep going. If you see the torches in the woods, keep going. If there's shouting after you, keep going. Don't ever stop. Keep going. If you want a taste of freedom, keep going."— Harriet Tubman

2605.   "... Experiencing deep sadness can, sometimes, heighten your ability to feel joy."— Markéta Irglová

2606.   "Too many of us are not living our dreams because we are living our fears."— Les Brown

2607.   "Anger does not solve anything; it builds nothing."— Thomas S. Monson

2608.   "One of the penalties of an ecological education is that one lives alone in a world of wounds. Much of the damage inflicted on land is quite invisible to laymen. An ecologist must either harden his shell and make believe that the consequences of science are none of his business, or he must be the doctor who sees the marks of death in a community that believes itself well and does not want to be told otherwise."— Aldo Leopold, A Sand County Almanac

2609.   "We are such spendthrifts with our lives, the trick of living is to slip on and off the planet with the least fuss you can muster. I'm not running for sainthood. I just happen to think that in life we need to be a little like the farmer, who puts back into the soil what he takes out."— Paul Newman

2610.   "Why am I compelled to write?... Because the world I create in the writing compensates for what the real world does not give me. By writing I put order in the world, give it a handle so I can grasp it. I write because life does not appease my appetites and anger... To become more intimate with myself and you. To discover myself, to preserve myself, to make myself, to achieve self-autonomy. To dispel the myths that I am a mad prophet or a poor suffering soul. To convince myself that I am worthy and that what I have to say is not a pile of shit... Finally I write because I'm scared of writing, but I'm more scared of not writing."— Gloria E. Anzaldúa

2611.   "So many things are possible as long as you don't know they are impossible"— Mildred D. Taylor, The Land

2612.   "Now, five years is nothing in a man's life except when he is very young and very old...- Wang Lung"— Pearl S. Buck, The Good Earth

2613.   "He who despairs is wrong."— Victor Hugo, Les Misérables, tome I/3

2614.   "when you don't create things, you become defined by your tastes rather than ability. your tastes only narrow & exclude people. so create."— Why The Lucky Stiff

2615.   "It is better to fill your head with useless knowledge than no knowledge at all."— Jim Hinckley, Route 66 Backroads: Your Guide to Scenic Side Trips & Adventures from the Mother Road

2616.   "Nothing is so much calculated to lead people to forsake sin as to take them by the hand and to watch over them in tenderness. When persons manifest the least kindness and love to me, O what pow'r it has over my mind."— Joseph Smith Jr.

2617.   "Through the reciprocation of energy, always, and every time, we will get exactly what we put out there to others. Like Karma, whatever we do will indefinitely come back to us in some way shape or form.
When goodness is given, it is likely to returned.
When you support someone, you will be supported.
When you Love, you will be Loved.
If you give someone your last dollar, someone will help you equally.

This is the law of the universe. What selfless characteristics do you portray to benefit your reality? Expand."— Will Barnes, The Expansion of The Soul

2618.   "But if the gods do not exist at all - then we are lost,' I said.
On the contrary - we are found!' said Aesop.
But when we are afraid, who can we turn to, if not the gods?'
Ourselves. We turn to ourselves anyway. We only pretend there are gods and that they care about us. It is a comforting falsehood."— Erica Jong, Sappho's Leap

2619.   "The way to move out of judgment is to move into gratitude"— Neale Donald Walsch

2620.   "I tried to make meat loaf out of the girl but it becomes too frustrating a task and instead I spend the afternoon smearing her meat all over the walls, chewing on strips of skin I ripped from her body"— Bret Easton Ellis, American Psycho

2621.   "Sometimes you've got to be able to listen to yourself and be okay with no one else understanding."— Christopher Barzak, One for Sorrow

2622.   "Never kick a fresh turd on a hot day."— Harry S. Truman

2623.   "The symbol of Goddess gives us permission. She teaches us to embrace the holiness of every natural, ordinary, sensual dying moment. Patriarchy may try to negate body and flee earth with its constant heartbeat of death, but Goddess forces us back to embrace them, to take our human life in our arms and clasp it for the divine life it is - the nice, sanitary, harmonious moment as well as the painful, dark, splintered ones.
If such a consciousness truly is set loose in the world, nothing will be the same. It will free us to be in a sacred body, on a sacred planet, in sacred communion with all of it. It will infect the universe with holiness. We will discover the Divine deep within the earth and the cells of our bodies, and we will lover her there with all our hearts and all our souls and all our minds."— Sue Monk Kidd, The Dance of the Dissident Daughter: A Woman's Journey from Christian Tradition to the Sacred Feminine

2624.   "Though I do not believe that a plant will spring up where no seed has been, I have great faith in a seed. Convince me that you have a seed there, and I am prepared to expect wonders."— Henry David Thoreau

2625.   "There is loveliness to life that does not fade. Even in the terrors of the night, there is a tendency toward grace that does not fail us. "— Robert Goolrick, The End of the World as We Know It: Scenes from a Life

2626.   "We are built for the valley, for the ordinary stuff we are in, and that is where we have to prove our mettle."— Oswald Chambers

2627.   "Some of God's greatest gifts are unanswered prayers."— Garth Brooks

2628.   "Unhappiness does not come from the way things are, but from the difference between how things are and how we think they should be"— Creflo A. Dollar

2629.   "The straight path must sometimes be crooked."— Carole Wilkinson, Dragon Keeper

2630.   "I think we agree, the past is over."— George W. Bush

2631.   "Do you know that one of the great problems of our age is that we are governed by people who care more about feelings than they do about thoughts and ideas."— Margaret Thatcher, Margaret Thatcher

2632.   "When you take risks you learn that there will be times when you succeed and there will be times when you fail, and both are equally important."— Ellen DeGeneres, Seriously...I'm Kidding

2633.   "Talent is a gift, but character is a choice."— John C. Maxwell

2634.   "Do not sabotage your new relationship with your last relationship's poison."— Steve Maraboli, Unapologetically You: Reflections on Life and the Human Experience

2635.   "You can't connect the dots looking forward; you can only connect them looking backwards. So you have to trust that the dots will somehow connect in your future."— Steve Jobs

2636.   "We are the cosmos made conscious and life is the means by which the universe understands itself."— Brian Cox

2637.   "The book was turned to the page with Anne Frank's name, but what got me about it was the fact that right beneath her name there were four Aron Franks. FOUR. Four Aron Franks without museums, without historical markers, without anyone to mourn them. I silently resolved to remember and pray for the four Aron Franks as long as I was around."— John Green, The Fault in Our Stars

2638.   "I've learned recently to love imperfection a lot because it shines such a big light on God's grace. And if someone has grace for you that's when you feel their love the most and they see you for who you are and they love you anyway."— Lacey Mosley

2639.   "When you are used to the kind of life -of never getting anything you want- you stop knowing what it is you want."— Haruki Murakami, The Wind-Up Bird Chronicle

2640.   "I don't think you should wait. I think you should speak now."— Taylor Swift, Taylor Swift: Speak Now

2641.   "No great wisdom can be reached without sacrifice."— C.S. Lewis, The Magician's Nephew

2642.   "It's better to have a few faithful friends than numerous shallow friendships."— Jonathan Anthony Burkett, Friends 2 Lovers: The Unthinkable

2643.   "One of the mistakes many of us make is that we feel sorry for ourselves, or for others, thinking that life should be fair, or that someday it will be. It's not and it won't. When we make this mistake we tend to spend a lot of time wallowing and/or complaining about what's wrong with life. "It's not fair," we complain, not realizing that, perhaps, it was never intended to be."— Richard Carlson, Don't Sweat the Small Stuff ... and it's all small stuff: Simple Ways to Keep the Little Things from Taking Over Your Life

2644.   "Selflessness and Bravery aren't that different~ Tobias/Four"— Veronica Roth, Divergent

2645.   "Never give a sword to a man who can't dance."— Confucius, The Analects

2646.   "Fear and realization of ignorance, strong medicines against stupid pride."— Garth Nix, Sabriel

2647.   "Who is it who decides that one man should live and another should die? My life wasn't worth any more than his, but he's the one who's buried, while I get to enjoy at least a few more hours above the ground. Is it chance, random and cruel, or is there some purpose or pattern to all this, even if it lies beyond our ken?"-Roran"— Christopher Paolini, Inheritance

2648.   "If you don't want a generation of robots, fund the arts!"— Cath Crowley, Graffiti Moon

2649.   "It is foolish to tear one's hair in grief, as though sorrow would be made less by baldness."— Marcus Tullius Cicero

2650.   "I'm not afraid of dying. I'm afraid I'll never get a chance to live!"— A.A. Bell, Diamond Eyes

2651.   "In the time you will live, there will be heroes around. Simple men, honest men who work two jobs, go to school, raise a family, and serve our God. An older couple who have the courage to seek out the truth while enduring the scorn and ridicule of their children and friends. A young man, a special spirit, who will take on a body that is deformed- and yet you will never see him unhappy or without a smile on his face. A young mother who will care for a daughter while she suffers a painful death, and yet never doubt or loose faith that her Father loves them both.
In your world famous people will be hard to find. But you will be surrounded by heroes; you will meet them every day. They will be the simple people who struggle but never give up, those who strive to be happy despite the cares of the physical world, those who dream of the day when they will find the truth, those who search for understanding as to why they were born, why there is pain, or what it all means, and yet continue to endure, knowing in their soul, somewhere deep inside, that there has to be an answer.

These are the heroes that our Father needs down on earth. And you will be a hero. We already know that."— Chris Stewart

2652.　　　　"All men will die. All men will be called upon to pass through the veil. But only a few, only a few special men, only those who have been worthy to answer a calling from God, are given the honor to die for a cause.
And in this life, in these times, all of us will be called on to make a sacrifice. When, or in what manner that sacrifice may be required, only God knows. All we can do is wait and prepare and pray that when our time comes, we will be ready to complete the task that he gives, so that when it is over, when we have done all we could, we might look to the Lord and say the same words he said: 'I have fought my way through, I have finished the work Thou didst give me to do.'"— Chris Stewart

2653.　　　　"By space the universe encompasses me and swallows me up like an atom; by thought I comprehend the world."— Blaise Pascal

2654.　　　　"Tomorrow is not another day; tomorrow is today's backup plan."— Ian Coburn

2655.　　　　"Because dreams are the difference between living...and existing..."— Danielle Ackley-McPhail

2656.　　　　"Live with an Attitude of Faith. Have faith in GOD for every dream. Dream Big."— C.F. Baker

2657.　　　　"Truth builds trust."— Marilyn Suttle

2658.　　　　"You can't go home again"— Thomas Wolfe

2659.　　　　"Is there some lesson on how to be friends?
I think what it means is that central to living
a life that is good is a life that's forgiving.
We're creatures of contact regardless of whether
we kiss or we wound. Still, we must come together.
Though it may spell destruction, we still ask for more--
since it beats staying dry but so lonely on shore.
So we make ourselves open while knowing full well
it's essentially saying "please, come pierce my shell."— David Rakoff

2660.　　　　"It's a beautiful day in this neighborhood, A beautiful day for a neighbor.
Would you be mine?
Could you be mine?
It's a neighborly day in this beauty wood, A neighborly day for a beauty.
Would you be mine?
Could you be mine?
I've always wanted to have a neighbor just like you.
I've always wanted to live in a neighborhood with you.
So, let's make the most of this beautiful day.
Since we're together we might as well say: Would you be mine?

Could you be mine?
Won't you be my neighbor?
Won't you please, Won't you please?
Please won't you be my neighbor?"— Fred Rogers

2661.   "Finding the center of strength within ourselves is in the long run the best contribution we can make to our fellow men. ... One person with indigenous inner strength exercises a great calming effect on panic among people around him. This is what our society needs — not new ideas and inventions; important as these are, and not geniuses and supermen, but persons who can "be", that is, persons who have a center of strength within themselves."— Rollo May, Man's Search For Himself

2662.   "Pet names are a persistent remnant of childhood, a reminder that life is not always so serious, so formal, so complicated. They are a reminder, too, that one is not all things to all people."— Jhumpa Lahiri, The Namesake

2663.   "Always be like water. Float in the times of pain or dance like waves along the wind which touches its surface."— Santosh Kalwar

2664.   "In this world love has no color yet how deeply my body is stained by yours."— Izumi Shikibu, Diaries of Court Ladies of Old Japan

2665.   "A poem begins in delight and ends in wisdom."— Robert Frost

2666.   "I've done my best, and I begin to understand what is meant by 'the joy of strife'. Next to trying and winning, the best thing is trying and failing."— L.M. Montgomery, Anne of Green Gables

2667.   "Your daddy is standing in a swimming pool out a little bit from the edge. You are, let's say, three years old and standing on the edge of the pool. Daddy holds out his arms to you and says, "Jump, I'll catch you. I promise." Now, how do you make your daddy look good at that moment? Answer: trust him and jump. Have faith in him and jump. That makes him look strong and wise and loving. But if you won't jump, if you shake your head and run away from the edge, you make your daddy look bad. It looks like you are saying, "he can't catch me" or "he won't catch me" or "it's not a good idea to do what he tells me to do." And all three of those make your dad look bad. But you don't want to make God look bad. So you trust him. Then you make him look good—which he really is. And that is what we mean when we say, "Faith glorifies God" or "Faith gives God glory." It makes him look as good as he really is. So trusting God is really important. And the harder it seems for him to fulfill his promise, the better he looks when you trust him. Suppose that you are at the deep end of a pool by the diving board. You are four years old and can't swim, and your daddy is at the other end of the pool. Suddenly a big, mean dog crawls under the fence and shows his teeth and growls at you and starts coming toward you to bite you. You crawl up on the diving board and walk toward the end to get away from him. The dog puts his front paws up on the diving board. Just then, your daddy sees what's happening and calls out, "Johnny, jump in the water. I'll get you." Now, you have never jumped from one meter high and you can't swim and your daddy is not underneath you and this water is way over your head. How do you make your daddy look good in that moment? You jump. And almost as soon as you hit the water, you feel his hands under your arms and he treads water holding you safely while someone chases the dog away. Then he takes you to the side of the pool. We give glory to God when we trust him to do what he has promised to do–especially when all human possibilities are exhausted. Faith glorifies God. That is why God planned for faith to be the way we are justified."— John Piper

2668.   "When I pray for another person, I am praying for God to open my eyes so that I can see that person as God does, and then enter into the stream of love that God already directs toward that person."— Philip Yancey

2669.   "Love does not traffic in a marketplace, nor use a huckster's scales. Its joy, like the joy of the intellect, is to feel itself alive. The aim of Love is to love: no more, and no less. You were my enemy: such an enemy as no man ever had. I had given you all my life, and to gratify the lowest and most contemptible of all human passions, hatred and vanity and greed, you had thrown it away. In less than three years you had entirely ruined me in every point of view. For my own sake there was nothing for me to do but to love you."— Oscar Wilde, De Profundis

2670.   "We are all these things [...]. Pride, desire, compassion, cleverness, belligerence, fruitfulness, loyalty...and guilt. But above it all stands love. And if we desire to be more than human, that is the star by which we must set our sights. "— Jacqueline Carey, Kushiel's Avatar

2671.   "Your dream is a reality that is waiting for you to materialize. Today is a new day! Don't let your history interfere with your destiny! Learn from your past so that it can empower your present and propel you to greatness"— Steve Maraboli, Life, the Truth, and Being Free

2672.   "You're never ready for what you have to do. You just do it. That makes you ready."— Flora Rheta Schreiber, Sybil: The Classic True Story of a Woman Possessed by Sixteen Personalities

2673.   "My dream is to dream, a dream."— Santosh Kalwar

2674.   "I am looking forward enormously to getting back to the sea again, where the overstimulated psyche can recover in the presence of that infinite peace and spaciousness."— C.G. Jung

2675.   "But what do I have? The things I'm told and the things I tell, that's all. And as far as I know, that never yet made anyone fly."— Mario Vargas Llosa, The Storyteller

2676.   "You can't make yourself happy by causing other people's misery-Tyler Perry The Family That Preys"— Tyler Perry

2677.   "We didn't start the fire
It was always burning
Since the world's been turning
We didn't start the fire

No we didn't light it
But we tried to fight it"— Billy Joel

2678. "Don't stop doing what you love.
Don't let your future be ruined by a bunch of loony sand monkeys."— Megan McCafferty, Second Helpings

2679. "Live life with a purpose and live it full out."— Steve Maraboli, Life, the Truth, and Being Free

2680. "If you concentrate always on the present, you'll be a happy man. You'll see that there is life in the desert, that there are stars in the heavens...Life will be a party for you, a grand festival, because life is the moment we're living right now."— Paulo Coelho, The Alchemist

2681. "Remember what I said about finding a meaningful life? I wrote it down, but now I can recite it: Devote yourself to loving others, devote yourself to your community around you, and devote yourself to creating something that gives you purpose and meaning."— Mitch Albom, Tuesdays With Morrie

2682. "It was on my fifth birthday that Papa put his hand on my shoulder and said, 'Remember, my son, if you ever need a helping hand, you'll find one at the end of your arm."— Sam Levenson

2683. "Life is like playing the violin in public and learning the instrument as one goes on."— Samuel Butler

2684. "To say that one waits a lifetime for his soul mate to come around is a paradox. People eventually get sick of waiting; take a chance on someone, and by the art of commitment become soul mates, which takes a lifetime to perfect."— Criss Jami, Venus in Arms

2685. "What we do for ourselves dies with us. What we do for others and the world, is and remains immortal."— Albert Pine

2686. "Do you know what you are?
You are a manuscript of a divine letter.
You are a mirror reflecting a noble face. This universe is not outside of you. Look inside yourself; everything that you want, you are already that."— Rumi, Hush, Don't Say Anything to God: Passionate Poems of Rumi

2687. "I hope to write someday and that's even more terrifying than performing. You don't just entertain the audience; you give them little bits of your soul."— Chris Colfer

2688. "The great secret of true success, of true happiness, is this: the man or woman who asks for no return, the perfectly unselfish person, is the most successful."— Swami Vivekananda

2689. "It's easy to forget things you don't need anymore."— Haruki Murakami, Kafka on the Shore

2690.   "This place is a dream. Only a sleeper considers it real. Then death comes like dawn, and you wake up laughing at what you thought was your grief."— Rumi

2691.   "What the mind can conceive and believe, and the heart desire, you can achieve."— Norman Vincent Peale

2692.   "But I'm not special", Bailey says, "not the way they are. I'm not anyone important. "I know", Celia said, "you are not destined or chosen. I wish I could tell you that you were if that would make it easier, but it is not true. You are in the right place, at the right time, and you care enough to do what needs to be done. Sometimes that is enough."— Erin Morgenstern, The Night Circus

2693.   "You can't control what others think. The only thing you can control is yourself. Some people will look down on you for your choices in life, no matter what they are. You can't do anything about that. The only thing you can do is decide how to live your own life. And to hell with everybody else"— Marie Sexton

2694.   "I wasn't sure what I'd done to deserve such a wonderful gift, and I wasn't sure if it was insolent, but I thanked God for fallen angels."— Jamie McGuire, Providence

2695.   "People who love themselves come across as very loving, generous and kind; they express their self-confidence through humility, forgiveness and inclusiveness."— Sanaya Roman, Living with Joy: Keys to Personal Power and Spiritual Transformation

2696.   "A man who knows how little he knows is well, a man who knows how much he knows is sick. If, when you see the symptoms, you can tell, your cure is quick.
A sound man knows that sickness makes him sick and before he catches it his cure is quick."— Lao Tzu, The Chinese Translations

2697.   "The most basic and powerful way to connect to another person is to listen. Just listen. Perhaps the most important thing we ever give each other is our attention.... A loving silence often has far more power to heal and to connect than the most well-intentioned words. "— Rachel Naomi Remen

2698.   "Twant me, 'twas the Lord. I always told him, 'I trust to you. I don't know where to go or what to do, but I expect you to lead me,' and He always did."— Harriet Tubman

2699.   "Better to do something imperfectly than to do nothing flawlessly."— Robert H. Schuller

2700.   "Everyone has the right to doubt everything as often as he pleases and the duty to do it at least once. No way of looking at things is too sacred to be reconsidered. No way of doing things is beyond improvement."— Edward De Bono, Use of Lateral Thinking, the

2701.   "Creative work is not a selfish act or a bid for attention on the part of the actor. It's a gift to the world and every being in it. Don't cheat us of your contribution. Give us what you've got."— Steven Pressfield

2702.   "Then the singing enveloped me. It was furry and resonant, coming from everyone's very heart. There was no sense of performance or judgment, only that the music was breath and food."— Anne Lamott, Traveling Mercies: Some Thoughts on Faith

2703.   "Never think that you're not good enough yourself. A man should never think that. People will take you very much at your own reckoning."— Anthony Trollope

2704.   "I have no time to justify you, fool, you're blind, step aside from me"— Dave Matthews Band

2705.   "If you think you are too small to be effective, you have never been in bed with a mosquito."— Betty Reese

2706.   "If you contemplate the Golden Rule, it turns out to be an injunction to live by grace rather than by what you think other people deserve."— Deepak Chopra, The Third Jesus: The Christ We Cannot Ignore

2707.   "We appreciate the complicated and wonderful gifts you give us in each other. And we appreciate the task you put down before us, of loving each other the best we can, even as you love us."— Kate DiCamillo, Because of Winn-Dixie

2708.   "Restlessness is a fickle catalyst; it can drive you to achieve or it can coax your demise, and sometimes the choice isn't yours"— Slash, Slash

2709.   "The world lies in the hands of those that have the courage to dream and who take the risk of living out their dreams - each according to his or her own talent."— Paulo Coelho

2710.   "Today is Your Day to Dance Lightly with Life. It Really Is."— Jonathan Lockwood Huie

2711.   "It was as if hope had appeared out of nowhere to settle beside her and it wasn't going anywhere, it wasn't going to desert her now."— Alice Hoffman

2712.   "You are the gold and Love is within your heart."— Judy Azar LeBlanc

2713.   "...there ain't no journey what don't change you some."— David Mitchell, Cloud Atlas

2714.   "There is a relationship between the eye contacts we make and the perceptions that we create in our heads, a relationship between the sound of another's voice and the emotions that we feel in our hearts, a relationship between our movements in space all around us and the magnetic pulls we can create between others and ourselves. All of these things (and more) make up the magic of every ordinary day and if we are able to live in this magic, to feel and to dwell in it, we will find ourselves living with magic every day. These are the white spaces in life, the spaces in between the written lines, the cracks in which the sunlight filters into. Some of us swim in the overflowing of the wine glass of life, we stand and blink our eyes in the sunlight reaching unseen places, we know where to find the white spaces, we live in magic."— C. JoyBell C.

2715.   "I don't look for love. Love looks for me." "Why?" "Because it needs me. Because I'm not afraid of it."— C. JoyBell C.

2716.   "Whether a thought is spoken or not it is a real thing and has powers of reality."— Frank Herbert, Dune

2717.   ".."I don't even know her yet. But if she could see me right now, I'd want her to know that I love her..." ~E.L.~"— Eric Ludy, When Dreams Come True: A Love Story Only God Could Write

2718.   "I will take the Ring", he said, "Though I do not know the way."— J.R.R. Tolkien, The Fellowship of the Ring

2719.   "Have faith have faith. When you have nothing else have faith."— Francine Rivers, A Voice in the Wind

2720.   "Allow yourself to enjoy each happy moment in your life."— Steve Maraboli

2721.   "Why am I seeking? I am the same as he. His essence speaks through me. I have been looking for myself"— Rumi

2722.   "Instead, what I was beginning to understand was that however things unfolded from here on, whatever the next chapter was, my life could never be the sum of one circumstance. It would be determined, as it had always been, by my willingness to put one foot in front of the other, moving forward, come what may."— Liz Murray, Breaking Night: A Memoir of Forgiveness, Survival, and My Journey from Homeless to Harvard

2723.   "All these things are miracles. It is a miracle if you can find true friends, and it is a miracle if you have enough food to eat, and it is a miracle if you get to spend your days and evenings doing whatever it is you like to do."— Lemony Snicket, The Lump of Coal

2724.   "Simplify your life. You don't grow spiritual, you shrink spiritual."— Steve Maraboli, Life, the Truth, and Being Free

2725.   "Speak when you are angry, and you'll make the best speech you'll ever regret."— Laurence J. Peter

2726.   "My home is in Heaven. I'm just traveling through this world."— Billy Graham

2727.   "Sometimes change was good. Sometimes it was even exactly what you needed."— Jenny O'Connell, Plan B

2728.   "Each friend represents a world in us, a world possibly not born until they arrive, and it is only by this meeting that a new world is born."— Anais Nin

2729.   "Don't believe everything you read. It's very difficult to be accepting of our own bodies. This topic deserves its own book, but since I'm not qualified to write it, I won't. Instead I'll just say this: The pictures staring out at you from the supermarket checkout stands, the images we are all supposed to aspire to? They lie"— Ally Carter

2730.   "Be undeniably good."— Steve Martin

2731.   "Live Today! Do not allow your spirit to be softened of your happiness to be limited by a day you cannot have back or a day that does not yet exist."— Steve Maraboli, Unapologetically You: Reflections on Life and the Human Experience

2732.   "Life means nothing without love, You learn lust from love, And you learn your lessons from, The love you lost."— Kelly Boulden

2733.   "Disappointments are like weeds in the garden. You can let them grow and take over your life, or you can rout them out and let the flowers sprout."— Wanda E. Brunstetter, A Cousin's Challenge

2734.   "From now on I'll connect the dots my own way."— Bill Watterson

2735.   "There is something good in all seeming failures. You are not to see that now. Time will reveal it. Be patient."— Sivananda Saraswati

2736.   "Make a pact with yourself today to not be defined by your past. Instead, shake things up today! Live through today. Don't just exist through it - LIVE through it!"— Steve Maraboli, Unapologetically You: Reflections on Life and the Human Experience

2737.   "Do not despair. Do not give up. Look for the sunlight through the clouds."— Gordon B. Hinckley

2738.   "In the times of trouble, be like the strong wall. In the times of joy, be like the smiling sun."— Santosh Kalwar

2739.   "Don't forget, a person's greatest emotional need is to feel appreciated."— H. Jackson Brown Jr., Life's Little Instruction Book: 511 Suggestions, Observations, and Reminders on How to Live a Happy and Rewarding Life

2740.   "...And we pray, not for new earth or heaven, but to be quiet in heart, and in eye clear. What we need is here."— Wendell Berry

2741.   "Leaders live by choice, not by accident."— Mark Gorman

2742.   "Do not lose hold of your dreams or aspirations. For if you do, you may still exist but you have ceased to live."— Henry David Thoreau

2743.   "True love is boundless like the ocean and, swelling within one, spreads itself out and, crossing all boundaries and frontiers, envelops the whole world."— Mahatma Gandhi

2744.   "I wish I could make him understand that a loving good heart is riches enough, and that without it intellect is poverty."— Mark Twain, The Diary of Adam and Eve

2745.   "You can't build your life around hurts from the past"-Tyler Perry The Family That Preys"— Tyler Perry

2746.   "You're water. We're the millstone.
You're wind. We're dust blown up into shapes.
You're spirit. We're the opening and closing of our hands. You're the clarity.
We're the language that tries to say it.
You're joy. We're all the different kinds of laughing."— Rumi, The Essential Rumi

2747.   "No ideology can help to create a new world
or a new mind or a new human being --
because ideological orientation itself
is the root cause of all the conflicts and all the miseries.
Thought creates boundaries, thought creates divisions and thought creates prejudices; thought itself cannot bridge them. That's why all ideologies fail.
Now man must learn to live without ideologies religious, political or otherwise.
When the mind is not tethered to any ideology, it is free to move to new understandings. And in that freedom flowers all that is good and all that is beautiful."— Osho

2748.   "We do not inherit the planet from our ancestors; we borrow it from our children."— Native American Saying

2749.   "Emotions were like wild horses and it required wisdom to be able to control them"— Paulo Coelho

2750.   "Adversity, if for no other reason, is of benefit, since it is sure to bring a season of sober reflection. People see clearer at such times. Storms purify the atmosphere."— Henry Ward Beecher

2751.   "A revolution is coming – a revolution which will be peaceful if we are wise enough; compassionate if we care enough; successful if we are fortunate enough – but a revolution which is coming whether we will it or not. We can affect its character; we cannot alter its inevitability."— John F. Kennedy, Profiles in Courage

2752.   "Flow down and down in always widening rings of being."— Rumi

2753.   "The same wind that uproots trees makes the grass shine.
The lordly wind loves the weakness and the lowness of grasses.

Never brag of being strong.
The axe doesn't worry how thick the branches are.
It cuts them to pieces. But not the leaves.
It leaves the leaves alone."— Rumi, The Essential Rumi

2754.   "A woman who surrenders her freedom need not surrender her dignity."— Wally Lamb, The Hour I First Believed

2755.   "It ain't no sin to be glad you're alive."— Bruce Springsteen

2756.   "Cautious, careful people, always casting about to preserve their reputation and social standing, never can bring about a reform. Those who are really in earnest must be willing to be anything or nothing in the world's estimation, and publicly and privately, in season and out, avow their sympathy with despised and persecuted ideas and their advocates, and bear the consequences..."— Susan B. Anthony

2757.   "Bird by bird, buddy. Just take it bird by bird."— Anne Lamott, Bird by Bird: Some Instructions on Writing and Life

2758.   "I am buoyant and expansive and uncontainable--but I always was so, only I never knew it!"— Chitra Banerjee Divakaruni, The Palace of Illusions

2759.   "Don't you know how sweet and wonderful life can be?"— Marvin Gaye

2760.   "I don't care how impossible it seems."— David Byrne

2761.   "Fingerprints are like values--you leave them all over everything you do"— Elvis Presley

2762.   "I'm not sure this will make sense to you, but I felt as though I'd turned around to look in a different direction, so that I no longer faced backward toward the past, but forward toward the future. And now the question confronting me was this: What would that future be? The moment this question formed in my mind, I knew with as much certainty as I'd ever known anything that sometime during that day I would receive a sign. This was why the bearded man had opened the window in my dream. He was saying to me, "Watch for the thing that will show itself to you. Because that thing, when you find it, will be your future."— Arthur Golden, Memoirs of a Geisha

2763.   "An opinion should be the result of thought, not a substitute for it."— Jef Mallett

2764.   "Float like a butterfly, sting like a bee."— Muhammed Ali

2765.   "YOU ARE AN ARTIST OF THE SPIRIT
Find yourself and express yourself in your own particular way. Express your love openly. Life is nothing but a dream, and if you create your life with love, your dream becomes a masterpiece of art."— Miguel Ruiz

2766.   "The heart that gives thanks is a happy one, for we cannot feel thankful and unhappy at the same time.
The more we say thanks, the more we find to be thankful for.
And the more we find to be thankful for, the happier we become.
We don't give thanks because we're happy.
We are happy because we give thanks."— Douglas Wood, Secret of Saying Thanks

2767.   "Being truthful when you know it will cost you, Is the true test of honesty."— Dave Weinbaum

2768.   "No, this is not the beginning of a new chapter in my life; this is the beginning of a new book! That first book is already closed, ended, and tossed into the seas; this new book is newly opened, has just begun! Look, it is the first page! And it is a beautiful one!"— C. JoyBell C.

2769.   "Only two things can reveal life's great secrets: suffering and love."— Paulo Coelho, Aleph

2770.   "When something is important to you, you make sure it's safe."— Amanda Hocking, Switched

2771.   "We have no right to express an opinion until we know all of the answers."— Kurt Cobain

2772.   "The majority of people have successfully alienated themselves from change; they tediously arrange their lives into a familiar pattern, they give themselves to normalcy, they are proud if they are able to follow in auspicious footsteps set before them, they take pride in always coloring inside the lines and they feel secure if they belong to a batch of others who are like them. Now, if familiar patterns bore you, if normalcy passes before you unnoticed, if you want to create your own footsteps in the earth and leave your own handprints on the skies, if you are the one who doesn't mind the lines in the coloring book as much as others do, and perchance you do not cling to a flock for you to identify with, then you must be ready for adversity. If you are something extraordinary, you are going to always shock others and while they go about existing in their mundaneness which they call success, you're going to be flying around crazy in their skies and that scares them. People are afraid of change, afraid of being different, afraid of doing things and thinking things that aren't a part of their checkerboard game of a life. They only know the pieces and the moves in their games, and that's it. You're always going to find them in the place that you think you're going to find them in, and every time they think about you, you're going to give them a heart attack."— C. JoyBell C.

2773.   "Life is short. Kiss slowly, laugh insanely, love truly and forgive quickly"— Paulo Coelho

2774.   "Friendship is thinking of the other person first."— George Alexiou

2775.   "I feel infinite."— Stephen Chbosky, The Perks of Being a Wallflower

2776.		"When you are unsure about the future, keep doing what is in front of you with all your heart and with love, and what is meant for you will find you."— Guru Mayi Chidvilasananda

2777.		"Become the leader of your life. Lead yourself to where you want to be. Breathe life back into your ambitions, your desires, your goals, your relationships."— Steve Maraboli, Unapologetically You: Reflections on Life and the Human Experience

2778.		"It's not over if you're still here," Chronicler said. "It's not a tragedy if you're still alive."— Patrick Rothfuss, The Wise Man's Fear

2779.		"When you stop being afraid you feel good"— Spencer Johnson, Who Moved My Cheese

2780.		"Remembering that you are going to die is the best way I know to avoid the trap of thinking you have something to lose."— Steve Jobs

2781.		"Bring something incomprehensible into the world!"— Gilles Deleuze, Thousand Plateaus: Capitalism and Schizophrenia

2782.		"A child may not know how to feed itself, or what to eat, yet it knows hunger."— Daniel Keyes, Flowers for Algernon

2783.		"How would your life be different if...You were conscious about the food you ate, the people you surround yourself with, and the media you watch, listen to, or read? Let today be the day...You pay attention to what you feed your mind, your body, and your life. Create a nourishing environment conducive to your growth and well-being today."— Steve Maraboli, The Power of One

2784.		"The only easy day was yesterday."— US Navy SEALs

2785.		"It is our failure to become our perceived ideal that ultimately defines us and makes us unique. It's not easy, but if you accept your misfortune and handle it right your perceived failure can become a catalyst for profound re-invention."— Conan O'Brien

2786.		"The universe is a million billion light-years wide, and every inch of it would kill you if you went there. This is the position of the universe with regards to human life."— Martin Amis

2787.		"Hope and courage and risk dwell inside of us on an uncharted island and if we learn to look for it and tap into it, our possibilities are endless."— Katie Kacvinsky, Awaken

2788.		"Cake is happiness! If you know the way of the cake, you know the way of happiness! If you have a cake in front of you, you should not look any further for joy!"— C. JoyBell C.

2789.		"I went to the school and put it to William, particularly, that if you find someone you love in life, you must hang onto it, and look after it, and if you were lucky enough to find someone who loved you, then you must protect it."— Diana Princess of Wales

2790.   "I have a dream." "Is your dream very big?" "No." "Well is it very grand?" "Not either." "Neither?" "Neither." "What is it then?" "It is very shiny."— C. JoyBell C.

2791.   "Beauty is finding the right fit, the natural fit. To be perfect, you have to feel perfect about yourself. Avoid trying to be someone you're not."— Rick Riordan

2792.   "meditation vs. prayer = listening vs. talking"— Elizabeth Gilbert, Eat, Pray, Love

2793.   "You are a firework!"— Katy Perry

2794.   "In the land where excellence is commended, not envied, where weakness is aided, not mocked, there is no question as to how its inhabitants are all superhuman."— Criss Jami, Venus in Arms

2795.   "Someone once told me that we move when it becomes less painful than staying where we are"."— Anne Hines, The Spiral Garden

2796.   "It is born in mind that the tragedy of life does not lie in not reaching the goal. The tragedy of life lies in having no goal to reach."— Benjamin E. Mays

2797.   "To protect themselves, the weak focus on the "bad" in people. Conversely, the strong, who fear little, focus on the "good"."— Iimani David

2798.   "Heaven wheels above you, displaying to you her eternal glories, and still your eyes are on the ground"— Dante Alighieri

2799.   "You cannot shake hands with a clenched fist."— Mahatma Gandhi

2800.   "There's no such thing as im-POSSIBLE, Hiccup, only im-PROBABLE. The only thing that limits us are the limits to our imagination"— Cressida Cowell, How to Cheat a Dragon's Curse

2801.   "I am not a victim. No matter what I have been through, I'm still here. I have a history of victory."— Steve Maraboli, Unapologetically You: Reflections on Life and the Human Experience

2802.   "Man is a being in search of meaning."— Plato

2803.   "You soak up my soul and mingle me. Each drop of my blood cries out to the earth. We are partners, blended as one."— Rumi

2804.   "There is no such thing as a great talent without great willpower."— Honoré de Balzac

2805.   "How fortunate for governments that the people they administer don't think"— Adolf Hitler

2806.　　"As I go clowning my sentimental way into eternity, wrestling with all my problems of estrangement and communion, sincerity and simulation, ambition and acquiescence, I shuttle between worrying whether I matter at all and whether anything else matters but me."— Stephen Fry, Moab Is My Washpot

2807.　　"NOTHING goes exactly as planned. Make your OWN destiny"— Tate Hallaway, Almost to Die For

2808.　　"Lose your mind and come to your senses."— Frederick S. Perls

2809.　　"I know how it feels to be completely alone and helpless, and the last thing you want to hear in that situation is, 'It's going to be OK.' "The only thing that seems to really help is that someone else who has felt that low expressing those feelings to you."— Evanescence

2810.　　"The power to change your life lies in the simplest of steps."— Steve Maraboli

2811.　　"Your mind can be either your prison or your palace. What you make it is yours to decide"— Bernard Kelvin Clive, Your Dreams Will Not Die

2812.　　"The desperate usually succeed because they have nothing to lose."— Jodi Picoult, Vanishing Acts

2813.　　"Whoever thought that he had understood something of me had merely construed something out of me, after his own image."— Friedrich Nietzsche

2814.　　"I have seen sights and travelled in countries you cannot imagine. I have been afraid and I have been in danger, and I have never for one moment thought that I would throw myself at a man for his help."— Philippa Gregory, The Queen's Fool

2815.　　"Some of this book—perhaps too much—has been about how I learned to do it. Much of it has been about how you can do it better. The rest of it—and perhaps the best of it—is a permission slip: you can, you should, and if you're brave enough to start, you will. Writing is magic, as much the water of life as any other creative art. The water is free. So drink. Drink and be filled up. "— Stephen King, On Writing: A Memoir of the Craft

2816.　　"Beauty Lures the Stranger More Easily into Danger -Septimus Heap"— Angie Sage

2817.　　"Follow your heart. Just don't get lost."— Ilsa J. Bick, Draw the Dark

2818.　　"A lack of clarity could put the brakes on any journey to success."— Steve Maraboli, Life, the Truth, and Being Free

2819.　　"We need to forgive ourselves and everyone else for NOT being perfect."— Linda Masemore Pirrung, Explosion in Paris

2820.   "Sometimes really, really bad things happen to people, and there is no explanation and no reason whatsoever."— Sarah Dessen

2821.   "You know what I noticed when I was with Jacob? In your world, people can reach each other in an instant. There's the telephone, and the fax - and on the computer you can talk to someone all the way around the world. You've got people telling their secrets on TV talk shows, and magazines that publish pictures of movie stars trying to hide their homes. All those connections, but everyone there seems so lonely."— Jodi Picoult, Plain Truth

2822.   "Your agreement with reality defines your life."— Steve Maraboli, Life, the Truth, and Being Free

2823.   "What you have learned from experience is worth much more than gold. If you have a house it may burn down. Any kind of possession can be lost, but your experience is yours forever. Keep it and find a way to use it."— Somaly Mam, The Road of Lost Innocence: The True Story of a Cambodian Heroine

2824.   "I just never let anything bother me, man. I know myself really well. Nobody's opinion of me can shake my opinion of myself."— Ruben Studdard

2825.   "You know, it's interesting. Children learn much more, far more quickly than adults. Do you know why that is?" Elizabeth assumed there was some scientific explanation for it, but shook her head. "Because they're open-minded. Because they want to know and they want to learn. Adults"—he shook his head sadly—"think they know it all. They grow up and forget so easily instead of opening their minds; they choose what to believe and what not to believe. You can't make a choice on things like that, you either believe or you don't. That's why their learning is slower. They are more cynical, they lose faith, and they only demand to know things that will help them get by day by day. They've no interest in the extras. But, Elizabeth," he said, his voice a loud whisper, eyes wide and sparkling, and Elizabeth shivered as goose pimples rose on her arms. She felt as if he were sharing the world's greatest secret with her. "It's the extras that make life." "That make life what?" she whispered. He smiled. "That makes life." Elizabeth swallowed the lump in her throat. "That's it?" Ivan smiled. "What do you mean, that's it? How much more can you get than life, how much more can you ask for than life? That's the gift. Life is everything, and you haven't lived it properly until you believe."— Cecelia Ahern

2826.   "Where ignorance lurks, so too do the frontiers of discovery and imagination"— Neil deGrasse Tyson

2827.   "You were born together, and together you shall be for evermore...But let there be spaces in your togetherness...Love one another, but make not a bond of love. Let it rather be a moving sea between the shores of your souls. Fill each other's cup but drink not from one cup. Give one another of your bread but eat not of the same loaf. Sing and dance together and be joyous, but let each one of you be alone, Even as the strings of a lute are alone though they quiver with the same music."— Kahlil Gibran

2828.   "I shut my eyes in order to see."— Paul Gauguin

2829.   "I attribute my success to this - I never gave or took any excuse."—
Florence Nightingale

2830.   "The institutions of human society treat us as parts of a machine. They
assign us ranks and place considerable pressure upon us to fulfill defined roles.
We need something to help us restore our lost and distorted humanity. Each of
us has feelings that have been suppressed and have built up inside. There is a
voiceless cry resting in the depths of our souls, waiting for expression. Art gives
the soul's feelings voice and form."— Daisaku Ikeda

2831.   "Wise men put their trust in ideas and not in circumstances."— Ralph
Waldo Emerson

2832.   "To be happy you must have taken the measure of your powers, tasted
the fruits of your passion, and learned your place in the world."— George
Santayana

2833.   "Failure? I never encountered it. All I ever met were temporary
setbacks."— Dottie Walters

2834.   "Naw, Jem. I think that there is just one kind of folks. Folks."

2835.   Jen turned and punched his pillow. When he settles back his face was
cloudy. He was going in to one of his declines, and I grew wary. His brows came
together; his mouth became a thin line. He was silent for a while. That is what I
thought, too," he said at last, "when I was your age. If there is just one kind of
folks, why can't they get along with each other? If they're all alike, why do they go
out of their way to despise each other? Scout, I think I am beginning to
understand something. I think I'm beginning to understand why Boo Radley
stayed shut up in the house all this time...it's because he wants to stay inside"—
Harper Lee, To Kill a Mockingbird

2836.   "The most wasted day of all is that during which we have not
laughed."— Nicolas Chamfort

2837.   "He, who is more mindful of one, loses the love and the faith of
both."— Kahlil Gibran, The Prophet

2838.   "Without you the instruments would die. One sits close beside you.
Another takes a long kiss. The tambourine begs; Touch my skin so I can be
myself. Let me feel you enter each limb bone by bone, that what died last night
can be whole today. Why live some soberer way, and feel you ebbing out? I
won't do it. Either give me enough wine or leave me alone, now that I know how it
is to be with you in constant conversation."— Rumi, Night and Sleep

2839.   "You can't base your life on other people's expectations."— Stevie
Wonder

2840.   "Only the children know what they are looking for. They waste their
time over a rag doll and it becomes very important to them; and if anybody takes
it away from them, they cry..."— Antoine de Saint-Exupéry

2841.   "Loosen up. Relax. Except for rare life-and-death matters, nothing is as important as it first seems."— H. Jackson Brown Jr., Life's Little Instruction Book: 511 Suggestions, Observations, and Reminders on How to Live a Happy and Rewarding Life

2842.   "It's okay to be afraid. It's not okay to let the fear STOP you."— Cupcake Brown, A Piece of Cake

2843.   "There's no time for hatred, only questions. Where is love? Where is happiness? What is life? Where is peace?"— Jeff Buckley

2844.   "Go make your mark on the world. Be a world changer! Live bold for Christ no matter the cost."— Crystal Woodman Miller

2845.   "Our life is like a land journey, too even and easy and dull over long distances across the plains, too hard and painful up the steep grades; but, on the summits of the mountain, you have a magnificent view--and feel exalted--and your eyes are full of happy tears--and you want to sing--and wish you had wings! And then--you can't stay there, but must continue your journey--you begin climbing down the other side, so busy with your footholds that your summit experience is forgotten."— Lloyd C. Douglas, The Robe

2846.   "Nobody is just anything... everyone is of equal value, regardless of their station"— Tim LaHaye, Left Behind Series

2847.   "He was free to enjoy the breathless glee that overwhelmed him: the speed, the clear cold air, the total silence, the feeling of balance and excitement and peace."— Lois Lowry

2848.   "There are things you do sometimes, actions that you take by obeying sudden impulses, without stopping for even a fraction of a second to think, and then you spend the rest of your life either lamenting it or thanking yourself for it. They are rare, unique, and perfect moments."— Irene Gonzalez Frei

2849.   "A king who trusts no man is weak."— Patricia Briggs, Dragon Blood

2850.   "The dream is like a river, ever changing as it flows and the dreamer just a vessel that must follow where it goes. We must learn from what's behind us never knowing what's in store keeps each day a constant battle just to stay between the shore"— Garth Brooks

2851.   "In some not too distant tomorrow the radiant stars of love and brotherhood will shine over our great nation with all their scintillating beauty."— Martin Luther King Jr., The Autobiography of Martin Luther King, Jr.

2852.   "The Bible makes it clear that every time that there is a story of faith, it is completely original. God's creative genius is endless."— Eugene H. Peterson

2853.   "LIFE is four letters so is FCUK, LOVE is four letter so is PAIN."— Santosh Kalwar, Quote Me Everyday

2854.	"The one help we all need is given to us freely though the Atonement of Jesus Christ. Having faith in Jesus Christ and In His Atonement means relying completely on Him-trusting in His infinite power, intelligence, and love."— Dieter F. Uchtdorf

2855.	"When people first discover beauty, they tend to linger. Even if they don't at first recognize it for what it is."— Sherwood Smith

2856.	"If you're a nobody, if your work has no impact, then it deserves to be praised. If, however, you climb out of that state of mediocrity and are a success, then you're defying 'the law' and deserve to be punished."— Paulo Coelho, The Zahir

2857.	"It does not matter how long you are spending on the earth, how much money you have gathered or how much attention you have received. It is the amount of positive vibration you have radiated in life that matters,"— Amit Ray

2858.	"you must be careful never to allow doubt to paralyze you. always take the decisions you need to take, even if you're not sure you're doing the right thing. You'll never go wrong if, when you make a decision, you keep in mind an old German proverb: 'The devil is in the detail.' Remember that proverb and you'll always be able to turn a wrong decision into a right one."— Paulo Coelho, Brida

2859.	"If you are not the hero of your own story, then you're missing the whole point of your humanity."— Steve Maraboli, Unapologetically You: Reflections on Life and the Human Experience

2860.	"the future belongs to those who believe in the beauty of their dreams"— Theodore Roosevelt

2861.	"There is a time to live and a time to die but never to reject the moment."— Lao Tzu

2862.	"You can't change the wind but you can set your sails."— Billie Joe Armstrong

2863.	"You and your purpose in life are the same thing. Your purpose is to be you."— George Alexiou

2864.	"It is a serious thing to live in a society of possible gods and goddesses, to remember that the dullest most uninteresting person you talk to may one day be a creature which, if you say it now, you would be strongly tempted to worship, or else a horror and a corruption such as you now meet, if at all, only in a nightmare. All day long we are, in some degree helping each other to one or the other of these destinations. It is in the light of these overwhelming possibilities, it is with the awe and the circumspection proper to them, that we should conduct all of our dealings with one another, all friendships, all loves, all play, all politics. There are no ordinary people. You have never talked to a mere mortal. nations, cultures, arts, civilizations - These are mortal, and their life is to ours as the life of a gnat. But it is immortals, whom we joke with, work with, marry, snub, and exploit - immortal horrors or everlasting splendors."— C.S. Lewis, The Weight of Glory

2865.   "You can sacrifice and not love. But you cannot love and not sacrifice."— Kris Vallotton

2866.   "One more dance along the razor's edge finished. Almost dead yesterday, maybe dead tomorrow, but alive, gloriously alive, today."— Robert Jordan, Lord of Chaos

2867.   "Wherever the art of Medicine is loved, there is also a love of Humanity."— Hippocrates

2868.   "Hope springs forever."— J.K. Rowling, The Tales of Beedle the Bard

2869.   "Hope like that, as I thought before, doesn't make you a weak person. It's hopelessness that makes you weak. Hope makes you stronger, because it brings with it a sense of reason. Not a reason for how or why they were taken from you, but a reason for you to live. Because it's a maybe. A 'maybe someday things won't always be this shit.' And that 'maybe' immediately makes the shittiness better."— Cecelia Ahern, The Book of Tomorrow

2870.   "You will see that the things you desire most are the very things that bring you the greatest sorrow."— Christopher Pike, Phantom

2871.   "From what we get, we can make a living. What we give; however, makes a life."— Arthur Ashe

2872.   "Arrogance on the part of the meritorious is even more offensive to us than the arrogance of those without merit: for merit itself is offensive."— Friedrich Nietzsche

2873.   "Why does each thing on the earth war against each other thing? Why does each small thing in the world have to fight against the world itself? Why does a fly have to fight the whole universe? Why does a dandelion have to fight the whole universe? For the same reason that I had to be alone in the dreadful Council of the Days. So that each thing that obeys law may have the glory and isolation of the anarchist. So that each man fighting for order may be as brave and good a man as the dynamiter. So that the real lie of Satan may be flung back in the face of this blasphemer, so that by tears and torture we may earn the right to say to this man, 'You lie!' No agonies can be too great to buy the right to say to this accuser, 'We also have suffered."— G.K. Chesterton, The Man Who Was Thursday

2874.   "I am striving to give back the Divine in myself to the Divine in the All."— Plotinus

2875.   "Live today as if you were going to live forever, for you surely shall."— Gordon B. Hinckley

2876.   "And I will show that there is no imperfection in the present, and can be none in the future, And I will show that whatever happens to anybody it may be turned to beautiful results, And I will show that nothing can happen more beautiful than death, And I will thread a thread through my poems that time and events are compact, And that all the things of the universe are perfect miracles, each as profound as any."— Walt Whitman

2877.   "We are the Bibles the world is reading; we are the creeds the world needs; we are the sermons the world is heeding."— Billy Graham

2878.   "Our hearts have been made for you, O God, and they shall never rest until they rest in you."— Augustine of Hippo

2879.   " — This world is full of trouble, umfundisi.
— Who knows it better?
— Yet you believe?
Kumalo looked at him under the light of the lamp. I believe, he said, but I have learned that it is a secret. Pain and suffering, they are a secret. Kindness and love, they are a secret. But I have learned that kindness and love can pay for pain and suffering. There is my wife, and you, my friend, and these people who welcomed me and the child who is so eager to be with us here in Ndotsheni – so in my suffering I can believe.
— I have never thought that a Christian would be free of suffering, umfundisi. For our Lord suffered. And I come to believe that he suffered, not to save us from suffering, but to teach us how to bear suffering. For he knew that there is no life without suffering.
Kumalo looked at his friend with joy. You are a preacher, he said."— Alan Paton, Cry, the Beloved Country

2880.   "I will remember what I was, I am sick of rope and chains -
I will remember my old strength and all my forest affairs.
I will not sell my back to man for a bundle of sugar cane; I will go out to my own kind, and the wood-folk in their lairs.
I will go out until the day, until the morning break –
Out to the wind's untainted kiss, the water's clean caress;I will forget my ankle-ring and snap my picket stake.
I will revisit my lost love and playmates master less!"— Rudyard Kipling, The Jungle Books

2881.   "He doesn't have to say it, I feel it too; it's not subtle - like every bell for miles and miles is ringing at once, loud and clanging, hungry ones and tiny, happy, chiming ones, all of them sounding off in this moment. I put my hands around his neck, pull him to me, and then he's kissing me hard and so deep, and I am flying, sailing, soaring…"— Jandy Nelson, The Sky Is Everywhere

2882.   "And as for going into a bookstore and not finding a book suitable for your 13-year-old…maybe you should do some research before you go in? And I'm being serious here. There are a bunch of great blogs that will tell you the content of books. Reading Teen is one of them, and I've seen others, and I love what they do because they make YA books feel safe to protective parents. There are plenty of YA books that celebrate joy and beauty. Now, I would argue that many of them are also the "dark" books to which the article refers, and that saying they aren't suggests a pretty inattentive reader...but that's neither here nor there. I'm not trying to bicker with the careful parents. I'm just saying: do some research and you'll be surprised what you find. So, that's what I'm going to say about it."— Veronica Roth

2883.   "The typical expression of opening Friendship would be something like, 'What? You too? I thought I was the only one!"— C.S. Lewis, The Four Loves

2884.   "Dream, Dream Dream
Dreams transform into thoughts
And thoughts result in action."— A.P.J. Abdul Kalam

2885.   "Be wise enough not to be reckless, but brave enough to take great risks."— Frank Warren

2886.   "LAW 38
Think As You Like But Behave Like Others
If you make a show of going against the times, flaunting your unconventional ideas and unorthodox ways, people will think that you only want attention and that you look down upon them. They will find a way to punish you for making them feel inferior. It is far safer to blend in and nurture the common touch. Share your originality only with tolerant friends and those who are sure to appreciate your uniqueness."— Robert Greene, The 48 Laws of Power

2887.   "God uses broken things. It takes broken soil to produce a crop, broken clouds to give rain, broken grain to give bread, broken bread to give strength. It is the broken alabaster box that gives forth perfume. It is Peter, weeping bitterly, who returns to greater power than ever."— Vance Havner

2888.   "May my heart be kind, my mind fierce, and my spirit brave."— Kate Forsyth, The Witches of Eileanan

2889.   "Once time is lit, it will burn whether or not you're breathing it in. Even after smoke becomes air, there is the memory of smoke. I am seeing as if by the light of a match, a glimpse of my life and having it feel right."— David Levithan, The Realm of Possibility

2890.   "One of the sanest, surest, and most generous joys of life comes from being happy over the good fortune of others."— Robert A. Heinlein

2891.   "Stop searching the world for treasure, the real treasure is in yourself."— Pablo

2892.   "Stop just cheering for others who are living their visions. Commit yourself to your own success and follow the steps required to achieve it."— Steve Maraboli, Life, the Truth, and Being Free

2893.	"You can lose your MONEY. You can lose your FRIENDS. You can lose your JOB and you can lose your MARRIAGE...and still recover...as long as there is HOPE. Never lose HOPE."— John Paul Warren

2894.	"Thriving. That's fighting... Surviving is barely getting by."— Jillian Michaels

2895.	"Too many locks, not enough keys."— Sarah Dessen

2896.	"I believe absolutely in my own free will and my own power to accomplish - and that is the belief that moves mountains."— Jean Webster, Daddy-Long-Legs

2897.	"The master observes the world but trusts his inner vision. He allows things to come and go. He prefers what is within to what is without."— Lao Tzu

2898.	"Negative desires can cause no evil if you do not allow yourself to be seduced by them."— Paulo Coelho, Maktub

2899.	"In the end, you feel that your much-vaunted, inexhaustible fantasy is growing tired, debilitated, exhausted, because you're bound to grow out of your old ideals; they're smashed to splinters and turn to dust, and if you have no other life, you have no choice but to keep rebuilding your dreams from the splinters and dust. But the heart longs for something different! And it is vain to dig in the ashes of your old fancies, trying to find even a tiny spark to fan into a new flame that will warm the chilled heart and bring back to life everything that can send the blood rushing wildly through the body, fill the eyes with tears--everything that can delude you so well!"— Fyodor Dostoyevsky, White Nights

2900.	"Let today be the day you stop having conflict between your actions and your goals and finally align your greatest intent with your purposeful actions, creating a universal symphony serenading your success!"— Steve Maraboli, Life, the Truth, and Being Free

2901.	"I used to think that if I were a certain kind of person I would spend all my time creating something beautiful. Well, it turns out I am, and I am."— Jason Letts

2902.	"I think there's no greater joy than completing a song out of thin air. It's like inventing something, but it's invisible, you know? It's weird. It amazes me. You can send it out in the world, and that's the joy. It's like giving birth to all these songs and letting them go like they're your kids."— Jason Mraz

2903.	"... just because [butterflies'] lives were short didn't mean they were tragic... See, they have a beautiful life."— Lisa Genova, Still Alice

2904.	"For the Jesus Revolutionaries, the answer was clear: Jesus would not be out waging "preventative" wars. Jesus would not be withholding medicine from people who could not afford it. Jesus would not cast stones at people of races, sexual orientations, or genders other than His own. Jesus would not condone the failing, viperous, scandalplagued hierarchy of some churches.

Jesus would welcome everyone to his table. He would love them, and he would find peace."— David Levithan, Wide Awake

2905.   "We have been moving along at such a fast pace that we no longer know what we are doing. Now we have to wait until our soul catches up with us."— Paulo Coelho, Maktub

2906.   "Some of the greatest battles will be fought within the silent chambers of your own soul."— Ezra Taft Benson

2907.   "The boy reached through to the Soul of the World, and saw that it was part of the Soul of God. And he saw that the Soul of God was his own soul. And that he, a boy, could perform miracles."— Paulo Coelho, The Alchemist

2908.   "[A young adult novel] ends not with happily ever after, but at a new beginning, with the sense of a lot of life yet to be lived."— Richard Peck

2909.   "When you truly embrace your human impermanence you connect with the power you have, and influence you have, over the time you have."— Steve Maraboli, Life, the Truth, and Being Free

2910.   "Stories change us; they change the world. People are stories of themselves."— Karen Healey, Guardian of the Dead

2911.   "Sometimes I dance, alone, to music no-one can hear but me. When I dance I feel the beat of the earth's own heart rise through my feet and legs, through my loins and belly and into my chest, until my own heart beats in time with the earth's. Then I wonder if you feel it too, beneath that portion of the earth's crust where you stand, or walk, or lie, or dance too. Because always, when I'm dancing, I'm dancing with you."— Sarah Bower, The Book of Love

2912.   "maybe there is more to a person than a body and a mind. maybe something else figures into the mix— not a soul, exactly, but a spirit that hints you might one day be greater, stronger than you are now. a promise; a potential."— Jodi Picoult, Keeping Faith